Dr Clarence J
Bellevue Polyclinic

Advice from a Failure

ADVICE

FROM

SD .STEIN AND DAY / *Publishers* / New York

A

FAILURE

BY *Jo Coudert*

for

NINI R. VAS DIAS

not to pay a debt
but to acknowledge it,
with affection
and gratitude

TABLE
OF CONTENTS

7

PART III: TO ACT

8

ADVICE FROM A FAILURE

T HE qualifications of an author for writing a book of non-fiction are customarily set forth on the dust jacket, and they may be on this one when the book comes to be printed. But they will not be true, or, at least, what is true will be magnified and what is inconveniently also true will go unmentioned. The publisher is in his right, and very good, mind, and he is not about to convince you to buy a book on how to lead a more intelligent, less troubled life by confiding that the writer of it comes from divorced parents, has an alcoholic mother who is now in a state mental hospital, is divorced herself, has a precariously healed ulcer, and has spent the last ten years being a playwright the even tenor of whose career is undisturbed by a single success.

Advice from a Failure

My relish for these humiliating facts is slight enough to keep me from mentioning them in ordinary circumstances. Like everyone else, I prefer appearing in the best possible light, and I conceal the evidence that clouds that light as imaginatively as I am able. But I have discovered, through sad experience, that if I conceal it from myself, I have not a chance of making the future turn out any better than the past. I have, then, spent a fair amount of time, far more than someone with a better record than mine, in hunting around for where things went wrong, how and why, and what in heaven's name I intend doing about it.

The happy, to borrow Arthur Koestler's phrase, are rarely curious. They do not need to be. There is no more incentive for a contented person to go mucking about in the works than there is for a motorist to stop and lift the hood when the engine is ticking smoothly. But the unhappy had better be curious or it is going to be a long, rough life.

So, at least, it has seemed to me, and I have subjected myself to four and a half years of psychoanalysis and double that of self-analysis in trying to get a look at the works and make what adjustments seem possible. As someone has wittily remarked, the trouble with self-analysis is that the countertransference gets in the way. Without yet having written this book, I know I shall try to convince you, between the lines, that I am a charming, generous, gentle person, for, as the analyst of myself, that is my countertransference, that is the way I view myself. If you believe me, it does not matter. This book is not to say that, God forbid, you should be like me, but to describe the tools I have used to find out what I am like and how better to manage my life.

Nietzsche has been quoted as saying, in effect, that if you can read your own life, you can understand the hieroglyphics of universal life. Emerson noted, in another context, that "what is true for you in your private heart is true for all men," and Polly Adler, whose passkey to this company is that she quotes Henry James, speaks of the "terrible algebra" of one's own life. These people seem to be saying that the algebra of one life, deeply understood, is the algebra of all lives, that we are all far more alike than different.

Is this so? I hope it is, because this is why, a failure, I presume to write about living. I have tried to understand my own life; if I have, and if I tell you how I have, perhaps your life is not so different from mine and you will gain some keys to decoding the algebra of your own. This is not to say that you are me or I am you, only that, while I cannot read the book for you, with luck I can describe ways of using the library to find the information that may be useful.

The Business We Are In

Having listed some biographical facts, I hope to set down as few more as possible, even those that might be mitigating, for what concerns me is how a self can be examined by the self, how a life can be understood by the one who is living it. There must be ways of living a life with grace and intelligence. How can they be found? There must be ways of moving in the world that are not abrasive. There must be ways of integrating the self, the unacceptable parts of the self, so that exhausting efforts to reject or repress can be given up. There must be ways of knowing what one is, and then, knowing, being what one is.

Although I am not above a play on words, "being what one is" is not meant to be such. There are people who are angry who never express their anger. There are people who are dependent who never lean on anyone. It is not unattractive to be conciliatory or to be self-reliant, but to be these things in all circumstances because you do not know or cannot accept that you are also their opposite is costly. It takes an enormous amount of energy, creative energy withdrawn from the total economy of the person, to hold a trait underground, and, unfortunately, needs and drives do not go underground alone; they carry with them useful parts of the personality, depriving it of richness and the possibility of a variety of response.

Time magazine once ran a piece on corporate planners, a new breed of executive whose job it is to figure out what business the corporation they work for is in. On the face of it, this appears to require no thought at all, but, put in the way the planners elucidate it, the task assumes more relevancy. If, they say, buggy makers had known they were in the transportation business, they would still be in business today—as automobile manufacturers.

While I hesitate to use the phrase because Americans are accused of being materialistic, nevertheless it seems graphic to say that we are, each of us, in the business of living and that it is vital, if not to the fact of existence, to the meaning of it, to recognize this. To say, to believe, that one is a pilot, a wife, an actor, a designer, a father, a machinist, a mother, an accountant, a secretary, a baseball player, is to mistake attributes for essence, to mistake what one does for what one is, and, thus, quite often, not to know what one is.

15

If carriage makers had lifted their eyes to the wider frame of reference, they would have shifted their ground when an improved mode of transportation came along rather than having it cut out from under them. If we identify that we are in the business of living, we can look for ways to make a go of it, to sort out irrelevancies, to weigh alternatives, to make choices. It surely is clear that, although the analogy is business, none of this has anything to do with money. As an example, I received a letter yesterday asking if I would be interested in a job as managing editor of a new medical magazine. I make my living as a medical editor, so I could do the job, and I now work free-lance and only occasionally, so my income would go from four to twelve thousand a year. If I think I am in the business of medical editing, I cannot turn down the job; if I think I am in the business of living, I cannot take it, for it is not the way I want my life to go.

The Well-Lived Life

My grandfather often spoke, when he was very old and I was very young, of the leather factories he had owned years before. A favorite reminiscence was of the time one of his salesmen obtained a huge contract for buggy whips. It meant building an additional factory for their manufacture, and my grandfather refused the order, already, he said, seeing Henry Ford's handwriting on the wall. But he lost his factories anyway because he kept on making harnesses. It is not enough to see. You must be able to act on what you see.

To act, you must have goals. Is happiness a reasonable goal? Alas, I suspect it is not. I suspect it is the last thing to aim for, that when most aimed for, it is most likely to be missed, when most pursued, it is most elusive, for it is a by-product, a thing that appears when you are engaged in some other task, a thing that disappears when you set out after it, like a cat, who, pursued, will hide; coaxed, will stride indifferently over to the neighbor's yard; but ignored, will come and lean on your leg as you work or climb in your lap as you sit reading.

Happiness, if not the goal, can nevertheless be fall-out from a well-lived life. To get through life with all the courage and decency and equanimity and acceptance and joy we can muster is the business we are fundamentally in. Nobody promises us luck. Nobody even promises us what we deserve. It is not to be regretted. If we all got our just desserts, none of us would be eating ice cream. Given the deaths and disappointments and failures inevitable in a life, how does one achieve the posture of a human being? Given the capriciousness of time and chance, whose favors cannot be solicited but whose disguises may go unpenetrated, how does one maneuver to undergo as little unhappiness as can be managed while, at the same time, hopefully, making a few people pleased to have one around?

I am going to argue that all that really counts, all that is truly decisive, in the well-lived life is the individual's relation to himself. Not to other people. To himself. Not to events or beliefs or groups, for what he thinks of events and beliefs and groups, how he acts toward other people, how loving or hateful, how grasping or withdrawn, how generous or mean, is governed by how he sees himself. If he is not friends with himself, he will be no one else's friend. If he has no love for himself, he will love no one else. If he does not see himself as worthy of love and respect, he will not leave off defending himself against their absence long enough to accord them to another. The self refracts one's view of the world, and the world reflects one's view of oneself.

You Will Never Be Asked

It is not an easy world to live in. It is not an easy world to be decent in. It is not an easy world to understand oneself in, nor to like oneself in. But it must be lived in, and in the living there is one person you absolutely have to be with. I have never known anyone who did not have some family, whether near or distant, some friends, including one close one, but family can be forgotten and friends can be lost and still you have with you your self.

Martin Buber, in an interview which, regrettably, I did not clip and so cannot quote accurately, told of a sentence spoken by an old rabbi, let us call him Golden. "God will never ask me why I was not Moses," said the old man in these or similar words, "but He will ask me why I was not Rabbi Golden."

To be yourself, you must know yourself. And that is the difficult thing. It can be accomplished by anyone more readily than you, for no one else has anything like as large a stake in maintaining your fictions as you do, even, or perhaps especially, if you are uncomfortable with yourself. No matter how vicious, unprincipled, or selfish we darkly suspect ourselves to be, we remain our own most unswerving admirers. No matter how stupid our conduct, we know the most excellent and compelling justification for it. We know why we deserve to be loved and the unassailable reasons why we do not love. We know all the potentialities that the surface accomplishments are merely a slight indication of. We are generous to a fault, provided only that it is our own.

Can the self be known? I shall be honest and say that I believe the answer is: only marginally. I remember a psychologist commenting that a person who distorts no more than ninety per cent of the time is doing very well indeed. That leaves ten per cent. Is it worth trying to achieve sway over ten per cent? I shall say: yes, because it is *my* answer. I have made enough of a mess of things not to want to go stumbling on, pushed by dimly understood compulsions through a wasteland strung with barbed wire I can't see until I am tangled in it and mines laid I don't know where until I have exploded them. Your answer? I can quote Socrates and argue that the unexamined life is not worth living. But if you are managing well enough, nothing will persuade you to rummage through the "pernicious contraries," that marvelous phrase with which

18

the wastepaper industry describes irritating objects mixed in with the salvagable.

Since you are prevented from knowing what you are by knowing what you might be, including not only the good possibilities but the unacceptable, the disastrous, and the bad —for example, to find that you are loving, if to be loving, you believe, means to be swallowed up, can be disastrous—why not ask an onlooker? Well, perhaps it will be transparent to him that somewhere you are loving and he will tell you that you hide it. You will not believe him because you fear that love means annihilation, so you cannot afford to believe him. The other possibility is to ask a trained observer, a psychoanalyst. Knowing in advance that you will not believe him, he will not attempt to tell you what you are. He will sit with you three times a week for as many years as it takes you to tell yourself, now and again asking a question or making a comment in order to turn your search in this direction or that, but he knows that this is the one area in which the only usable education is self-education.

The Givens of a Life

Psychoanalysis, to its great credit, respects the human body as a place to live in, but the housecleaning it knows it must leave to the occupant. If pernicious contraries are cluttering up the place, it is the patient who will cart them out into the open, sort among them, and dispose of what he can do without. The psychiatrist will oversee, but the main task is not his.

Can pernicious contraries be discerned without the expert testimony of the psychiatrist? I am not sure, but I have set down the ways I know of making a try at it. To whatever degree they can be used with success, does change then automatically follow? There are, of course, many givens in a life. It is probable that each of us is born with a particular emotional set, a depressive set, for instance, which determines that we will live with a slight damper on our spirits, or a hypomanic set which determines that events will be ridden out with some bounce. But you can learn your set, your characteristic approach, learn the situations that intensify it, and in this way, and to some extent, control rather than be controlled.

Each of us has a history, and, as Santayana has said, "Those who cannot remember the past are condemned to repeat it." I cannot claim without question that if you understand the past, you will never make the same mistakes again, for there are people who understand their neurotic drives very clearly but are powerless to short-circuit them. There are also people who change without understanding why. Good things happen in life as well as bad, as a friend of mine occasionally points out with some wonder, and congenial circumstances may extinguish deficit behavior. But I find in my own thinking the conviction that Stein and Vidich have discussed in *Identity and Anxiety* as emerging from Shakespeare's plays ". . . that men can grow, that choices matter, that man is both determined and self-determining." Given that men grow, choices matter, and that the self can determine the self—these are the givens that interest me. The area of autonomy, the area in which one can be master of one's own house, may not be without limits (one is determined as well as determining) but to default an inch of freedom to act that can be seized back from unexamined, automatic, repetitive behavior is, to me, to abdicate something of what it means to be alive, to be a person.

Feedback from a Conscious Endeavor

One's life is, of course, external as well as internal, and while "in touch with reality," "reality-oriented," and "contact with reality" are frequently used terms in the delineation of mental health or illness, it is not a matter of there being an imprisoned person looking out through two slits in the wall of his skin at the reality around him; there is a flow back and forth between reality and the person, an interpenetrability between the external and the internal. You signal and the

20

environment acts. The environment acts and you react. You act, the environment reacts, you react, the environment reacts.

Let us say that you walk into a party and into the midst of many strangers, which makes you a bit nervous. You light several cigarettes in a row, which makes you aware you are nervous, which leads you to an effort to control your nervousness, which makes you postpone lighting another cigarette. By forcing your hands to hang naturally at your side, you indeed become less nervous because you are not signaling yourself you are nervous by behaving in a nervous manner. And you have ceased to signal the environment, so that it then begins to act quite differently toward you.

Much of this book will consider, not just ways of knowing and being the self, but ways of moving and acting and being in the world. For you are what your actions are: you may think murder but you are not a murderer until you have murdered in the world. Actions take place in the world, not within the self. You are not only the actor of your actions but the observer of them, and the feedback of what you observe yourself doing will tell you, in some measure, who you are and what you are. Successful actions, like not lighting another cigarette, signal to you that you are better off than you thought. So, it is very important to have all the successes you can achieve. To handle things just as well as possible at one time means to handle them better the next.

How long does it take before you arrive at being a competent, comfortable, well-functioning person, able to meet most situations well and able to salvage the most from muffed or impossible ones? How long will you live? A feedback mechanism is a device for returning information to an electrical or mechanical system which allows the system to regulate itself. A hot water heater, for instance, does not unceasingly heat water; information about its own functioning, in terms of how hot the water in the boiler already is, comes back to it; the flame goes up or down as needed to maintain a constant temperature. Continual adjustments are made in its functioning according to information received. As long as you live, there will be output—you acting—and as long as you live, there will be input—information about your actions coming back—in the light of which you can regulate your further actions.

Thus, the well-lived life is a process, not a destination. How well lived depends on how accurately input is appraised and how much flexibility in action is available. Bursitis overtakes one's character with age, just as surely as calcium deposits limit range of motion in one's shoulder.

To behave relevantly rather than in stereotyped fashion, to grow, to be always becoming rather than prematurely arrived, options must be open. This is partially a problem of identifying and, insofar as possible, breaking character adhesions, and partially a much more simple matter of just thinking about the main areas of life. Much repetitive behavior is not the consequence of inner necessity but of inattention. My most elegant friend, for example, has a theory that many people are cases of arrested development in the clothes they choose: the thirty-year-old woman who wears the same sweaters and skirts she wore in college, the fifty-year-old who ties a ribbon in her hair, the middle-aged executive who wears a blazer. The probability is not that they are trying to appear young but that, at a successful time in their lives, these were the successful clothes they wore and they have not rethought the subject since.

This book is not to give answers. You have already run quickly through in your mind: "How do I dress? What stage am I arrested at? It does not hold for me. But, Sam, now with those boyish bow ties . . ." It may not hold for you; I have no way of knowing. But you have now thought about your clothes, and you may have added a dimension to your view of Sam. And that, if I can do it, is all I have set out to do: crack the familiar subjects open so that they are accessible to examination, and thus to choice and decision.

PART I

TO

KNOW

"Why were you not Rabbi Golden?"
"Because I did not know who Rabbi Golden was."

One
THE WELLSPRINGS
OF BEHAVIOR

HERE is a succinct theory of playwriting that goes like this: in the first act the writer gets the hero up a tree, in the second he throws stones at him, and in the third he brings him down. Less crisply put, it is in the first act of a play that the characters are introduced, relationships are established, and the seeds of the events to come are planted, with the second and third acts being given over to action. If you, as a theatre-goer, by any chance miss the first act, or if perhaps you are in the theatre but doze through the first act, only coming awake at the start of the second, it is difficult to understand what is taking place—why the hero is behaving as he is, why the other characters are opposing him, why he is enmeshed in the situation he is struggling with.

The Stones are Flying

Baffled and irritated by your inability to make sense of what is going on, you may risk making a nuisance of yourself to inquire of your neighbor: Why is the old man wandering around in a storm? Why didn't he leave a third of his kingdom to the other daughter? Why does he believe she doesn't love him? Why is that young man pretending to be someone he is not? Even if your neighbor gives you answers, they are not likely to be clear ones. Although he witnessed the first act, he cannot quickly fill you in on all that happened. His reconstruction will be sketchy. He will remember well only what roused echoes in him. And he will be too absorbed in the on-going drama to care about clearing up your confusion.

Each of us is the story of our lives. And each of us, to our confusion, dozed through the first act. Characters were introduced, relationships established, and the seeds of future events planted, but we slept, to come awake only when we are already up the tree and the stones are flying.

What then? Well, some of us duck, erect defenses, shield ourselves from the risk of bruising blows as best we can. Some of us catch the stones and hurl them back. Some of us cry. Some of us cry out. And most of us, in any respite we get, hunt for a way down.

One possibility of finding a way down is an attempt to retrace the steps of the way up. We were dozing, not sound asleep, through the first act, and occasional events can be dimly recollected, occasional words remembered, occasional feelings re-evoked. Is it worthwhile to try to reconstruct what was missed, to try to piece together some understanding of the first act?

Since the first act motivates the second and third, the key to all present actions is missing without a knowledge of it. But the task of retracing our steps, if rewarding, is also both difficult and frightening. If we undertake it, it is in spite of what we expect to find, not because of what we expect to find. The only truly heartening fact I know is that we will find nothing so strange that it is not also alive in other pasts, nothing so exotic that it does not furnish out other minds as well.

This may strike you as small reassurance if you sense you will uncover that once upon a childhood, crucial people failed you and you reacted with despair or murderous rage, that once you were unbelievably demanding and selfish, that once you were dirty and cruel and quite capable of the most unacceptable thoughts, and that once you were helpless. But it is really not small comfort to know that so, once, were we all.

I have heard people remark that they would not consider entering group therapy because it would involve exposing their most private thoughts to others. But I have been told that, in practice, this proves to be one of the greatest assets of group therapy. Again and again, people confess their relief to discover, when finally they bring themselves to tell

26

of a shameful happening or an ugly wish, that the other patients simply nod; they have been there too; they can match the thought, the experience; and they are not surprised or repelled. Apparently, to discover one's common humanity can be no less reassuring than to appreciate one's unique identity.

So often, we feel alike in our goodness but alone in our badness. Although not reasonable, this is understandable in that we display our goodness and hide our badness, and there is no chance to find out the startling universality of our most fervently disowned thoughts. We have all been born, have had a long and helpless infancy, have had parents, have been fed and taught and punished and toilet-trained. Our experience, no matter how different in particulars, is nevertheless the same in broad outline, and so what we have thought and done during that experience cannot be outside all other's knowledge.

We are in good company, or if not good, at least in company as numerous as the world's. I once encountered a fellow to whom this discovery was so important that he had changed his name to honor it. He was a patient at a mental hospital, and when he was presented at a staff conference, he announced that we were to call him Havelock. He had changed his first name when he was in his teens, he said, because he had come across a book by Havelock Ellis in which masturbation was described as ubiquitous, normal under all but exceptional circumstances, and a source of absolutely no damage to body or brain. His relief was so intense at finding that he was not alone, not strange, not freakish, that he honored his deliverer from isolation by adopting his name.

The Meadows of Infancy

Emboldened by an awareness that the first acts of all lives bear a close family resemblance to one another, you may be able to persuade yourself that your own contains no unbearable surprises. You may resolve that it is worth be-

27

coming further acquainted with because, far from being over and done with, it is exerting a lively influence on the second and third acts. You may even hope for the same intense relief as the homonymous Havelock found. But you will then encounter another problem: the first act has long since been rewritten for publication, and the revisions have been made by the person who loves you best in the world, the person most interested in sparing you hurt and saving your pride. Details have been changed, incidents have been suppressed, time and action have been rearranged, the starring role has been tailored to fit as though you were the most temperamental of aging movie stars. By whom? Yourself.

How do you get hold of the original script? You have to outwit your own self-love. In one sense, the reward for succeeding at this is grim, for there lives on in every one of us the vulnerable, hurt child and the rebellious, poorly controlled adolescent we once were, and you will come face to face with these alive and kicking shades of earlier times. It is not a pretty sight, not when you believe yourself grown and in control. But it is a necessary confrontation.

It is a necessary confrontation, that is, if the object is more than to place blame, if it is more than to come face-to-face and say: this is what I am, and I am what I am and I cannot change; I am what I am because my mother did this, my father did not do that, and a brother was born. If you stop there, just as certainly as if you never undertake the task of confronting the past, all of your life will be a re-enactment, for there is a fundamental tendency toward repetition in human life, a fundamental tendency to repeat past experience and past attitudes, particularly those early established.

A new worker is hired in the office and the rivalrous birth of your brother takes place again. Your boss fails to praise you and, once more, your father withholds his approval. The co-worker on whom you depend for understanding takes an inexplicable fancy to the newcomer and, yet again, you perforce share your mother's love.

The brain has been likened to a meadow. The first perception cutting across it leaves the trace of a path, like the slight flattening of grass in a meadow. The second perception that follows the path wears it down a little more. Others coming the same way incise it deeper, until the path is engraved on the meadow and perceptions routinely follow it rather than seek out a new and more relevant route.

The more deeply the path is etched, the more it is used, and the more it is used, the more deeply it is etched. It is a circular process of repetition and reinforcement. With this in mind, it is easy to understand why, despite the myriad pathways there come to be in the brain, it is the few laid down early that continue to carry the most traffic, and why, because they carry the most traffic, they do not fade out. Attitudes derived from recent experience are not difficult to revise because they have not received constant reinforcement over the years, but attitudes formed in the infancy of a life are extremely resistant to change.

A Hen Sitting on China Eggs

Early attitudes are persistent not because, by accident, the same things keep happening to us but because, by unknowing design, we structure the things that happen to us to fit the old pathways. The world does not provide reinforcement; we provoke reinforcement from the world. We find what we expect to find. We experience what we expect to experience. We do not see the world as it is but as we are.

Like a computer that can rapidly select a matching fingerprint out of millions, the mind can remark resemblances in an instant. Unlike the computer, it is satisfied with a fractional fit if that fraction is well known to it. A friend of mine told of encountering a frumpy, sixtyish, domineering, and opinionated woman at a dinner party to whom she immediately reacted with feelings of anger and fear. S____, my friend, a most attractive and ordinarily urbane woman, described herself as knowing her face had set in sullen lines and of deciding quite consciously that if she said anything at all during the evening, it would be something quite biting in order to punish her escort, whose friend the unpleasant woman was, for "exposing me to such people." But her anger and fear were so out of proportion that they caught her attention, and when she left off her defensiveness long enough to examine them, she was able to make the connection her unconscious mind had leaped to instantly. Her ex-husband had been a driving, tyrannical man whom she had feared because of his swamping qualities and whom she had fought in anger to prevent him from reducing her to a cipher.

Operating in an unlit world, the unconscious mind is a brilliant detective. To detect the resemblance between a frumpy, elderly shrew and a handsome young man is insightful and clever; it is also stupid, for thrust out of consideration is every other parameter on which the shrew and the tyrant differ. The shrew, simply an inconsequential woman on a casual evening, is perceived as being as great a threat as the tyrannical husband, and the anger and fear surge back in all their original intensity, but completely inappropriately.

S____ might perhaps have told herself that she, well-dressed and young and cultured, had aroused the frump's antagonism and that her own anger and fear were a reasonable response to the unreasonable attack of the frump. Instead, she turned her intelligence on herself, put it in the service of her need to understand, not to conceal, and, regaining her poise, went on to outmaneuver the woman, blunting her weapons of force with a correct and mocking courtesy. Thus, while pathways are not established by intelligence, they can be closed to traffic by it.

An example of the converse is a man, a long-time friend of mine of whom I am very fond and whom I treat very badly. R____ has moved across the country now, and when he telephones, he says, "I don't suppose you know my voice any more," and I reply, "No, I don't. Who is this?" When I had a book published at a time he happened to be in town, he said, "I could stop at a bookstore on my way down and buy a copy," and I said, "Oh, for heaven's sake, do you think I wouldn't give one of my best friends a copy?" He came, and I remembered it was my last copy and, though

I could buy more at author's discount, I told myself he had more money than I, and I did not give him a copy.

R____ expects to be treated badly. And he is. We who are his friends frequently disappoint him, but we never disappoint his expectations. When first he knew each of us, there was nothing in our behavior to suggest we would reject him. He had no present reason for expecting rejection from us. But he had every past reason. People who should have loved him once conveyed, by their failure to love him, that he was unworthy of love, and we who love him now consistently treat him unlovingly. Our behavior confirms his experience of the world as unloving and ungiving, and who can say his experience is wrong, for we do indeed walk all over him. But he makes it virtually impossible for us not to do so.

Because present happenings tend to travel the same route as past perceptions, and because the pathway of, let us say simply, masochism was laid down early in R____'s life, his perceptions of other people tend to travel in that groove. He then quite rightly acts in accordance with what he perceives. Thus does uneconomic, unrewarding behavior perpetuate itself, and thus is R____ prevented from finding out that the past is not the present. A person who hugs his own notions long past their time of accuracy and relevancy has been likened to a brood hen sitting on china eggs, and this, alas, seems an accurate description of R____. It is his fate always to be incubating china eggs.

If we think of a simpler animal than a human being, though, we might wonder why this is so. Take the experiment of a rat placed in a cage with two levers. One lever, when pressed, releases a pellet of food; the other produces an electric shock. The rat will learn to discriminate between the two levers and will press only the one that releases the food. But the rat will not remember this indefinitely. If the electric shock is turned off, if there is not reinforcement of what the rat has learned by the same event recurring through time, the rat will forget, the pathway will fade out. R____ learned, when his world was new, that it was a cold and

31

humiliating place. But the world is not always a cold and humiliating place. Successes happen. Generous people exist. Kindnesses are offered. Why did this learning not fade through time?

Unfortunately, R―― provides his own reinforcement. He structures his world so that he repeatedly relearns what he already knows. His behavior skews other people's behavior toward him. He acts like a doormat, and he gets stepped on. He needs no experimenter to provide electric shocks. His actions cause the electric shocks that cause his actions. Thus, his early learning is never extinguished. It may be argued that, surely, not everyone R―― meets can be induced to reinforce his masochism. But, then, not everyone R―― meets does he make friends with. Too, there are probably very few people who do not have, somewhere within them, the propensity for pushing other people around, and R―― finds this area, presses the lever, and gets the shock. We all respond to part-aspects of others, as S―― responded to the domineering quality of the frump and missed other aspects that made S――'s escort value her friendship. When S―― brought her intelligence into play, her vision became more accurate. R――, on the other hand, moved across the country, fleeing the friends who treated him as he expected to be treated.

A Constant Fate

It is said that actions can be divided into the broad categories of fight or flight. R―― chose flight; S―― chose to fight. They are equally intelligent, and, if anything, R―― has the greater technical knowledge of psychology. Part of the answer perhaps is that S―― harked back to a marriage six years previous, while R―― was perpetuating a pattern laid down in infancy and, as has been noted, early established reaction pathways are the most difficult to extinguish. But it cannot be the whole answer, for S―― had reasons for marrying the man she did and these reasons must have come out of a pattern also established in infancy.

But there was a willingness to stop and examine on S____'s part. Aside from what went into this willingness, whether it was that she was not so incapacitated by anxiety that she could not think or that she did not feel herself so threatened that every defense came into play, the encouraging fact is that she was not impotent, she could turn a light on the unlit world of the unconscious, and she could modify her behavior by gaining insight into it. But she did need, first, the willingness; and this she got because, baldly, she did not like her behavior. She did not like the picture of herself as frightened and angry, and she made herself aware that her response had taints of the irrational in it. As much as she disapproved of the other's behavior, she was also able to disapprove of her own.

This willingness to become aware is a long step. Many a person who is uncomfortable with other people will never manage to alter how they treat him because he is not uncomfortable with himself. He agrees with his own actions; he approves of them. Since he does not question them, he remains unaware that they are also unprofitable, repetitive, and reinforcing, bringing about exactly that which makes him uncomfortable.

To break the cycle of repetition, reinforcement, and repetition, it is necessary to be willing to become aware of responses in yourself that you would recognize as inappropriate if you saw them in someone else. Tracking them to their source is far from easy, but an awareness that much of what you feel toward figures in the present is transferred from emotions you felt toward figures in the past often is enough in itself to permit obligatory behavior to become optional behavior, to short-circuit repetition and prevent repeated reinforcement.

Willingness to become aware, thus, is crucial, willingness to listen to the self's explanations and excuses but then to keep going and look behind them. To do this, you must be convinced that the past is alive in the present, that it is characteristic of the human mind to interpret present experience in terms of past experience. Perhaps you can satisfy yourself that this is so by remembering a cocktail party at which you knew few of the guests. If the distracted host put a drink in your hand and abandoned you, you may have looked over the guests and quickly categorized them: the bleached blonde, the bohemian sitting on the floor, the too-loud wife, the aggressive female, the childlike mother of four, the businesswoman; and the salesman, the lecher, the well-preserved tennis player, the alcoholic, the slick guy, the nice guy. You know the types because you have pulled out of the filing cabinet of your memory the cards headed "bleached blonde" and "salesman." Details remain to be filled in, but you already have an opinion based on past experience and you immediately know whom you will maneuver to talk to and whom you will maneuver to avoid.

This comparison of past and present is useful and necessary. If every situation were totally strange, every experience would take place in a foreign country, with a good deal of time and energy taken up with simply orienting oneself. When it goes on within awareness, the instant matching is subject to revision as further evidence comes in: the bleached blonde may turn out to be demure and the salesman an introvert. It is when the matching goes on outside of awareness, in subterranean channels, that it resists revision and gives rise to stereotyped reactions.

To open up the question of whether your own reactions are stereotyped, it is useful to consider whether you seem to be subject to a rather constant fate. Are you always the one to pick up the check? Are you always the one the boss blames? Are you always the one who loves but is not loved? I know a woman who occasionally remarks that she is constantly doing something for someone else, while no one does anything for her. But E___ never goes for a visit without taking her sewing machine, three sponge cakes, and a ham, and the minute she arrives, she is in the kitchen washing up the dishes. It is her fate, she says, to "do for others."

But the world and the people in it are infinitely varied, and if your fate is constant, it is likely that the consistency is not in the world but in you. E____ was deputized to care for a younger sister during her childhood, and she learned too thoroughly that the way to be accepted, praised, and loved was to look after people. And because, of course, she could not help but have mixed feelings about having to drag a little sister with her everywhere she went, she now has ambivalent feelings toward the people she does so much for.

Many a Live Coal

Before Dr. Janet Travell became famous as President Kennedy's physician, I was sent to her because of a pain in the back of my neck. She hunted around and found a spot under my shoulder blade which, when she pressed it, reproduced the pain. I was not aware of any hurt in the original spot, in the trigger area, but only by treating that area could Dr. Travell cure the referred pain in my neck. She injected the trigger area with novocaine so as to interrupt the circuit of pain impulses from mid-back to neck to mid-back again, but she remarked that it was sometimes sufficient just to press the trigger area very hard with her thumb, as though the intense discharge of impulse this produced exhausted the trigger area and caused it to become quiescent.

The trigger areas of psychological pain are located in early childhood, the mechanism of their action in the present being "transference." Transference is defined by the *Psychiatric Glossary* as "the unconscious attachment to others of feelings and attitudes which were originally associated with important figures (parents, siblings, etc.) in one's early life." Another definition, this one put forward by Dr. Otto Fenichel in *The Psychoanalytic Theory of Neurosis*, is that the individual "misunderstands the present in terms of the past; and then instead of remembering the past, he strives, without recognizing the nature of his action, to relive the past and to live it more satisfactorily than he did in childhood. He 'transfers' past attitudes to the present." Dr. Aaron Stein remarks that,

35

"It is generally agreed that transference is a universal phenomenon. It develops rapidly—sometimes instantaneously—in almost all relationships and situations . . ."

In thinking of the problem of R____, his transference of past emotions to persons in the present is not difficult to see, and it might be questioned why one of us, as his friends, did not function as Dr. Travell and point out and put pressure on the trigger area to interrupt the circuit. Indeed, one friend did, and R____ broke with her immediately, explaining that she was an aggressive, attacking female with whom it was impossible to maintain a friendship no matter how kind and forgiving one was. R____, you see, has a tremendous investment in being kind and forgiving. He has put his life into this way of behaving, and he somewhere senses that to be deprived of it would bankrupt him. And well it might. Only if he himself withdrew his investment in small amounts, trying out new ways of behavior while, if they failed, he still had old savings to fall back on, would change be possible.

He would have to put his finger on his own trigger area. This he could do only by searching for the points of constancy in his fate and then raking through the ashes of his childhood to uncover the many a live coal still burning there. It is not in the near yesterday that he will find the beginnings of attitudes, because there has not been time for enough repetition to have set them firmly; it is in the very far yesterday, in the first act.

But the near yesterday can provide clues as to where to start. I was standing at the sink washing dishes one evening, feeling depressed and wondering why I felt depressed, for I had been to the doctor the day before and he had said there was nothing wrong with me, that I should just ignore the collection of symptoms I had. It occurred to me that the trouble was that I did not believe him, that that was why I had felt depressed ever since I left him. But I went on thinking and realized that I always felt depressed when a doctor told me there was nothing wrong with me. I could recall time after time when this was so, and also the happy

36

relief on the occasions when the verdict was: well, you've got this or that and it has got to be taken care of.

Even I could appreciate that this was a paradoxical way to feel, and as I thought about it, suddenly a sentence popped into my mind just as clearly as though the man speaking it were standing behind me. It was my father's voice saying, "For God's sake, do you want the child to die!" Tears came to my eyes, and I remembered, for the first time in all the long intervening years, when he had said it—even that he had said it. I had been sick for several days, but my mother believed that only her own illnesses were serious and left it to my father finally to call a doctor. The doctor came, made his examination, and went away with a blood sample, then telephoned to say I had acute appendicitis and must be brought to the hospital at once, that there was not time to send an ambulance. My mother sat down at her dressing table and began putting her make-up on, and my father, trying to bundle me in a blanket, shouted to her, "For God's sake, do you want the child to die!" My mother answered that she could not go out without combing her hair, and I heard her answer as, "Yes, I want the child to die."

One does not live with such knowledge and I forgot it immediately, but the knowledge lived on in me. As an adult, I went to the doctor, and when he said there was nothing wrong with me, somewhere out of my awareness I transferred the feeling to him that he was going to let the child die, and I became depressed. Even now, I cannot write about the memory without a feeling of despair, so remembering does not end the emotion, but its influence on my life is over. Four years ago, I saw a doctor about what seemed a silly thing: a fifty-cent-sized area in the back of my head that echoed hollowly when I brushed my hair. As I expected, he laughed and dismissed it with a joke about my having a hole in my head. The fact that, when finally investigated, it proved to be a tumor that had gone through the skull and was beginning to invade the brain, although fascinating to me, is not important in this context except to say that I had not expected interest and care and I did not get it, but in a parallel, though less serious, situation this past winter, I now knew my characteristic way of behaving, ordered myself not to behave in that way, and got immediate, effective treatment.

There are differences in competence and thoroughness among doctors, of course, but I do not really believe that was so much the case in these two experiences as the difference in me. My unconscious communication—you won't take this seriously; you will take this seriously—was perfectly understood, unconsciously, by the two doctors.

Is the moral of this tale that, if you come to understand your transferences, the life you save may be your own? Perhaps, in a way, it is, even if it is usually one's psychological life that is being saved, not one's physical life. Your life may indeed be your own, to direct as you will, not as you unconsciously remember, if you can find the live coals of the past. To free the self from automatic, repetitive, reinforcing behavior based on transference of past attitudes to present-day people is to come into full possession of the self. To stop behaving in what has been called an "as if" fashion: as if the past were the present, as if the people of the past were demons with the power to assume the shapes of current loves and current enemies, is to enable the self to act imaginatively and appropriately and discriminatingly.

We fight old battles so long after peace should have been declared. If we hold our ground and stay with the struggle, we are defeated. If we give up the struggle and flee, the demons simply bide their time until a new friend is made, a new love is found, and then they go to live in the new bodies. And so it goes, unless, with luck, we learn that demons cannot be defeated; they can only be confronted and laid to rest.

T o reconstruct the first act of a life takes active digging through the strata of childhood, and it is tricky to distinguish a genuine find from an artful reproduction. A memory of clarity and force may simply be a screen in front of a deeper event. A recollection convincing in its ugliness may be a false lead planted to encourage digging in a neutral area. As natives "salt" an ancient location with modern artifacts, so the landscape of memory may be salted to send the tourist away happy at having dug up "the real thing" when, in fact, he has been decoyed from the original ruins.

A small story about A_____ shows how the trappings of authenticity can be misleading. A_____, who had her problems and knew it, reconnoitered the present rather thoroughly and decided that memories of her younger brother were a promising site for excavation. She was elated when she succeeded in digging up a memory of bathing him at a time when he was an infant and she guessed herself to be four or five. Dragging the memory into the light, she pieced it together: he had been wet and slippery and had squirted from her grasp, falling to the floor and rolling into a corner. It was clear why she had forgotten this event, for it showed that she had so longed to have her parents' love all to herself that she had gone to the lengths of near murder. Remembering this, she felt that her days of being competitive with men and guilty about it were over. But they were not. She was haunted by the memory of an atrocious deed, and she felt angry toward men for arousing guilt in her. This was disappointing, for she felt that she had made an honest effort to face her past and the honest effort had not released her. It was not for quite awhile that she realized there were discrepancies in the story. Why had the baby, crashing to the floor, remained unhurt? And what was she doing bathing the baby in the first place? At such a young age she would not have been allowed to. She asked her mother if she remembered the incident, and her mother laughed and said it had never happened. Then A____ remembered the true incident. She had been playing with a cake of soap while her mother washed the baby, and it was the soap that had squirted out of her hands and rolled into the corner. And with that, her guilt ended, for a wish is not an action, and one can forgive oneself a small child's understandable wish.

Reconstructing the first act may seem comparable to digging at random in the deserts of the Middle East for the remains of biblical cities. But the sandy wastes are not featureless to the educated eye, and things are known that are common to all cities: they must be near some source of water and they come into being on traveled routes. Likely sites can be identified before the digging is undertaken. And so can they also in infancy and childhood, for all of us had requirements in common and all of us passed through the same stages. If the requirements and stages are known, it can immensely simplify the question of where to dig.

The Adventures of X

The life of a baby being a subject that interests me almost not at all, I shall stave off discussing it by recounting instead the adventure that befell X. I call him X because, when his story starts, X was a victim of total amnesia. He did not remember his name nor his previous life nor how he had gotten where he was. The best guess was that he had been a flyer and there had been an accident. When he came to, he seemed to be in a dark cave, and apparently there were no broken bones because he could move his limbs, but his brain was barely functioning and he soon slipped back into unconsciousness. How long he remained in the cave he had no idea. Weak and helpless, he dozed, moved a little, dozed again. Since he was warm, not hungry, and perfectly comfortable, he made no effort to rouse himself. He was content to let things be as they were.

But paradise is lost as well as gained, and one day he woke to find himself being hauled unceremoniously into the light. Anxiety flooded through him, and he screamed in terror. For the first time since the accident, he feared for his life. It was a primitive, consuming fear that washed through every cell, every capillary. Coming out of darkness, his brain was seared with glare and his eyes blinded. Sounds beat at his ears. Cold penetrated every pore. For all he knew, the natives who had yanked him from his hiding place had yanked him into hell.

Apparently, though, they did not intend to kill him. They covered him and laid him down, and, exhausted, X fell asleep. He slept most of the next days and weeks. He was too weak even to lift his head; all his energy was concentrated inward on the effort to stay alive. Unable to speak and at the mercy of the natives for his every need, he called out when he woke, cried helplessly when no one came. This may not seem very admirable behavior, but put yourself in his shoes: he was feeble and helpless; he was surrounded by strangers whose ways and intentions he did not know; his mind was barely working; his eyes scarcely saw; he knew little beyond that he was alive and totally dependent.

But gradually his panic began to subside and his mind emerged fitfully from its haze. As he gained a little strength, his attention flickered outward for brief moments, and he tried to gather some clues as to where he was and whether the natives were friendly. He noticed that apparently one native in particular had been deputized to look after him and that it was usually she who came when he needed something, although occasionally it was her assistant, a man. Since she was gentle enough in handling him and even seemed to be rather fond of him, he began to feel somewhat reassured about his situation. His longing for the serenity and simplicity of the cave did not end, but it grew less intense. His new environment more and more engaged his attention. And he had one success, which encouraged him to believe he might be able to learn to get along. He noticed the woman smiling at him, and he smiled back. This seemed to delight her, and she called other natives to come to see. He obligingly smiled at them, figuring that if this was what they wanted, this was what he would do.

As time went on, X gained strength, but it was a slow business and he still did little but sleep. In his waking moments, lying on his back and looking at the ceiling, he speculated about what kind of place he had landed in and what sort of people he would encounter when he was able to be up and around. He took it for granted that the woman who cared for him was typical of the natives, so he stored up every clue he could glean from her behavior. He listened to her tone of voice for hints as to whether she was happy or discontent. He noted how she handled him so as to guess whether he must be prepared to deal with a hostile people or a peaceful one. He counted how long it was after he signaled he was hungry before she came with food, so he would know whether, later, he would have to battle for sustenance or would obtain what he needed quite readily. He eavesdropped on the talk around him, although he could not understand the language, to learn whether this was a place where the people quarreled a good deal among themselves or whether they got along equably and enjoyed each other's company. He watched the woman's expression as she tended to his needs to find out whether they were a puritanical or a natural people.

Knowing that his life depended on whether or not the people would accept him once he was able to move about among them, he was most intensely interested in what the woman thought of him. He evaluated her behavior for clues as to whether he would be liked, whether he would be found personable and attractive, whether he would elicit sympathy and interest or be ignored. So preoccupied was he with this that he began to find acceptable in himself anything that she found acceptable and to dislike anything about himself that she disliked. Without realizing it, he came to use her as a mirror to reflect back what sort of person he was.

42

Being so dependent on her, when she went away he wondered desperately if she would ever return. Some of the early anxiety flooded back when he feared she had deserted him. He had so much of her attention that it took a long time for him to realize that she was a person with a life of her own, that her life did not center exclusively on his, that they were two different people. He had viewed her, at first, just as an extension of himself, the legs that could fetch for him, the arms that could bring things to his mouth. His weakness had made him terribly self-centered, as people who are ill are self-centered.

Being together so much, a closeness grew between X and the woman. They developed a language of their own of signs and sounds. She had always been empathic to his needs, but now he began to understand her better, to know her moods and read her expressions. They laughed quite a bit sometimes, and sometimes they were just quiet together. They played small games, and they teased each other. Once, when they were playing, he nipped her to show his increasing strength. He was startled when she pulled back and frowned and spoke sharply. He had not meant to hurt her. He decided it meant that the natives did not like aggressive behavior and that he had best keep any impulses in that direction under wraps.

With the man, whom he was also coming to like and trust as he saw more of him, he could play more roughly, and he enjoyed this because it gave him needed exercise. From them both, he learned how love was expressed in this culture, and he tried to imitate them, for he realized that it was their loving behavior that meant the difference between life and death for him. If he could not make these people who knew him most intimately care about him, he would have to expect little goodwill from the other inhabitants, and so he was alert to any clues and he tried hard to please them.

It was clear by now both that he would survive and that he would be spending a long time among these people, so X set about learning the language. This had both welcome and unwelcome consequences: the increased ease in communicating was satisfying but he had a sense of loss that the direct, wordless communication between himself and the woman was gone. He was nostalgic for that, as he had been nostalgic for the cave and as he was to be for other warm closeness as he grew more competent and better able to look after himself, but he knew he could not remain helpless and dependent always.

The woman knew it too, and she began to point out his responsibility for keeping himself clean. For the first time since he had been with them, X found that he had the upper hand, that he could choose to comply or not. There was some pleasure in testing out this area of autonomy, and a battle of wills seemed to be in the offing. But the woman made an effort to remain good-humored and relaxed, and X, valuing her affection and approval, decided to do his best to meet her wishes.

It is not surprising that, with X becoming more of a person, one of his first acts as a person was to fall in love with the woman. He asked her to marry him, but she pointed out that, not only did he still need a long period of care before he would be able to be on his own, but that she was already married to the man. He considered the first objection no more of a drawback than does the patient who decides to marry his nurse. As for the second, he settled on a straight-forward approach. He told the man he planned to marry the woman and that he would appreciate it if he did not come to the house any more. The man laughed and went right on returning each evening. Brooding on the problem and won-dering if he would have to resort to violent means to get the man out of the way, X considered the possibilities. A most unexpected realization was that the man, being far more powerful and perhaps able to divine his intentions, would strike first and render X impotent to take his place. This threat of castration, although existing entirely in X's mind, so frightened him that he abandoned any plan to take the man's place. Indeed, he went somewhat to the opposite extreme. On the theory that if you cannot beat them, join them, he set about identifying with the man and attempted to become more like him. This episode ended with their be-coming good friends and joint admirers of the woman.

44

X had been with them for about four years at the time of this contretemps, and he learned from it that he had best begin to widen his horizons. Accordingly, he began to venture farther from the woman's side. Initially, of course, he had not been able to walk at all, but as his muscles strengthened, he had tried short steps with the woman's help, and now he was walking fairly well without her aid. He sallied forth to see something of the village, but still stayed close enough to call for help if he needed it. He became acquainted with the natives in the surrounding houses, observed their mores, increased his vocabulary, and acquired some new skills. As far as he could see, he had been right to assume the woman was typical of the other inhabitants, and he confirmed many of the conclusions he had drawn when he had had only her to go on. One of the most pleasing ones was that other people also found him attractive and likable, and this gave him a happy confidence in himself. He made friends easily with the natives. They liked his smile and his sturdiness. They approved of his efforts to learn and to master the world he found himself in.

Each success gave him courage to try for a further success, and the man and woman had taught him well enough so that when he failed, he learned from it and went on. It was satisfying to X to be increasingly self-reliant after his long period of helplessness, and because his problems were few, it was a tranquil time. His keepers were proud that he was learning the ropes and they did not try to hold him back. But they were there when he exceeded his strength or his capacities, and thus he had the best of both independence and dependence.

The culture was not the simple one X had expected. He tended at first to make easy generalizations about the people and their life, but eventually he became able to accept complexity and contradiction. He stopped looking solely for answers and became interested in the questions. He realized that it was more useful to draw inferences than conclusions. He became an avid collector of facts.

And so time passed, and X got along very well. If he remembered the early time at all, it was only on the rare occasions when something threatened to go wrong and some of the anxiety came seeping back. Having learned so much in the twelve years he had been there, X began to feel that he had learned everything, and he was startled to discover that the woman and man, who had once seemed to him to be omniscient, really did not know so much after all. It was clear that he had grown beyond them and they had outlived their usefulness to him. He found his strength and his enthusiasm, not in them now, but in friends. His friends understood him, understood his moodiness, his rapidly changing interests, his concerns, his impatience. He felt guilty that he was turning his back on the man and woman who had saved his life, but he told himself that he had not asked them to bring him into their world.

As tranquil as the previous time had been, this one was stormy. It was not until after it was over and he looked back on it that X knew it had had to be this way. The stirrings within him that had given rise to his rebelliousness were the promptings of knowledge that he must turn outward, must leave this home, must wean himself from this woman and this man if he were ever to find who he really was and where he belonged. It had been a trial time of sailing while still tied to the dock. His old gratitude to the man and the woman came back. He saw that they were wise, and when not wise, they were generous. He saw that they had done their best and that they loved him. He saw that he loved them, and it did not lessen him but enrich him. They had sheltered him for twenty-one years, and now they knew they must let him go. Their job was over. It was up to him now to find his own people.

X never did anything harder in his life than leave them.

The Journey Had Five Legs

If I have a little knowledge, I like to show it off, so now that I have related the story of X, I would like to point out that psychoanalytic labels could be attached to the successive chapters in his adventure. The earliest time was clearly an oral phase. Being fed was the central experience, a passive taking in of food supplied. Since X was given food soon after he notified his world that he was hungry, and since the food was warm and good and agreed with him, he extrapolated this to mean that the new world was a satisfying place and he was justified in taking an optimistic view of it. He expected to be well treated, to have no particular difficulty in obtaining the necessities of life, and to enjoy the love and attention of other people. And, indeed, it worked out this way.

If, on the other hand, X had cried and cried before food arrived, he would probably have decided that the world was heartless and depriving. He would not have expected good things. He would have been pessimistic about his chances, and he might well have decided he was not worthy of being given to. This is a discouraging point of view, and X might have lived his life haunted by a depression he could not shake, finding current reasons for it in fancied inadequacies of his own and the ungenerous behavior of others, never realizing its early roots.

Had the woman looking after X been overly solicitous and offered him food before he had a chance to become aware he was hungry, X might have emerged a lazy, selfish person who expected the world to give and give without any effort on his part. He might have become an endlessly passive spectator, uncommunicative with others except to indicate that he intended being supplied with love and affection whether or no he reciprocated. He would expect the world, in short, to be a huge supplying mother, and if it turned out not to be, he might decide to ignore the real world and create a fantasy one that met his specifications, which would land him in severe trouble indeed.

Another possibility was that X might have been fed sometimes before he was hungry and sometimes long after. In this event, he would not have known what to think of the world. He would have been considerably confused. Should he consider it friendly or hostile? Would it supply or withhold what he needed? Should he be optimistic or pessimistic? He might have spent the rest of his life not knowing what to expect.

In the succeeding phase, when he realized he had teeth and could bite with them, the episode in which he used his teeth and was scolded for it taught him that attacking, biting, sarcastic words were forbidden and he became a rather soft-spoken person who seldom was rude or aggressive. In fact, he leaned too far in this direction and did not stick up for himself in an argument. If the woman had been even more emphatic in her disapproval and had repeatedly scolded him, he might forever have abandoned any idea of fighting back, which would have rendered him helpless in the face of onslaughts of others, too timid to speak his mind, too fearful to claim ideas as his own, too afraid of criticism to speak up. He might have fallen back on his earlier, more successful phase of passive dependency and become stuck with this way of behavior all his life. He might have continually offered the world a nonaggression pact which only he was prepared to observe.

But the woman did not go to this extreme, nor to the other extreme of encouraging him to bite more and harder. Had she done the latter, it is quite possible that hostility would have become an important part of his behavior, a quite acceptable way of behavior to him, as it is to someone I know who has a quick, sharp tongue and a talent for the sarcastic appraisal that cuts a personality to shreds. Make a mild observation to this one and you are liable to find yourself a nonvolunteer assistant in a knife-throwing act, pinned to the wall by verbal darts.

The second period of X's experience was an anal phase, the psychoanalytic label for the time of toilet-training. X, again, was fortunate in his handling. The woman did not institute her requests for cleanliness until his muscular control had advanced to the point where it was not difficult for him to comply. Thus, he did not develop a sense that demands would be made on him discouragingly beyond his ability to meet. And because the woman was relaxed, he learned a relaxed attitude that carried over to other tasks. He could accomplish what he had to. He could conform when it was relevant, but could

48

avoid slavish conformity. He did not overvalue what he himself had created. He was able to throw away things that had lost their value, including ideas. He was flexible, neither too easily swayed nor too rigid. He was able to complete what he started. He was neither frugal nor spendthrift. He was orderly and neat, but not compulsively so.

Had there developed a tense battle of wills between him and the woman, he might have turned into a possessive, withholding person, perhaps a stingy one. He might have come to value money very highly indeed, been interested in the accumulation and retention of it, and been unable to spend it with enjoyment. As well as holding on to money, he might have pursued hobbies such as coin or stamp or antique collecting, hoarding his treasures and gloating over their possession. And he would have been likely to hoard ideas as well, to be rigid in holding to what he believed to the point of obstinacy, to have a stubborn, closed mind. This means, of course, he would be set in his ways, unbending and tending to place a great deal of value on his own opinions, on his own work, on his own accomplishments. He would drive himself, setting high standards of performance and being exacting in his demands on others. The opposite of generous and relaxed, he would have been a precisely neat, clean, and tidy man, like a friend of mind whom I dropped by to wish a good trip to on the day before she was leaving for Europe; her suitcases were open on the floor, and every blouse, every shoe, every piece of underwear was wrapped in a separate piece of tissue paper, as neatly as if she were going to a party and her possessions were presents.

All of this assumes that, had there been a battle of wills, X was, in some measure, not the ultimate winner because he would become toilet-trained but the winner in the sense that he felt it was his own choice to comply, which would give rise to the feeling that he was powerful, and thus he might have become a strongly self-willed person, apt to be more interested in having his own way than in cooperating. If, on the other hand, he had lost the battle of wills, he would probably have tended to give in all of his life, to be compliant and submissive and able to be ordered about. But underneath his compliant behavior, rebellion would have lingered on, and he would have been angry and defiant deep inside. He would have behaved one way but felt another, and thus have been in a state of continuing conflict. He would have taken orders but resented them, been yielding but truculent. He might have been like a friend of mine who does his work well but balks every step of the way, resenting his boss, resenting the demands made upon him, staying home from work often but getting his work done; he has never had a job in which he did not feel put upon even though they have all been well within his capabilities, and he has never had a boss he did not think was unreasonable and dictatorial even though, to their faces, he is affable and docile.

If the woman had instituted his training too soon, before he was physically ready to meet her standards, X might have come to feel himself a failure, a person who tried hard but was doomed to be unsuccessful, and he might have come to despair over his incapability, feeling himself helpless to meet the demands made upon him. If, in contrast, the woman had waited too long beyond the time when he was physiologically ready, X might have become a self-indulgent person who believed standards and deadlines were not for him, that conformity was for the meek, that authority existed to be flouted. He might have become the type of man who strews his clothes about the house and takes it for granted someone else will do the picking up, like a man I once knew all too well who slopped water all over the bathroom floor and then left towels and dirty underwear lying around in it. For X perhaps, as was true for this man, other people's wishes would have come to count for very little, restrictions on his behavior would have been resented, and he would have considered himself a fine, powerful fellow and not to be treated like one of the herd.

But X and the woman apparently negotiated this phase without swinging to one extreme or the other, and X's attention, freed from this area by his growing competence, focused next on the genital area and he entered the phallic or oedipal phase. He, as we saw, fell in love with the woman and wished to have her to himself. Because she was shocked neither by this proposal nor by other manifestations of his interest in sexuality, he did not acquire a fear of, nor a distaste for, this side of himself. He did not consider himself bad or depraved. He did not suppress his interest and he did not feel guilty about it. It was not a secret vice to be hidden, but a natural and enjoyable part of life. Because the woman did not forbid him to express what he felt, he did not have to be furtive or feel ashamed, and he was able to accept with grace the few prohibitions she laid down.

She handled with understanding his desire to marry her and remained loving and kind, thus showing him that love included the sexual but was not confined to it. Since she did not make fun of him, he did not, in later years, come to view himself as inadequate as a lover. He did not insist on proving himself with each woman he met, and he was not preoccupied with sex, nor did he go to the opposite extreme of disclaiming interest in it. He did not look for rejection, but he took it with good grace when it came.

Since the woman did not threaten him with reprisal for nasty thoughts, since she did not punish him, X did not come to view women as castrating creatures to be feared and placated or shunned. When he was opposed in later years, he knew he was opposed fairly and that his masculinity was not being threatened. And since the man did not treat him as a rival and attack him, he came to expect, too, to be treated fairly by men. The castration he had fantasied from the man taught him only to be realistic, to respect other people's rights, and to look to the wider world for pleasures. Nothing the man did or said substantiated this fear, so X could recognize it for the fantasy it was and thus work his way free of it. Nor did he have the bad luck to undergo such an experience as having his tonsils out at this time, so no other event took on the symbolic meaning of castration, which might have rooted it deeply as a lifelong fear.

It is interesting that nothing was said or done to plant the fear of castration in him, that X came upon the thought himself. However that may be, it spurred X to imitate the man and start on a path of accomplishment and attainment. His interest ceased to focus on sexuality, and he entered a latency phase in which it was present but not preoccupying. With his attention turning away from his body, X ventured forth to explore, to learn, to master by trying out situations in play. Neither the man nor the woman tried to restrict his exploration, so they did not communicate fears to him that he would be hurt or overwhelmed if he did not stay under their wing. They had confidence in him, and so he gained confidence in himself. He became stronger, more able, and he never again felt timid about new situations. His experience carried over into all his later years, and he was always able to face the unknown, sure of his ability to master it or, if he failed, to pick himself up and try again.

Had the man and woman held him back, X might have felt that unnamed terrors existed that he was not equal to. Or he might have acquired the view that he was incompetent and not to be trusted to handle himself properly. He might have given up the idea of looking after himself and making his own decisions. Or he might have rebelled and always been foolhardy in an effort to prove something, always looking for challenges to demonstrate that he could meet them, always moving on to other adventures—restless, doubting himself, immature, proving, proving, proving.

Knowing that X had had a long period of helplessness, the man and the woman did not consider that their task in caring for him was at an end but that it had shifted from providing a home to providing a home base, a place from which he could sally forth and a place to which he could retreat. Had they pushed him out, he might forever have felt himself helpless in a hostile world or he might have attacked a world that refused him nurture and successful experiences. He might have grown old without growing up. He might have felt that he must always be independent, even at times when it would be appropriate to be dependent, like a woman I encountered in a hospital. She was a strapping, hearty Scandinavian woman, and she kept coming into my room and exhorting me to get out of bed and walk around. "Walk up and down, up and down, like me," she said. "I've had six operations, and the minute I come to, I start walking. That way you get strong. That way you get well." I asked what her operations had been for. The first had been an abdominal operation; the other five had been hernia repairs.

The woman and the man were easier on X, and thus he was easier on himself than my Scandinavian acquaintance. He was not expected to strain beyond the limits of his competence. He was not faced with tasks that were too much for him. He, and they, were satisfied with one step at a time. Given time to rest, to consolidate his gains, he did not afterwards come apart at the seams when demands were made upon him.

"There is a time to squander and a time to reap." This time of latency was both for X. He seemed to be just living, to be wasting time on games, but he was learning and he was testing. It was preparation for the years when he would be on his own. He widened his knowledge of people by making friends. He distinguished himself further from the man and woman, moved out of their shadow while staying in their warmth. He gulped quantities of facts, for, free of tensions, relatively free of body concerns, and eager to master his environment, education was a delight to him. He had a sense of himself, and he wanted a sense of his world.

It was nothing the man or woman did that nudged him out of latency and into puberty. It was his own growth. The sexuality that had been quiescent came to the fore again, stimulated by biological changes in his body. And now began the final time of testing himself and his ability to be on his own, the final breaking away from dependency, the destruction of the united front the woman, man, and he had presented to the world. So difficult and painful was this to do that he often seemed to attack the man and woman to drive them apart from himself, as though, ambivalent about making the break himself, he would force them into it. There was little they could do to help him now. They could only be patient and trust they had done their early job well enough to allow him to weather this time.

He had learned in the oedipal phase that incest was prohibited, so he had to find other outlets for his sexual drives. Masturbation was one, but it was insufficient, and he had neither the opportunity nor the poise to essay true sexual expression. Thus, by a process of sublimation taking place outside his awareness, he channeled his sexual energy into intellectual pursuits and sports. But since this was only partially effective, he often acted as though driven by an erratic motor, with abrupt changes of direction and speed. He was the soul of helpfulness one day, the image of indifference the next. He cared only for books; he would not open a book. He played baseball avidly one season, considered it a silly game the next. He traveled in a pack; he locked himself in his room alone. He lived in cyclonic disorder; he straightened and cleaned and scrubbed. He dressed as though his name headed the casualty list; he was groomed to the point of elegance.

He became absorbed in abstract questions about truth and beauty, religion and philosophy. He was frequently selfish in practice but altruistic in bent. Social causes, iniquity, injustice engaged his sympathies. He insisted on his prerogative to the the symbols of maturity: cigarettes, alcohol, an automobile. But particularly was he intent upon establishing his own individuality, on separating himself as a person in his own right from the man and the woman.

Because the man and the woman did not fight this, he succeeded and returned to them. As an equal now, he saw they were neither the giants of his early years with them nor the pygmies of the recent ones, but persons as he was a person. They had not been infallible, but they had never failed him by design or neglect. They had cared for him and they had cared about him. They had been able to let him go, and he came back as a friend, the five legs of his journey completed.

Three
THE PERSISTENCE
OF THE PAST

What a pity it is that we were not all as lucky as X,
that we did not come out of our childhoods Sanforized so that,
as adults, we could get in hot water without shrinking. We
all went over the same course. We all went through the same
five, oral, anal, oedipal, latency, and adolescent phases. But
most of us emerged with derivatives that make our lives small
and mean. We pull back from variety. We have, not a wide
range of behavior open to us, but a few tight modes. We are
fearful and anxious and insecure. We find harm where there
is none intended, rejection where there is neutrality, threat
where there is challenge, withholding where there is indifference, monsters where there are people. And we do not know
why.

The Cuffed Flamingoes

A cruel joke has been played on us. We are fated always
to remember what we learned but never to recall the experiences that taught us. Who can remember being born? Yet,
it is possible to speculate that anxiety has its roots in this experience, that dread of abandonment, fears of separation, intol-
erable loneliness go back to this moment. Who can remember
being cared for as an infant? Yet, the model for future give
and take was established then, for being able to love and to
accept love, for optimism or pessimism, for expectations of
satisfaction or disappointment. Who can remember being
toilet-trained? Yet, the mock-up for control of self and manipulation of others, for mastery or submission, for hoarding or
spending, for ambition or resignation was put together then.

55

Who can remember the attachment which developed to the parent of the opposite sex? Yet, this set a pattern for relationships with one's own and the other sex, for rivalry and competitiveness, for reactions to authority, for thoroughgoing or partial acceptance of one's own sexual identity, for fear of passivity or fear of aggression. We cannot remember. But what we have forgotten lives on dynamically. We are racked by the traces of these times, but we have no conceptual labels to put to them.

Because they came first in time, the oral, anal, and oedipal periods were by far the most influential in shaping us. We stored up impressions rapidly, as X did, when new to this world, so as to learn what to expect of it and what it expected of us. Of necessity, we accepted our experience as gospel, and of necessity, we evaluated it with the mind of a child. And therein lies the difficulty. We could not weigh, judge, and discard. We could not compare. We could not search out precedents. We could not understand that an experience might be atypical, that it might be isolated, that it might be meaningless. We could not know that a parent might have failings, inadequacies, vulnerabilities that had nothing to do with us. We could not know that we did not know enough to know.

Our plight was like the plight of young flamingoes shown in a television documentary of African wildlife. Hatched out on a soda lake, the baby flamingoes pittered about on their matchstick legs in the shallow waters of the lake, knowing no other environment and unknowing that a prolonged drought was evaporating the waters of the lake. The soda concentration became so high that, as they stumbled playfully along, cuffs of soda formed on their legs. The cuffs grew, becoming ankle irons. Too young to get away from their inimical environment, the baby flamingoes slogged on, becoming exhausted from the weight of the accretions they were carrying. Thousands fell and could not get back on their feet and go on.

We, too, slog on, weighted by the accretions of childhood. We, too, fall and struggle back to our feet and fall again. Because we do not remember when the accretions formed, we think they are truths. Really, they are just opinions. And because they are opinions that were arrived at with the narrow vision of a child, they are a heavy burden to carry. As psychologist Lawrence K. Frank has written, ". . . it is what the child hears and understands and believes that enters into his emerging personality. He builds up his own private frame of reference, with all the gaps, misunderstandings, distortions, and misconceptions of a three, four, or five year old and incorporates them in his basic concepts and assumptions. Most of us go through life trying to fit all our subsequent experience and learning into this early private frame of reference. Unless someone helps us, we rarely revise or reconstruct our early private version of life and reformulate it in adult terms."

The Army of Occupation

I know a woman, N——, the best time of whose life was spent in a concentration camp. On the way there, in a cattle car, she who had always been high-strung was quieted and shielded by a man who saved her from committing suicide, and in the camp he got food to her and bits of clothing and warnings when there were to be selections. Having lived her life until then in the envelope of her parents' rejection and her husband's contempt, she felt, for the first time, cherished; and in the unspeakable conditions of the camp, she thrived. But when I met her, she had slipped on her old mantle of worthlessness with the resumption of her marriage. She explained this by saying, with guilty nostalgia for that terrible time, that she did not know how to live with happiness, that she could only rise to awful occasions.

And in England shortly after the war, I commented to a Londoner what a relief it must be to have the bombings ended. "Oh," she said, "it was a marvelous time. You forgot about yourself and you did what you could and we were all in it together. It was frightening, of course, and you worried about getting killed, but in some ways it was better then than now. Now we're all just ourselves again." So, it would seem that circumstances of massive assault on the personality chip away the shackles, only for them to re-form when there is a return to the familiar.

Freud spoke of the journey through infancy and childhood being comparable to the advance of an army. As new territory is gained, part of the army remains behind to occupy the commanding heights, that is to say, occupational forces are left at the oral, anal, and oedipal stages. These forces remain very much a part of the army, and there is a strong tendency to fall back on them whenever the weakened army runs into opposition, so long, of course, as extraordinary circumstances have not cut off the line of retreat altogether. But even when this happens, as in the case of the woman in the concentration camp, as soon as the route has been reopened, retreat in the face of difficulty may again be utilized. Retreat, or regression, as it is called, is most readily observed in children. I expect all of us have known a two-year-old who went back on the bottle in reaction to the birth of a sibling, or a three-year-old who regressed to the need for diapers in reaction to his mother's being in the hospital. But regression is also apparent in adults. I have watched a gentleman of my acquaintance run a great many meetings. When B——— wants to carry his view against opposition, he leaves off arguing and exerts a boyish, winning charm that is reminiscent of nothing so much as the delightful blandishments of a nine-year-old boy who wants you to take him to the ball game. While this is not an unappealing way of behavior, other instances of regression can be exasperating, as witness the person who screams or sulks to get his own way and to whom one is likely to burst out with: "Oh, stop being so childish!" Some instances can also be quite disconcerting: I was present at a medical conference because I was responsible for editing the proceedings, and in the course of conferring with the three doctors whose names would be on the book, I remarked that I hoped the material would be in better shape than the previous batch they had given me. One of the doctors, a woman, promptly burst into tears. I soothed her with, in

58

effect, "There, there, don't cry, I didn't mean it," just as hastily as her mother must once have done.

This type of regression is a falling back on a phase of childhood that was effective and satisfying, a use of devices that worked then and an attempt to restructure present situations to resemble those of the earlier and more successful time. But there may be quite an opposite reason for regression. At another scientific meeting, after the papers were delivered and the socializing had begun, a psychologist friend of mine went to the ladies' room with a woman so famous in her field that to identify it might identify her. My friend congratulated the woman on the paper she had given, and the latter, a little tipsy, announced that what she was proudest of in her life was not her scientific achievement but the fact that she had been married three times and each husband had been stolen from a wife he was already married to.

This is reminiscent of the anecdote of the country boy visiting Coney Island and putting coin after coin in a nickelodeon to watch a one-minute strip-tease film. Asked why he was wasting his money, he said the danged machine kept stopping just as the girl was about to remove the last of her clothes. Apparently, the lady scientist could no more get to the denouement of the oedipal period than the country boy could get to the last scene of the film. Stealing one husband did not tack a resolution on the oedipal period; she ran the film over, stealing a second, and ran it again, stealing a third. This urge to re-enactment, this compulsion to live a time over again exists when the period was stormy and a great many troops were tied up in the battle originally. But the film always goes to black before the final scene. The initial frustration is a repeated frustration.

Once More, From the Top

As well as troops being left behind to garrison the various strongholds, fresh troops are recruited from the area to march

59

on with the main army. If a great many troops were recruited at one stronghold, instead of melding into the whole, they may march along but preserve their characteristic identity and exert a powerful and continuing influence. I remember one summer weekend spent with a couple who were dedicated beer drinkers and spurned the use of glasses; as we sat in brilliant sun on the lawn, they tipped back their bottles and drank and their eight-month-old son tipped back his bottle and drank, and suddenly there was very little to choose between parents and child. It was not that the couple regressed to oral modes of behavior so much as that the oral traits had marched right along, through the years the contents of the bottle changing from milk to Coca-Cola to beer but, always in hand, the bottle.

Fixation, like regression, can have its source in a time so gratifying that we cherish its souvenirs the rest of our lives. Or it can have its source in a time so frustrating that it is as though we are helplessly mired in it. It can be baffling to see a person with a troubled and difficult relationship with his parents break away, only to return over and over because he cannot shake free of his dependency needs. O____, the sister of friends of mine, could not wait to go away to college but transferred after a year to a college in the city and lived at home; graduated and took a job in Denver and wangled a transfer back home; quit and persuaded the State Department to send her to Italy and requested a transfer back home; went to Los Angeles and married and brought her husband back home. Those of us watching this yo-yo effect were inclined to lose patience and grumble, "O____ knows she can't get along with her parents. Why doesn't she have the sense to stay away?" But it is *because* she cannot get along with them that she cannot stay away. The relationship has always been bankrupt, but she is driven to return again and again to try to collect on the unpaid debts of her childhood.

The man O____ married is an immature soul whom she caters to and supports and mothers. It is as though she is showing her parents how she should have been taken care of, as though she identifies with him and takes care of herself in him as she wishes she had been looked after, supplies him as

60

she should have been supplied. This is not infrequently the source of our loving care of others. We see ourselves in the other, and we give ourselves in the other the understanding and tenderness we once should have been granted but were not. One way or another, we run through scenes from the first act again and again, all but saying, as a director says to actors when a scene has gone badly, "All right, let's take it once more from the top, and, for God's sake, let's get it right this time!"

The Clock Mechanism

Sometimes we try it with the original cast; sometimes with understudies. We force others into parental roles, or having been "parentified" ourselves by parents who could not be parents and so could not let us be children, we put on a one-man show, simultaneously playing the part of inadequate, unloving parent and inadequate, unloved child. We scarcely know ourselves for what we are, and we rarely know other people. We attribute to them feelings they do not have, attitudes they have not expressed, traits they have not shown. We evaluate them incorrectly, and we respond to them inappropriately.

And we somewhere know we are doing this, but we do not know how to stop because the source of our behavior is unconscious and we have many ingenious defenses to screen feelings that would be unacceptable to us if we became aware of them. One such defense is a reaction formation, that is, a display of the opposite of what is actually so. This is familiar in terms of the common observation: "He acts so superior because he's really got an inferiority complex." C. G. Jung, the Swiss psychoanalyst and theoretician, suggested a diagram of the mind as a circle with a line dividing it in half across the middle, the top half signifying the conscious mind, the bottom half the unconscious. If an x were to be marked at, say, twelve o'clock for a trait that is very prominent in the personality, a second x may be put at six o'clock to stand for its opposite. Let us say that the x at twelve o'clock represents aggression; the x at six o'clock would then represent passivity. The hypothesis is that any trait that is exceedingly emphatic in the personality must needs be so strong because it is defending against the appearance in consciousness of its opposite. In this instance, aggression would be so large a part of the personality because passive wishes were very strong but unconscious and unacceptable. If the passive wishes were less strong or more acceptable, they might be at four o'clock; in which event, aggression would appear at ten o'clock on the top half of the circle, that is, aggression could be correspondingly less prominent because not as great force was needed to hold passive wishes out of consciousness. Another trait in the same personality may seem sufficiently less intense to justify placement at two o'clock; that is, if ambition is present but not consuming, fears of insignificance are present but not too strongly defended against in the unconscious. If dependency wishes are at three o'clock and the drive to be independent at nine o'clock, then both are of ordinary strength and neither needs to be defended against, and both are conscious or very nearly so.

I remember a close friend of mine calling on the telephone and starting off in such a high key, in such a pressured tone, that I said, "Hey, take it easy." She good-naturedly said, "Oh, am I coming on like gang-busters again?" She knows just how aggressive she is apt to sound—and be; her aggressiveness is conscious and acceptable. She has lately been asked by a man she loves to marry him, and her hesitation has been based on the most surprising point. Having previously paid little attention to her material welfare, she now speaks again and again of her doubts whether he can take care of her, whether he can supply everything she needs, coming back repeatedly to the statement: "I don't mind depriving myself, but I am not going to let someone else do it to me." Not only is the worry about money uncharacteristic of her, it is also unrealistic, since the man makes twenty thousand a year. Perhaps it becomes explicable, though, if the aggression that is such a visible part of her personality is seen as a defense against a very strong, but deeply repressed, wish to be passive. In this light, her doubts seem a symbolic expression of her fear that to be passive, to be dependent, means to put herself in a position to be failed, to be hurt.

62

Substitution, a second type of defense mechanism, involves allowing ourselves to be conscious of one feeling as a defense against becoming aware of another feeling. We may admit to ourselves, for example, that we feel depressed when the fact of the matter is that we are frightened. Or we may become quite angry when, in truth, we are hurt. Each of us has emotions that we will allow ourselves to feel and others that are unacceptable. Objectively, one emotion may be quite as painful as another, or even more so, but one fits our picture of ourselves and the other does not.

Another device for warding off awareness of unacceptable emotions is projection. I used to go to visit a friend of mine, and time and again, on the drive from the station, he would say something like: "You didn't look very happy when you stepped off the train." This never failed to baffle me because I thought I felt happy, but when I said this, he would answer sadly, "You just say you want to come, but you don't really." I hate to confess how long it was before I realized that it was he who did not want me to come, but it is really extremely difficult to unmask projection. You protest that you do not feel what you are accused of feeling, but, of course, the more you protest, the more unconvincing it sounds, and you end up believing that the other person may know you better than you know yourself. Besides, projection often masquerades as an enviable degree of insight. I long admired a friend of mine who was able to detect, about mutual acquaintances, that one was "a very hostile man" and another was a person with "a tremendous need to be liked." I could not imagine how I was so obtuse as not to have noticed these striking traits until at last it dawned on me that everybody was either one or the other in her eyes and that the person she was really describing was herself.

Aristotle noted that: "Anyone can become angry—that is easy; but to be angry with the right person, and to the right degree, and at the right time, and for the right purpose, and in the right way—that is not within everybody's power and is not easy." For "angry," read any other emotion. We so often respond inappropriately to a situation or to a person because the defense mechanisms of denial, repression, substitution, or projection are operating to skew our own reactions and to cause us to misjudge those of others. Unhappily, we do not expand into adulthood; we narrow into it. We do not increase and refine our range of responses; we limit them. Our defenses form a carapace around us, as the shell encases the crab, and we end by becoming as constricted as the crab.

The Institute for Delinquents

I was with a friend and her child in a bakery when the boy, G——, told several times that he could not have a chocolate eclair, threw himself on the floor and kicked and screamed. His mother asked for a chair, sat down, placed the child over her knee and spanked him, thoroughly and dispassionately. G—— has not had a temper tantrum from that day to this. That kind of response, wild anger in the face of frustration, has been eliminated from his repertory of available responses. He may deny consuming anger, repress it, substitute a feeling of helplessness for it, or accuse a vis-à-vis of it, but he will not feel rage even if the occasion should be appropriate for it.

Since we have all seen a screaming child get slapped and go right on screaming, clearly it is not just corporal punishment that caps the well of rage. Something more has happened. That something more is a subtle, but nonetheless present, threat of losing the mother's love. G——'s mother spanked him so matter-of-factly, so without any anger of her own in a situation in which she might well have shown anger, that she communicated how deeply she disapproved of rage. She did not use it to get her own way, i.e., to have G—— stop screaming, and she indicated that she would not stand for his using it to get his own way. It was unacceptable to her, and if he himself was not also to be unacceptable to her, he must rule rage out as a possible response. The screaming child who gets slapped by an equally screaming mother, on the other hand, has received no such communication. He has been told to stop screaming for this moment, but not for all time.

Loss of love is a powerful threat which parents utilize, albeit usually covertly, to socialize their children. The child is so dependent on being loved and safeguarded that he will disavow emotions that bring disapproval down on him. Soon, the admonition need not even come from the parent; the parent's spanking hand and scolding voice are, so to speak, internalized. They have set up shop within the child and make the same prohibitions upon the child as the parent even if the parent is not present. Thus is conscience born, or, in other terms, the superego.

The superego becomes an internal judge of behavior in the same fashion as the parents are an external judge of behavior. The prohibitions the parents set up are the prohibitions the superego takes over and enforces. The types of behavior the parents reward are the types of behavior the superego rewards. And the superego uses the same means of enforcement: the reward of love and the punishment of loss of love. If the feelings are approved of, there is a rise in self-esteem. If the feelings are disapproved of, there is a fall in self-esteem. Since it is acutely painful not to like oneself, the defenses come into being to ward off the disapproved-of emotions. G_____ represses rage because he would like himself considerably less if he let it come through in behavior, he would feel guilt and anxiety, but he is cavalier in considering other people's sensitivities because his mother approves of going one's own way. My aggressive friend is well aware that coming on like gang-busters irritates other people, but she experiences no fall in her own self-esteem and so she makes no effort to tone down her driving qualities.

It is, of course, not quite so simple as a one-to-one correspondence between what the parents approve of and what the superego approves of. A parent may punish delinquent behavior, only to have the child persist in delinquent acts. This may be because such an activity as stealing symbolizes defiance to the child, and the need to express defiance, perhaps because of an experience in the anal period, overrides the parents' prohibition; the superego esteems the defiance and does not punish it with guilt or anxiety, even though the parents may disapprove of it vehemently. Or the parents may verbally disapprove of it but be secretly proud of the child's enterprise, and the child will pick up this unconscious communication. All too often children are manipulated, outside their own conscious awareness and that of their parents, into acting out emotions that the parents have repressed in themselves. I remember reading the case history of a fifteen-year-old girl whose promiscuity, which the parents deplored, ended the day she said, "My mother will just have to do her own running around from now on."

Attitudes derived from the parents, needs stemming from the experiences in the oral, anal, and oedipal phases, and a third factor structure the superego. This third factor is the strength of inborn, instinctual drives. We were not all born with the same quantum of aggressive drives or passive drives or sexual drives. It is an individual matter. One baby will reach out for toys energetically, grasping them and bringing them to his mouth; another will lie for a very long time just looking at toys before he tentatively reaches to touch them. This is a part of the baby's make-up, and the superego of a baby with strong aggressive drives will develop differently from that of a baby whose behavior is instinctively tentative and contained.

The instinctual drives and needs are collectively known as the id. The repository of self-preservative and sexual drives, the id is utterly imperious, demanding, indulgent, heedless, insensitive, uncompromising, and unaccommodating. And it remains so. The id drives go underground, but they never moderate. This is one of the reasons why we are afraid of self-exploration. We sense their existence, and we fear their exposure. We dread the possibility of being inundated by the irrational and the primitive. We do not wish to acknowledge the remnants of the infantile in ourselves. For most of us, though, the id is a toothless tiger, a tiger we can ride, not end up inside.

In infancy, the id has the field to itself, and the drives tumble forth into expression unimpeded. We scream when hungry without a thought about whether it is convenient for someone to feed us at that moment. But, eventually, we begin to realize that it does take someone to feed us. We realize that there is something other than ourselves. We become aware that there is a world and that it is larger than we are and that we are dependent on others to meet our needs. And this slight awareness of an environment, of an area that is not self, means a beginning awareness of a self. With awareness of a self, the ego comes into existence.

It is the ego's function to mediate between the id and reality, between the drives pushing unrestrainedly for satisfaction and the world that is not self in which the satisfaction must be obtained. The ego is assigned, in effect, the job of being gate keeper at an institute for delinquents, the middleman between the inmates and the surrounding countryside. Initially, it has not a chance of keeping the clamoring inmates inside; they rush past at will, swarming over the countryside and protesting rowdily if they do not get what they want. In its strategic position at the gate, however, with a view of the countryside and an opportunity to watch the comings and goings of the local residents, the ego begins to acquire a good deal of useful information, and the inmates fall into the habit of consulting it about the direction and timing of raids, the disguises they should assume, and how much the residents will stand for without retaliating. In the guise of helping the inmates to get what they want with the greatest effectiveness and the least trouble, the ego gradually establishes control over the traffic passing through the gate, although it is the precarious authority of the pirate captain who remains in command only as long as he can get sufficient plunder for his men.

With some sort of order having been imposed on the hitherto unruly inmates, the local residents authorize their representative, the superego, to take over the administration of the institution and to restrict and discipline the inmates further. The superego requisitions the control tower for its headquarters and lays down rules and regulations and establishes disciplinary procedures, delegating the ego as a deputy to carry them out. Having nothing to do other than to keep an eye on the inmates, the superego knows far better than the ego when the inmates are threatening to get out of line, but it charges the ego with the responsibility for making them behave and it is the ego that gets punished if they fail to. The superego calls the ego to account for any slip, making the ego feel guilty and incompetent and anxious. The ego, afraid of its boss, does its best, but it has not only the superego to satisfy; it must keep the inmates content by slipping some of them through the gate at reasonable intervals and it must be accurate in its judgment of how much the inhabitants of the countryside will stand for without complaining to the superego. How well the ego manages under these pressures depends on the benignity of the inhabitants, the tractability of the inmates, the strictness of the superego, and, most of all, on its own strength.

The Esteemed Self

The strength of the ego is determined by, in a word, love. The good opinion, the warmth, the approval, the affection of parents and people around the developing child give him confidence in himself. They are a warrant of help and protection should he need it, but they are also encouragement to autonomy because his protectors take pride and pleasure in his growing competence. The child who is loved can love himself. And the ego that is loved is a strong ego. It does not fear id insurrections; it does not fear superego retaliation; and it does not doubt its own ability to comprehend reality.

The superego, as it evolves in turn, can afford to be benevolent. Like an employer who has a trustworthy foreman, it need not be on the job every minute, overseeing, snooping suspiciously, seeking out signs of substandard performance. There is no need for the superego to become strict and punishing, to threaten with guilt, depression, anxiety, and loss of self-esteem.

68

But this happy state of affairs is not very common. Most of us fairly often experience guilt or anxiety or depression. Whether this is because we have been unloved, ambivalently loved, or inconsistently loved, the fact is that it causes us a good deal of suffering. Is the answer simply to do everything possible to stay on good terms with one's superego, that is, to avoid feelings, attitudes, and behaviors the superego punishes? This is the answer we try. This is the job that the carapace is designed to do.

If I may speak about myself, which is unavoidable because I do not have this kind of information about anyone else, I am an exceedingly pleasant, mild soul, most given to avoiding any hurt to others. Nonaggressiveness, indeed, is so prominent, so insistent a part of my personality that, on Jung's circle, an x standing for it would have to be placed at twelve o'clock in the conscious half, which means that another, standing for aggressive and hostile drives, must go at six o'clock in the unconscious. To be so deeply buried and so strongly defended against suggests that these drives are totally unacceptable. Thus, I must avoid any expression of them if I am to stay on comfortable terms with my superego. All well and good, but then there comes such a day as when I was asked to attend a meeting the purpose of which was to analyze a play written by one of the writers there. I had read the play carefully and had what I thought were intelligent comments to make about it, so it never occurred to me to make some excuse not to attend. I went, I listened to the other criticisms, and I waited for my turn. As it approached, my hands were suddenly dripping wet, blood pounded up the back of my head, and I thought I was about to faint. I was not sure I would be able to speak, but I managed to mutter a few words of praise and then said I had nothing to add in criticism.

My superego, knowing better than my ego that aggressive id drives were about to slide through, brought on a severe attack of anxiety. Well-intentioned and invited criticism was interpreted as an expression of aggression and was effectively inhibited. Since I had not known that it would so seem to me unconsciously, I had not been able to avoid the provocative

69

situation. But this inability always to predict the circumstance the superego will disapprove of is not the only barrier to simple avoidance as a means of staying on good terms with the superego. The superego has not only negative views but positive ones as well. My self-esteem was not restored by having mumbled a few noncommital sentences containing no hint of criticism. It remained shattered because I knew perfectly well that I had behaved like an idiot.

There is no constraint on the superego to be consistent. It can sharply punish behavior which, though adult, is unacceptable to it, and turn right around and punish unadult behavior. Self-esteem depends just as much on viewing ourselves as autonomous, adaptable adults as on not indulging in ruled-out behavior. There is a push in all of us toward self-actualizing, self-expressive behavior, toward growth and change and expansion. We wish to behave appropriately and adaptively, and when we cannot, we curse ourselves as failures. It is no answer for me, for example, to avoid all future such meetings. I would know myself to be childish and helpless, and I would have no way of liking myself in the face of that.

We make our world restricted and our behavior inflexible in order to avoid situations of threat to our self-esteem. And in such fashion do we lose our self-esteem. The attempted cure for anxiety produces anxiety, for we appreciate how implacably we block our own push toward easy and adult ways of reacting and behaving. The very act of side-stepping situations in which we sense we shall fail is an admission of failure which brings down upon us our own painful disapproval. There is no way of steering successfully between a failed situation and a failed self except by stopping and taking our bearings.

Four
TRACKS IN
THE CLOUD CHAMBER

T o watch the documentary film of the baby flamingoes was almost unbearably poignant. Thousands sank down, dead of exhaustion, and thousands pitched forward and drowned in an inch of water. It is poignant, too, to watch my aggressive friend drive away the man she loves with her endless, senseless questions about his ability to support her. I can say, "Look, old girl, this doesn't sound like you. It must be concealing some other feeling," but I cannot simply take a hammer and crack off the accretions, as men did to save the surviving flamingoes when their plight became known. My friend has spent the years since she was small energetically and insistently believing one thing about herself; if she is ever to disbelieve it, it must be through her own efforts. A crab can shed his carapace when he outgrows it, but he cannot survive having it peeled off by force.

Having described so glibly my own repression of aggression at the playwrights' meeting, it must sound as though I had found understanding it no problem, as though I had simply gone home and said to myself, "Now, Jo, the problem is that you are afraid of the aggressive drives in yourself and they threatened to slip out and you had an anxiety attack, and then you got anxious all over again because you felt you'd behaved stupidly and you were worried everyone else had noticed and probably made fun of you after you'd gone." On the contrary. I came home and kicked the cat and said, "Damn it, damn it, damn it, what's wrong with me! Why can't I behave like a reasonable human being!" I then sat down and went thoughtfully and intelligently over what had happened: nobody said hello to me when I entered the meeting, a snide crack about lady playwrights made me feel insecure, a fellow I never had liked blew clouds of cigar smoke in my face and almost made

71

me faint. It was obvious that it had not been my fault in the least. Thus did I ease myself off the hook and stop the bleeding.

But some fresh trauma reopened the wound, as had happened uncounted times before. This was only one, and the least humiliating, episode in an unending procession, and finally it came upon me with despair that there was to be no end unless I myself blew the whistle. Because this episode was in some ways the most amenable to dissection, for it did not involve complex and loving relationships that might drift into dust if probed, it seemed a possible place to start and I looked at it again. I admitted that I had been afraid to criticize the fellow's play. There was a sense of relief in recognizing this, and even a sense of pride, for the next comment was: "What's wrong with being a decent, kind human being? There are enough critics in the world."

In such fashion is a necessity turned into a virtue. I gave myself a pat on the back and went striding off confidently—to fall on my face again. Only when I told myself that I was trying to understand my behavior in order to understand it, not to judge it, only when I persuaded myself not to be interested in my opinion of what I was doing but simply in what I was doing, was I able to come up with the statement which opened the gate: "I am a crippled human being." But the gate was only unlatched, and the next question, "Crippled how?", did not get me through it. It proved as impossible to study my traits directly as it is to study subatomic particles directly. The characteristics of subatomic particles cannot be observed; they can only be inferred from the tracks their passage leaves behind in a cloud chamber: to make such and such a track, the invisible must have such and such properties. I turned away from, "Crippled how?" to ask, "Where does it show up?"

What Do A Potato and an Onion Have in Common?

A friend argues with me that I am an old-fashioned playwright because I am concerned, first of all, with the plot of a play, with what is happening, while she herself is not interested in what her characters do but in what they are. My claim is that plot *is* character: Macbeth is not known to be ambitious because he says he is but because he murders Duncan to become king himself; Othello is not known to be jealous because he says he is but because he strangles Desdemona. I have not convinced my friend but I have convinced myself that people are what they do, not what they say. For example, while hunting a nursing home for my mother, I talked to the proprietor of what looked to be an attractive and pleasant place and was favorably impressed by her description of how she and her charges were one big happy family, all eating together and living together, not in an institutional atmosphere, but in homelike companionship, and I had about arrived at a decision when a tiny old lady wandered out into the hall where we were standing and reached for the knob of the outside door. The proprietor snatched her arm, whirled her around, and gave her a push that sent her reeling. I thanked the proprietor for her time, said I would think it over, left, and was not heard from again in that quarter.

Her action, not her self-description, was what I believed. It was the track in the cloud chamber that allowed me to know her. And it seems to me that this is how we can know ourselves, not by asking: What am I like? but by asking: What do I do? This is not to imply that the question of why is unimportant but to suggest that the way to get at *why* is to start with *what*. When I started with: Why did I have an anxiety attack?, all I got from myself were rationalizations. When I asked: What was I doing?, I could reply that I was about to be critical and then I could think back to other times when it was appropriate to be critical and remember what my reaction had been.

A——, who mistook a cake of soap for her brother, made no headway with her problem with men until she searched for a common denominator in her ways of behaving toward them. She was a quite successful seller of mutual funds, a lively and dynamic woman who was attractive to men and had an active social life but somehow had not married despite a succession

73

of suitable candidates. She asked herself why she broke each engagement and answered that it was because she made more money than each of the men and this made her feel guilty, as though she were undermining their masculinity. But this was an insight without urgency and without usefulness. It happened that a new man was hired in the office, and her sales, which had slumped, began to boom. Not being involved with this man, she was better able to remark the coincidence. And it occurred to her, when she thought back, that it was not a coincidence, that her sales always went up when a new man loomed. What she was doing was working harder. What she was doing was competing. And competitiveness, once she had isolated it, proved to be the common denominator in her relationships with men. Knowing *what*, she could then assume, since it was habitual, that it had its roots in her childhood, and she could begin to look for the *why*.

The beginning of insight, the approach that makes the acquisition of insight possible, is acknowledgment of the probability that common denominators underlie our actions and that these will not be numerous but few. With this hypothesis, it is possible to cut through the trimmings and lay bare the base. What we are looking for is not what we have done differently each time but the underlying strata of consistency, not the springs that bubble to the surface but the underground stream that is their common source. To identify this stream is easier for some minds than others because some minds are given to extracting similarities, to seeing broad resemblances, while others focus more readily on points of difference. There is a question, for instance, on one of the widely used intelligence tests that is not the same as, but is very like, this one: In what way are a potato and an onion alike? One may answer, correctly, that they both have skins, or that they are both round, or that they are both eaten, or that they both grow underground, but the highest level of abstraction is that they are both vegetables. This answer categorizes them in the fullest way, not on a single point of resemblance. And that is what we are after: the broad category into which seemingly disparate behavior fits.

The Texan from New York

Out of all the welter of actions in our lives, which should be examined for clues to a common denominator? Perhaps the most obviously in need of exploration are those happenings which have been handled very badly, as my playwrights' meeting was. Such an incident is unequivocally a personal failure, and the reactivity must have a personal source. Because of the discomfort involved, the incentive is often greatest to analyze what has happened at such a time, particularly if it can be admitted that the incident is one of a series, as it theoretically must be to have caused a reaction so out of proportion to the stimulus. Overreactivity is a blatant sign that a buried, and characteristic, problem has been triggered into. Although it may seem on the surface to be an isolated incident, extraction of its common denominator will show it to be a spring fed by a main stream.

In the case of A____, on the other hand, it was a chronic, rather than an acute, situation that set her to thinking. The very fact that breaking an engagement was a repeated, not an isolated, incident eventually made it stand out, directing her attention to this area and making her ask herself what she was doing. Too great a consistency should make us suspicious of actions, for behaving in an invariable way suggests that we are responding not to outside stimuli but to inner promptings. It may be well, even if we are not aware of any particular dissatisfactions, to look at the broad areas of living, such as family relationships, marriage, friendship, career, sex, to see if a record of consistency is a disguised record of failure.

To complicate matters, it is just as necessary to be suspicious of an area of inconsistency. In every store visited by a friend of mine on her Saturday shopping rounds, she is greeted with a big, "Hi, Tex!" by the salespeople, who, when she first moved to town, assumed she must be from Texas because of her breezy, offhand manner and her habit of saying, "Howdy!" This would not be curious except that it strikes her friends as curious. We have never heard her say, "Howdy," a ld she is not breezy and offhand with us. I have no idea of why she needs to be seen one way by tradespeople and another by her peers, but if I were she, I would be interested in finding out, not in order to change the behavior, which does her no harm and brings pleasure to the dry cleaner, but because it is out of character, and what is out of character can throw light on what the character is. If "Tex" does look at the inconsistency and tells herself it is because she likes people or because she believes in democracy or because she is brightening the corner where she lives, she can throw such praiseworthy explanations out immediately. Isolated acts may have an impersonal motive, but a habitual mode of behavior comes out of personality, not theory.

While it is necessary to be suspicious of singular behavior which can readily be explained in global and self-congratulatory terms, it is equally essential to have a high index of suspicion for actions which cannot be explained short of excessive rumination. If you find yourself brooding about an event, your thoughts returning to it compulsively and getting ever more elaborate in an effort to come up with an interpretation that will allow you to dismiss it from your mind, stop thinking about why and turn to what. The more convoluted an explanation, the less likely it is to be true. It has been found in science that the tortuous explanation, the one that twists this way and that in order to cover all aspects, is the one that eventually proves to be wrong; and it is true in life, too, that the explanation elegant in its simplicity is, in all probability, the correct one. This is the law of parsimony: the simplest explanation that at the same time covers the greatest number of examples is most likely to be the correct one.

Remember at the time of the U-2 incident how a succession of statements was issued? Along about the third or fourth, I expect we all became convinced that we were not being told the truth. The more versions given out, the less likelihood that any one of them is accurate, a fact we are aware of when listening to other people's multiplying explanations but are apt to forget when judging our own. Someone I know said after one dinner party that the food had been too delicious to bother with distracting talk, after another that she had really been too tired to talk, after another that the conversation had centered on money so she had not bothered to join in, and after another that the people were too unintelligent to make it worthwhile to hunt for some common conversational grounds. This is a woman much too bright to be able to fool herself with an unvarying explanation and quite bright enough to come up with a new explanation each time she repeats the same maladaptive behavior.

To sum up, actions that are most likely to reveal a common denominator are those that are too consistent and those that are contradictory, those that can be flatteringly explained and those that must be overexplained, as well as those that make for discomfort, whether the form the discomfort takes is anxiety, guilt, or depression.

Paris or Bed

Several years ago, there was a description in *Time* magazine of a young girl born without the capacity to feel pain. As the story pointed out, before one gets too sunk in envy of a person who never has a headache, never is plagued by the throb of a cut finger, never is sorry she ate pickles and ice cream, the life-threatening side of the coin must be looked at: she can break a leg and not know it until the lameness is permanent, lower herself unsuspectingly into a scalding bath, walk around with a ruptured appendix. Pain, much as we dread experiencing it, has an indispensable warning function. That same warning function is served, on the psychological side, by anxiety, guilt, and depression. They are as useful as pain to signal that there is a threat to the integrity of the organism. While they are not pleasant, of course, and the impulse is to apply a poultice rather than probe them, if acknowledged and faced, they are extremely telling tracks in the cloud chamber. The difficulty, interestingly enough, may be in recognizing their presence. A gentleman I know plans a trip to Europe every

77

time a relationship grows close and warm, telling himself he is a wanderer and needs travel to renew and refresh himself. No trace of anxiety appears on the surface and he, I am certain, does not experience it, but I know by now that we have only to spend a particularly happy evening together for him to call Pan Am the next day and inquire whether there is a single seat available on a flight to Paris. Why the fear of closeness makes him anxious I do not know, but if he could allow himself to acknowledge the anxiety, he could watch for when it turns up and then look for the common denominator in the situations.

Another acquaintance of mine does not go to Paris; she goes to bed. She sleeps twelve, fourteen hours a night and, on weekends, from Friday night to Sunday afternoon. I have known her to do this six months at a time and then revert to a normal eight-hour schedule. She says she has finally gotten rested, but there is no degree of physical fatigue that is not alleviated by a few nights of sound sleep. It is mental fatigue from fighting off anxiety or depression that brings on this amount of exhaustion. Someone else I know does the opposite: exists on four hours of sleep a night and works indefatigably the other twenty hours. His reason is that he does not wish to live to be old, like his predecessors in his very long-lived family, and is determined to wear himself out by middle-age. True? I don't know. But I do know that you can ward off awareness of being anxious or depressed if you are never still. For myself, I seldom am aware of feeling depressed, but I often decide to give up writing for some other profession, and it turns out to be the same thing.

Does it matter if it is Paris or bed or a new profession instead of anxiety or depression or guilt? It matters for the same reason that it is better to have an X-ray than to take cough medicine for a persistent hack. A cough can be narcotized for stretches of time but it will return, and in the meantime the underlying disease process goes untreated. It sounds too sanguine to say we should be grateful for symptoms because they let us know when something is wrong, but if we can hold still until they work their way to the surface, rather than trying simply to escape their pain, they may be the vehicle of self-cure.

A real trap, though, is bravely to face the fact you are anxious when the truth is that you are depressed, or that you are depressed when the truth is that you feel guilty. It seems to me that the way to catch yourself out is, first, to become aware of avoidance impulses. When I find myself daydreaming of buying a farm or going to live in England, I know that something has gone wrong, not something realistic like having a producer drop the option on a play of mine, for that I respond to directly, but something in the realm of emotion, such as rejection or feeling unloved. Any thought that starts out: "Everything would be all right if . . ." should start a red light blinking, a signal that it is time to stop and say, "Okay, what happened to make me feel anxious?" A fellow I know believes everything would be all right if he had a college degree, and indeed, since he has been taking evening courses, he has seemed much more relaxed, but what is going to happen when he gets his B.A.? It is not the solution, any more than my buying a farm or going to England is a solution, for solutions to the problem of self are internal. The bandage of a B.A. is not going to patch up this fellow's feelings of inadequacy, and the old anxiety that he has fled from will return. Only if he can call it anxiety and not lack of education is there a possibility of freeing himself of it.

Each of us has a language that stands for anxiety or guilt or depression, and this language can be recognized by its repetition. If, aware of a slight feeling of disgust or boredom or dissatisfaction, you characteristically say, "What I need is to get away for a few days," or, "I feel like seeing a movie," these repeated responses can alert you to the possibility that you are avoiding a deeper feeling, and it is probably a good idea to postpone going away or to the movie until you have just sat quietly and let the warded-off feeling come up. This is a passive rather than an active process, a letting of the mind wander rather than an attempt to dig. Saying, "Am I anxious?" is not so fruitful as saying, "What has happened in the past few days?" The event that floats into consciousness may be quite unexpected: a minor telephone call, for example, not a major quarrel. To illustrate, on a day when I found I was working with one part of my mind but deciding what to plant on my nonexistent farm with the other, my directed thought went back to a luncheon with a theatrical agent which had involved several exchanges that were conceivably anxiety-producing, but my drifting thought kept rambling to a telephone conversation with a dear friend. I sat quite still and let myself feel, and what I felt was depression. Asking why brought no sensible answer; there was no reason. But when I asked what, what had she said, what had I said, the equation began to emerge. She was going to Puerto Rico. What difference did it make to me if she went to Puerto Rico? None. I had said, "You're lucky you don't have to work." But I have never minded working. The sequence is too long to detail, but the ultimate thought that slowly rose to consciousness was: "I work. I am conscientious. I do my best. R_____ irresponsibly goes off to Puerto Rico. I do what I should. She does what she wants. And I get no reward and she gets no punishment."

Such a small thing, and the minute it emerged into consciousness, I could laugh and forget it, saying, "Well, you've always known being a good child never got you anywhere. It's a pretty late date to start getting depressed about it now." But, if unknown and unexplained, the feeling of depression, fed by a hundred innocuous conversations, can give rise to a chronic state of depression, and the warning signal can finally become the disease, as the crippling of arthritis remains after the disease process itself has burned out.

The Hidden Quarry

N_____, whose husband became deeply involved in an affair with another woman, kept telling herself that she felt hurt. One day, entirely without warning and without any previous history of such an occurrence, while she was pleading with her husband to give up the other woman or, alternatively, to leave her, and he was saying helplessly that it was impossible for him to do either, N____ abruptly went into a major convulsion. The convulsions continued and she had to be hospitalized. When the convulsions were controlled with medication, she lapsed into a psychotic depression. Although an organic predisposition is probably necessary, convulsions can be interpreted as a sudden and massive discharge of damned-up anger which is prevented from reaching its target by the person's losing consciousness, and depression can be seen as a long-range means of inhibiting the acting-out of anger. It would be presumptuous to say categorically, but perhaps legitimate to speculate, that things might never have reached this pass had N____ questioned whether it was only hurt she felt. Had she been able to pry up the hurt to get a glimpse of the anger swarming under it, perhaps she might have been able to let some of the anger escape before it reached explosive proportions.

As I say, this is speculation, but it is often illuminating, even if there is no particular reason to be suspicious of the authenticity of an emotion, to raise with yourself the possibility that you may be feeling a second emotion unconsciously. Again, it is a search best carried out passively rather than actively. If you go crashing through the underbrush, the quarry has plenty of warning to hide, but if you sit passively and patiently, it may show itself. Anger at someone else may ease off, and a feeling of guilt for less than admirable behavior of your own may work its way close enough to the surface to be recognized. Or guilt you thought brought on by your mistreatment of someone else may have under it anger at his indifference to your own requirements. It is a sort of trying on for size of different alternatives, and it is not just an academic exercise; to call things by their correct names is to possess them rather than be possessed by them.

This questioning of what is being felt can be usefully extended to any strong emotion, not confined to just the painful ones. Elation, for example, may be serving to screen another feeling, and its enjoyableness should not allow it to pass unquestioned. An extreme example of this was a woman patient at a staff conference who laughed and told jokes and kissed the doctor and bounced in her chair like a sponge rubber doll, looking and sounding marvelously happy, but as she bounced, her bathrobe loosened and a large dressing over the area where she had had a breast removed came into sight. Her manic reaction overlay and held out of awareness feelings of depression.

One's sympathies go out in a situation like this, and the question comes up of whether elation is not preferable to recognition of the buried feelings. Temporarily, yes, but in the long run one has to come to terms with oneself, and this is only possible if feelings are identified for what they are. A good feeling that is inappropriate to the stimulus leaves one as little in command of oneself as an uncomfortable one and opens the way to oscillation in moods: an unwarranted elation may readily be supplanted by an unwarranted depression. Any reaction that is out of proportion deserves questioning, whether it is incommensurate in a positive or negative direction. And absence of feeling in a situation that ordinarily calls it forth is equally suspect; the person who does not react is as little in charge of himself as the person who overreacts.

Take Newhart

Jokes are made about the psychoanalyst falling asleep while the patient on the couch rambles on, and it is true, as I know from experience, that there is an inclination to wonder if the analyst is listening when an hour goes by without comment. We are accustomed to going to a physician and having him take some active measure, and we wish the psychoanalyst would intervene to stop the hurt, but what he is doing is listening passively with a free-floating attention, matching up in himself attitudes that the patient is expressing to see if they ring true and listening for the common denominator in descriptions of reactions. Where he does actively dig for clues, however, is in dreams and fantasies. These are extremely valuable as an expression in disguised form of the contents of the unconscious mind. Feelings too painful or too frightening to be allowed into awareness find an outlet masked in the seeming fiction of dreams and fantasies. Being fiction and being fleeting, they are a safety valve, allowing some escape of pressures, and problems that are otherwise beyond awareness can be tracked down by decoding their symbols.

Anyone can become usefully adept at interpreting the symbols of dreams if he accepts that dreams have much to tell him about himself. It is primarily a question of deciding to pay attention to them. Remembering them, surprisingly, can be achieved by consciously training yourself to. Spending the first few moments when you awake in the morning letting a dream float back into consciousness allows you to remember that you have dreamed and to catch hold of the dream itself. To counteract the tendency to dismiss a dream as senseless, it is helpful to get in the habit of writing them down. The more faithfully this is done, the more dreams will be remembered, and it is secondarily useful because the act of writing similar phrases or constructions or descriptions will call attention to recurrent symbols.

As in all efforts to track down the shape of the self, noting the presence of repetition provides the clearest clues. Whatever is repeated is dynamic in the personality, and symbols that are repeated in dreams are the most fruitful to explore. I had several years of dreaming about my apartment: that I had lost it, that I had been lured by seemingly excellent reasons into moving out of it, or that I had decided on my own volition to give it up. When I noted the recurrence, I realized the apartment must be a symbol standing for something else, and because of the feeling-tone associated with the dreams, I knew that whatever it stood for was extremely anxiety-producing. Some symbols, such as snakes or umbrellas or caves or water, are universal symbols and can be interpreted in much the same way for each person, although even with a familiar and obvious symbol, it is wise to be cautious for the person may be using it in an idiosyncractic way, but other symbols are peculiar to the individual, as my apartment was to me. I came to recognize that if I dreamed about it, I was troubled, but I did not know what it stood for. Indeed, I shied away from examining it, I suppose because I was frightened of what I would find behind it. When I thought about it, I got no further than saying, "I am not about to give up the apartment, so it is meaningless to dream about it." But, eventually, I let my mind drift, since active contemplation just led to dismissing the thought, and what I found myself thinking about was a theory I have concerning clothes, that they are a second boundary of the self: first, there is skin as the boundary of the self; next, there is the clothing. And it came into mind that the third boundary is the walls of one's home. The symbolism came clear: if I gave up my home, I was giving up my self; if I lost it, I was losing my identity; if it was taken from me, someone was depriving me of my identity. Indeed, this was completely pertinent to my problems at the time in a stormy relationship in which I felt menaced in ways and for reasons I could not fathom. Unconsciously, I was wrestling with intense fears of being overwhelmed, overridden, swallowed up, reduced to a pulp, without name, face, or will, and all of this was summed up in the ordinary symbol of my apartment. When I understood this, I extricated myself from the relationship, and the dreams ended.

To decipher your dreams and read the tracks in the cloud chamber, you can do for yourself what a psychoanalyst will ask you to do, that is, take a section of the dream and free-associate to it. Free-association is nondirected thought, noncensored thought. It is not discarding the association of "clothing" to "apartment" but following it to see what else comes to mind. No matter how far-fetched a series of associations may seem, if you can remain passive and let thoughts flow freely, the meaning may emerge, perhaps in a quite unexpected direction. It is a trick, it requires practice, and it may often turn up nothing, but it is worth trying, for dream analysis is one of the surest ways of finding where you are and what you are up to.

You may find that you are up to more good than you thought, for your unconscious mind may decide there is less to worry about than you consciously believe. I have been considerably worried about the form and shape of this book lately, whether it is worth writing, whether it will fall apart in the middle, whether I shall ever get to the end of it. Such fears are an occupational hazard of writers, surging up whenever work goes badly for a few days, but they are depressing all the same. Last night I dreamed that I was crossing the George Washington Bridge, walking along the center line on foot. I had been going along unconcernedly but suddenly became dreadfully worried about getting across. I dropped to my hands and knees, and then stretched full out, clinging to the pavement so as not to fall over the side. A state trooper, who looked like Bob Newhart, came and told me not to be afraid, to get up and keep going and I would make it to the end.

My first thought, when I remembered the dream this morning, was that the George Washington Bridge is at least six lanes wide; small chance of falling off of that, so my fears of not making it to the end are unjustified. Plus which, a patrolman arrives to tell me to pick myself up and go on, that is, to take "new heart" and I can make it. So, you see, messages from one's unconscious need not be discouraging.

It is said that so much is compressed in a dream that, were it to be analyzed to its ultimate extreme, it would reveal every aspect of the dreamer's life and personality. Clearly, no dream is analyzed that minutely, but it is useful to go beyond the manifest content, that is, the content that deals with the day's happenings, and to search for the latent meaning contained in the dream. This is, again, a question of looking for common denominators, of becoming acquainted with the symbols that stand for persistent concerns, of becoming aware of your own language, of your own repetitions. Freud has called dreams "the royal road to the unconscious," and his extraordinary book, *The Interpretation of Dreams*, which is available in the Modern Library edition of *The Basic Writings of Sigmund Freud*, is more than worth reading. Dreams are brilliant exercises in mental shorthand, and the more you can learn about transcribing them, the more access you will have to the self.

Among the psychodiagnostic tests, there is a projective technique called the Szondi Test, which requires only that the person being tested look at pictures of faces and choose from each set the two he likes best and the two he likes least. The faces are photographs of people each of whom suffers from one of eight categories of mental disorder, any one of which is assumed simply to be an extreme form of traits present in all of us: homosexuality, for example, is an exaggeration of the normal need to be loved and taken care of, while sadism is an exaggeration of the normal need to be active and aggressive in obtaining satisfaction of needs. By comparing the distribution of liked and disliked choices in the eight categories, the psychologist can assess which traits are accepted in the personality and which repressed, which are a source of tension and which find uncomplicated discharge in behavior.

The rationale of the test is that the subject unconsciously detects and responds with avoidance or attraction to the traits represented in the faces. Not every psychologist is comfortable with this assumption, but in the hands of effective interpreters, the test gives convincing results, and certainly, in everyday life, we all make intuitive use of this approach, appreciating that the person who objects violently to traits in other people is revealing his fear of the same traits in himself and that the person who accepts certain behaviors in others permits himself the same prerogatives. The audiences at Robert Anderson's play, *Tea and Sympathy*, had no difficulty in realizing that the more the insistently masculine teacher persecuted the boy accused of being effeminate, the more apparent it was that he was hounding the boy because he feared his own forbidden homosexual drives.

But can a trait be unconsciously perceived simply by looking at a face? I went to work in fairly large advertising agency and, in the course of my first day on the job, was taken around and introduced to perhaps thirty people working on the same floor. A few courteous words were spoken each time, but only one face made an impression on me; it was the face of someone who became one of the closest friends in my life. I know now why, but, somehow, everything I came to know about her, I already had unconsciously picked up in that first brief encounter. It is said that one should not trust first impressions, that they can be misleading, but I find that they are astonishingly accurate and that they come to seem misleading only because the conscious mind later is thrown off the scent by accepting the way the person wants to be seen and discarding the intuitive perception.

Holding on to first impressions long enough to examine them, aside from whatever use this may be in relation to other people, is a source of information about yourself, another set of tracks in the cloud chamber. A real dislike for an exhibitionistic person may suggest how strictly you forbid expression of your own exhibitionistic drives, while a feeling of attraction to an exhibitionistic person suggests that you would like to live out your own drives in this direction but are unable to. I, for instance, am afraid of and avoid aggressive people, but my friends, if I look for a common approach among them, are active, assertive people, suggesting I rule out overt aggression in others as I rule it out in myself but that I am also attracted to it, vicariously living out my repressed drives in my friends.

It is easier to pick up evidence relating to unconscious aspects of yourself from first impressions than from established friendships, but the latter is possible if you can, in effect, back off from the friendships, blurring out the very apparent individual differences and letting the underlying point of resemblance come to the fore, much as one sees the shape of a mountain when up close but the contour of the mountain range when far way. You will perhaps find your friends tend to be grouped into clusters: the motherly ones who are supportive toward you and to whom you look for acceptance and encouragement, the fatherly ones to whom you turn for advice and direction, the sisterly or brotherly friends with whom you are sometimes on the giving end, sometimes on the receiving end. I do not know how it is with other people—I suspect that

87

many people are much more consistent than I—but I find myself behaving quite differently with different friends. One, by constantly asking questions about what I think of this or that, puts me in the position of mother or teacher, while another, by reticence on the subject of himself and overinterest in the subject of me, reverses this, putting me in the position of child. They are responding to part-aspects of me, as I am responding to part-aspects of them.

Friends find in each other a chance to act out childhood needs for acceptance, love, satisfaction, and help, a chance to re-enact old strivings and live out old drives, a chance to re-run home movies with new actors in the original parts. All of this is unconscious, of course, but if it can be made conscious, if you can see the parts assigned to you by your friends and the roles you yourself apportion out as casting director, you are looking at the tracks in the cloud chamber made by a person who must have something very like the shape of yourself.

RRIVING tardily at a dinner party, the first sentence I picked up in the conversation was one guest saying to another, "Did you ever meet your uncle?" This struck me as a rather inane question, for who has not met his own uncle. The reply was equally uninteresting: "Yes, I first met him when I was six and Mother took us to Europe for Grandmother's birthday. He was very nice." The guest went on to tell a couple of pointless anecdotes about her uncle, that he had commented on how long one family member's hair showed no signs of graying and that he had called on her mother in knickers while on a walking tour, and the other guests listened with the closest attention. To tell the truth, I was getting bored, and finally, impatiently, I leaned over and whispered to the hostess, "Who, in heaven's name, was her uncle?" The answer bowled me over. "Don't you know?" my hostess said. "He was Sigmund Freud." It was as though I were in the same room with someone who had known Shakespeare, the other man in the history of the world whom I admire unreservedly. For me, these two were, not more than men, but the quintessence of men, and in some ways very much alike, having grandeur in their total acceptance of man's condition, equable, large-souled, and of a breathtaking dimension.

There has been too little time since Freud's death for him to be removed from all controversy, particularly since his name is used as a generic term for concepts which many people, not truly realizing that there is a whole body of monumental work behind them, find frightening or distasteful and reject. Freud's discoveries are spoken of as being a devastating blow to man's self-regard, man having considered himself, prior to this, master of his own mind, as he considered himself the center of the universe before Copernicus and a being unique in kind before Darwin. But Freud, as did Copernicus and Darwin, discovered; he did not invent. And any discovery of what is so, although it may seem initially to shrink man's dominion, in reality enlarges it, for what is understood can be mastered.

All that I have set down so far stems either directly or indirectly from Freud's work. The ideas do not seem to me threatening; indeed, when I first came to know of them, it was like light after light being turned on in a house I had thought haunted. To learn about repetition and reinforcement; transference; defense mechanisms; repression and fixation; the unconscious mind; the five phases of psychosexual development; and the id, ego, and superego, did not make me feel alien to myself but, for the first time, at home in my own house. They were keys to the riddle of self, which had long baffled me.

To use these keys is to engage in a process of uncovering, which is the very opposite of exhorting oneself to be this or that. There are books full of advice on how to suppress distressing aspects of the self: if you are frightened, whistle a happy tune; if you are timid, take dancing lessons; if you are angry, smile; if you want to be liked, smile; if you feel yourself a nonentity, smile. Following such precepts is like kicking a television set that is out of order: it may flicker back on temporarily, but the trouble is bound to recur. Although such writings should not be mentioned in the same paragraph with Freud's work, to be exposed to them and then to enter a world where the effort is not to tie leaves on the tree but to follow its roots into darkest ground is an extraordinary experience. Inevitably, to follow his thought is to engage in a parallel attempt to apply his concepts to an elucidation of the self, to make, perhaps for the first time, the effort to understand rather than to suppress, and thus to engage in self-analysis.

Amateur or Professional Analysis?

As you know, I myself went into psychoanalysis. It happened rather by accident. In talking to a friend just after returning from a Christmas visit to my mother, which had been made horrendous by her drinking and my ambivalent feelings of disgust and pity and love and hatred, I commented that if ever I had the money, I was going to go to a psychoanalyst and find out why I could neither cope nor pull free. It was an idle remark, for I had no money nor prospect of any, but my friend took it up and spoke to her analyst, who, still to my surprise and gratitude, volunteered to take me on, with the understanding that I would pay her when I was able. By one of those coincidences of life, in the same week in which I started in psychoanalysis I also obtained a job working with a psychologist, so my exposure to analytic theory was both as a patient and as, in effect, a student. Indeed, I also became a student, my identification with these two remarkable people leading me to decide to become a psychoanalyst myself, a course I pursued until its neurotic roots became evident and I went back to living my own life.

Because I was simultaneously in analysis while I was learning analytic theory, I cannot hold unequivocally that self-analysis is possible. I know that kicking the television set does no real good, but whether you should attempt to take it apart yourself or consult an expert repairman, I cannot say. Had I known, without undergoing psychoanalysis, the concepts I know now, would I have been able to use them to understand myself? I am not sure. I only know that, in the years since analysis they have been unendingly useful. They have been the tools for a depth of understanding and for a practical change in behavior that I was never able to achieve in analysis. I have pushed back and back the edge of darkness; I have taken charge of more and more of myself.

Let me enter a caveat here. I have an extremely verbal mind. Things come alive and are meaningful to me only when I have words for them. I used to be ashamed of my boredom with foreign movies and said nothing when people raved about this or that Italian or French film, until I realized that the photography they enthused about meant very little to me and that I sorely missed understanding the language. It is not pictures that bring the world to me but words. This is a physiologic fact stemming from a predominant type of brain wave, and another person, with a different type of predominant activity of the brain, may not be so grateful for verbal concepts as I am. It happened that a third person, also sent by the same friend, was in analysis with the same analyst at the same time I was, and she, who had only two years to my four, is managing her life with, I think, more skill than I am even though she is totally unable to verbalize the concepts of either her problems or her recovery from them.

Thus, the choice of self-analysis or professional analysis may hinge, to some degree, on the type of mind one has. If the concepts set forth in the previous chapters strike you as academic and remote, interesting enough but not viable, your choice, if you feel the need of therapy, will probably be to seek professional help. If, on the other hand, they have struck you with some force and have opened up avenues of insight, you may wish to have a go at self-exploration on your own. In this event, I can promise you that you need not fear that you will dismantle the television set and then be unable to reassemble it. The human mind protects itself from knowledge it cannot handle.

If you start in this way but what you catch hold of gives you no more than a tantalizing glimpse of the promised land of autonomy, you may decide then to go to a psychoanalyst. Excellent. I could not be more in favor of it. There is a saying in the theatre that everyone's second business is show business, but it must be unmistakable by now that I think everyone's second business is their occupation and that their first business is to know themselves. If living with yourself is acutely painful, however, I hope that you will not use this book to delay seeking help while you try to disentangle what has happened and what is happening to you. There is nothing sadder than the person who struggles on and on, his life an authentic agony as he desperately fights depression or overwhelming fears or feelings of disintegration, telling himself that he only needs to pull himself together. A friend has been calling me every day or so about a man she has been in love with who is going to pieces. She had gone to another state, where he had temporary business, to visit him and found him swamped by anxiety that he could not do the job and drinking a fifth of Scotch a day to fend off the anxiety; he alternately clung to L_____ and abused her, until, for her own sanity, she had to get out, at which point he drove to another state and married a girl he had picked up earlier in the evening in a bar. Returning here, he told L_____ he had done it because he had felt deserted by her and that he now feared himself so out of control that he might kill someone or himself. I gave L_____ the name of general hospitals in the city having psychiatric departments where the man could get immediate help, and she told him this and offered to go with him and promised that she would sign him out, if a signature was needed, the minute he wanted to leave. But he, although almost persuaded, ultimately said, "No, I am a man. I got myself into this. I've got to get myself out of it." Apparently, he considers it a sign of weakness to ask for help, although, as L_____ points out to him, he would think nothing of asking a professional to set a broken arm. Another friend of mine, on her way to see a psychiatrist for the first time, marshalled all the instances she could think of that might justify her seeking professional help, for she was fearful that her problems would be dismissed as too minor to require attention. Seated across from the psychiatrist, she listed them timidly and then waited to be told to go home and forget about them. Instead, the psychiatrist looked up from his doodling and said, "Well, you're not getting much fun out of life, are you? Let's go to work."

You do not have to be in deep trouble to see a psychiatrist, and if you are in trouble, you should not hesitate to see one. Don't think that it is an admission of failure. Call in a mediator if you are at war with yourself, for the bloodiest and most senseless of all wars are civil wars. Problems of mental health and illness are becoming better known, and there is less stigma attached to being under psychiatric care now than there was even a few years ago, and a few years from now, there will be less yet. Perhaps, someday, it will be an accepted part of everyone's education to learn about his inner world as we now learn about the outer world. I was hopeful that that day had come when the atom was split, for, not only did it seem indispensable to our survival to become aware of the irrational sources of our behavior, but I thought it was the only unexplored frontier left and, as such, could no longer be ignored. I was wrong, of course. We proved able to distract ourselves with exploration of space. But maybe the time will come.

Stopping the Action

There are many different approaches in psychotherapy, e.g., group therapy, supportive therapy, psychodrama, and directive therapy, and they may be employed singly or in combination according to the psychiatrist's judgment as to which approach is most likely to benefit the patient. An uncovering type of therapy, which is what psychoanalysis is, is not always indicated, but what, if it were to be recommended to you, would it be like? For one thing, it is a therapy in which the patient operates on himself. The patient talks. The analyst is silent. The basic rule of psychoanalysis is to say everything that comes to mind, not to try to organize or direct your thoughts but just to let them come out. The basic tool of psychoanalysis is transference. The analyst is, for the most part, silent and out of sight so that the person he is will not intrude on the person or persons you make him into, so that he will be a screen on which you project a parental image. If you accuse him of manipulating you, he will know, and you will come to know, that this is a feeling transferred from some other relationship. The images you make him over into will be the images you characteristically make other people over into. He will look for the repetition in what you perceive people to be like, and he will listen to the repetition in thoughts, e.g., "He doesn't appreciate me. She doesn't appreciate me. They don't appreciate me. You don't appreciate me," thoughts that may be widely separated in time but eventually call attention to themselves by their repeated appearance. Out of all the people in your life, you will return again and again to discussion of a few. Out of all the problems in your life, a few will come to the top and stay there. These will be the central relationships and the central problems. All other people and all other problems will in some fashion mirror these people and these problems. And they will be thrown into relief by your attributing to the analyst the characteristics of the central people, which he has not shown, and by your experiencing the central problems in relation to him, which he has not contributed to.

As an illustration of how this works, my analyst one day mentioned that someone she knew was looking for a person to do some work on Saturday afternoons and that it sounded like something I could do. I was in despair for the next three days, for here again was my mother telling me to look after myself, not to depend on her, not to expect love and care without paying for it (I took the mention of a job to mean that the analyst wanted money), not to hope that she would consider what I wanted and needed (I was working and going to school, and Saturday afternoons seemed like the last straw). At the next session, I started out by saying, "Look, if you want to be rid of me, just tell me so and I'll go away," and promptly burst into tears. It took an inordinate amount of time for the analyst to convince me that all she had had in mind was the knowledge that I was having trouble paying the rent and might want to earn some extra money, and gradually and gently she pointed out that I was inclined to interpret a great many things that people did as indicating that they did not care what happened to me and wanted to be rid of me. I had seen her as someone she was not and had attributed to her motives that she did not have.

The more unsatisfactory any childhood relationship, particularly with parents, the more difficult it is to pull free of it. This was true of my relationship to my mother, and almost all of the four and a half years I was in analysis was spent in trying to scrape off the gummy residue of that quagmire. Because I was not discharged from analysis but quit on my own decision, much else was left untouched, unexplored. Thus, when I found myself in almost as great difficulty as I had been in all

95

along, I determined to continue on my own to try to track down what I was doing and why I was doing it. My way of doing this was, and is, to keep a notebook.

"Keep" is too strong a word. It suggests a directed effort, an organizing effort, and there is nothing of this in it. The only effort I make is to set aside fifteen minutes at the end of my working day for writing in the notebook. I try not to think before I start to write and not to censor while I am writing. There is no effort to have it make any sense; certainly none to have it be literary or even coherent. All I ask myself is: where am I? what am I feeling? and I try to set this down as honestly as I can. I write as much as possible in free-association. Because thoughts easily outrace handwriting, all of them cannot be caught, but I try not to discard one in favor of another until I have considered it long enough to know what I am discarding and whether I am not choosing but defending. I try to set down what I did, not why I did it, and I try, above all, not to spare myself.

It is an outrageous document, for it describes despicable feelings and admissions of motives and behavior that I would never confess to under any other circumstance. It is a totally narcissistic document, for there is not a word in it that concerns anyone else except as he concerns me. If I take someone apart, it is because I want to know why he has done what he has done to distress me, not at all because I am interested in objective understanding of him. The notebook would unforgivably wound anyone who read it and found himself mentioned in it, for, if affronted or thwarted or hurt, I have screamed against him in the cruelest, most cutting of terms. The last thing I set out to be is fair or rational or reasonable; I try to behave well the rest of the time; these fifteen minutes belong to the infantile and irrational in me.

Because it is difficult to convey the flavor in descriptive terms, I have hunted through the notebook for a passage I might quote without too drastically compromising myself. The following is exactly as it was written five months ago.

Both E_____ and B_____ have the same problem: they're deeply afraid they're ordinary.

I have been enraged ever since E_____ called me yesterday. First, B_____ called to say that he would call, that he was in town. I wish I could catch now my reactions. I remember that I wanted not to answer the phone any more that afternoon. Thus, I strongly didn't want to talk to him—

Because he wouldn't give a hoot about me—

Because he just wanted to show off what he had become——

Because his becoming would take up so much room, would be so intrusive that there would be no space for me.

These same people demanding that I put myself in my pocket and be audience and support for them.

They think they are so fascinating, so important, that I should be happy to admire them. They don't realize that I honestly and deeply don't give a damn.

But I am not just indifferent—I am actively angry.

Sibling rivalry? E_____ is like P_____: anxious, cruel, sensitive to the slightest thing that affects himself, insensitive to others, thoughtless, bullying, basically a little dishonest, sly, and with it all well-loved by the mother. A phony, a fraud, will turn like a snarling cur if cornered but otherwise is bold, sycophantic. Pompous, inflated. Not worthy of love. To be seen through. The pulpy core. Rotten, a bit, like an apple. No flavor.

He expects I should love him, admire him.

It is E_____ I loathe, not K_____. Still loathe, although I do not care where B_____'s interest and affection go.

I haven't enough for myself, why should I give to you?

Demanding, pushing, boring, irritating, competitive.

Why should I care what's happened to him?

He thinks to honor me with a view of the great man.

I could be amused. Instead, I am angry. I hate and despise him for—what? That thoughtless, mean, arrogant little creature whom I knew to be sniveling and whining inside. He deprived me. He was accepted, in all his flawed state, as I was not in my wholeness and decency. We were rivals, but I could not fight, really, for fear of losing what little I had—and he could fight, knowing that even if he lost, he had a lot to fall back on. I lost if I won or lost. He won if he won or lost.

Why such contempt? For a dissociated part of myself? The mean, the sly, the cringing, the fearful, the tricky? Did I recognize myself in him and loathe him for it?

I have the same antipathy, revulsion almost, toward seeing P_____. About both I say that was the past and I couldn't care less what has happened, what will happen, to them. They are loved by D_____ and B_____ no matter how meanly they behave. I am not—I am simply used—no matter how well I behave.

97

Would my mother have liked me better if I were a boy? I don't think so, but she would certainly have had less control over me. I would have been freer, more separate. She would have seen me as a person, not just an extension of herself.

Oddly, every word of this is true, and yet none of it is true. I had completely forgotten the incident until I saw these pages again, and I can remember nothing of the telephone calls, which were perfectly innocuous as far as anyone listening might have detected. It is as though one lives on three levels: the person moving and speaking in the world, seen by both the self and others as a person with assets and flaws; the better and worse person one knows oneself to be in one's private mind; and the willful child screaming and kicking somewhere in the adult body. It is this last being who is conjured up in the pages of the notebook. And given voice. It is this child who is true and not true: not true the minute the feelings are given expression, terribly true as long as the feelings are held out of conscious awareness.

There was a family I often visited in the country on week ends, and they had a dog, a mutt, who would scratch and cry at the back door to be let in. Someone would finally go and grab him by the scruff and hustle him through the kitchen and shut him up in the cellar, where he howled and whimpered and barked and shredded anything he could tear apart with his teeth. I asked why he was not allowed in the house and was told it was because he had fleas and got on the furniture and chewed shoes. Being fond of animals, I borrowed the car, went to town and bought disinfectant soap and flea powder, and came back and gave the dog a bath. The poor thing shivered and shook all through the ordeal, having had so little attention in his short life that he thought any at all was inimical, but when it was over and he was beautifully combed and brushed and sitting at my feet in the living room, he gave a huge sigh, all but smiled, and from that moment on, set about becoming a responsible, integrated, beloved part of the family.

My notebook is like giving the dog a bath. The creatures whining and howling in the basement are allowed into the living room, and their behavior changes. Acceptance makes them easy to live with. Acceptance makes them a presence but not an intrusion. The minute I had written the foregoing, I forgot all about it. It was out, it was acknowledged, and it lay down and went to sleep. It was not whining and scratching and disturbing my peace. The passage quoted sounds so extremely forceful, as though I were ranting and gnashing my teeth, but it is designedly so, for I push what I feel to its limits so as to get it all out. Rather than say I am irritated, I say I am enraged, not trying to be accurate but to exaggerate, so the discharge of emotion is complete, like operating for cancer and making a radical excision so that no malignant cell is left behind to start a new growth. In both the theatre and in psychoanalysis, this is called catharsis, an explosion of emotion followed by a drained feeling and peace.

If a life is envisioned as a continuously running motion picture, the keeping of a notebook stops the action and allows a meaningful scene to be explored frame by frame. Searching the action to expose its causes is partially a continuing effort, perhaps woven in as it is in the quoted passage, sometimes coming at the end after I have set down what I did and begun to wonder why I did it. Partially it is a review effort. Occasionally, and almost always prompted by the fact that I am in more of a tangle than usual, I read back over the note book. What jumps out, what is unmistakable, is the repetition in it. Each day, while being lived, seems a new day, each encounter seems a new encounter, each friend and love seems unique, and yet, looked at again in the notebook, a few themes run like brightly colored threads throughout. They twist and turn, appear and disappear, show up in unexpected juxtapositions and combinations. They are what I am, and, following their progress, I see myself.

If self-analysis is feasible, and I think it is for many people, this is the vehicle of it. If you decide to undertake it, at first simply set down how you feel and the happenings and the people that apparently triggered these feelings. This in itself has some curative power because of the release it affords and because some understanding of your actions will spring from the page, presenting itself to your eye in the act of writing. Later, when the notebook is full, it is time enough to go back and read through it. Perhaps several readings will be necessary before common denominators begin to emerge, perhaps several notebooks as well, but eventually they will show up: repetitions in attitudes that will direct you to where conflicts are hidden and resemblances among people that will hint at the shape of your transferred feelings from past to present people. Knowing the concepts of repetition and reinforcement and transference, knowing the original sources of personality, may enable you to slip through your defenses and pull forth into the light at least some of the contents of your unconscious mind. The only caution is: do not go at it too vehemently nor too intellectually. It is like fishing: you bait the hook, but then all you can do is wait; if you dive in, you are going to come up empty-handed, or if you yank at the first tentative nibble, your prey will get away.

One of the eventualities which can cause formal psychoanalysis to bog down is the development of feelings on the part of the analyst for the patient, an emotional involvement in the problems of the patient, a liking for him, a welling up of sympathy or pity. This is called countertransference. If the analyst sides with the patient, he loses his usefulness to the patient no matter how comforting the patient may find it. The analyst must remain detached, nonjudgmental, completely interested and empathic but above the fray. This is a tall order when you are the analyst of yourself, and it is undoubtedly never totally possible, but there are some devices to achieve at least partial distance from the self. One is the simple physical act of writing at topmost speed. Although the description sounds suspect, I cannot delineate it better than to say I feel almost in a trancelike state, the words pouring out automatically from a self that is not my ordinary self, as though the superego is napping in the control tower, the ego has stepped aside at the gate, and the delinquents are rushing through. Knowing that no one will ever see what has been written helps very much in persuading the superego to close at least one eye to what is going on. Another aid is not rereading until weeks or months later. If you must face your irrationality and your incredible egocentricity immediately, you cannot help but dress up the account as you go along. But if it is not until much later that you take a look at the screaming child, time lends tolerance and you are much more apt to be simply interested rather than ashamed.

In rereading, it is well to take a look at every phrase in which you have blamed someone else, for it is here that you may spot your characteristic defenses against knowing yourself in action; and it is well to speculate whether an emotion expressed may be hiding a different, unacknowledged one. The impossible opposites can be tried out, just as an interesting exercise, to see if there is an unsuspected fit. If a reaction has been strikingly out of proportion to an action, pay dirt may be struck by asking whom from one's childhood the author of the action most closely resembles. In fact, it is helpful to ask this about any figure appearing in the pages of the notebook. If the answer is not forthcoming, take a fresh sheet and write down whatever comes into mind; the free, uncontrolled associations may lead you through the labyrinth to a sight of the original. The juxtaposition of thoughts, no matter how seemingly unrelated, is of significance, for there is always a connection between them even if the thread is seemingly invisible. But do not push for understanding. Do not go impatiently hunting for answers. It would be like forcing a friendship. Understanding must be allowed time, and, if given time, it will float up of itself. All you want to do is open a door so that, one by one, the unacceptable parts of the self can drift up and into the light. Indeed, the only danger in keeping a notebook is if it is used to codify behavior, to excuse, explain, forgive, or rationalize it. There will be a temptation to do all these things, and if it is not detected and squelched or bypassed, you will simply have added a notebook to your other defense mechanisms. Remember that what you are after is not how you have sinned and been sinned against. You are after you.

You are a person. You have a right to exist. You are not interested in justifying that but in seeing how you exist.

In my notes, I headed this section "the slippage of insight," and this describes what has been my experience: I know, I understand, and I forget. The insight slips away from me, and I must come upon it again and again. Does this sound discouraging? Did you hope to know, and, knowing, to know for all time? Regrettably, it cannot be. Life is on-going. The self lives through time. And insight has to be a journey, not a destination.

Describing psychoanalysis, Fenichel called it ". . . a chronic process of working through, which shows the patient again and again the same conflicts and his usual way of reacting to them, but from new angles and in new connections." And this is what keeping a notebook does. What one writes down are new angles and new connections; what one reads, in going back over it, are the old conflicts and the old reactions. The conflicts, the reactions, the transferences must be unmasked time after time after time. Just as the cells of the body are continually being replaced, so must the psyche be kept in constant repair.

While the penalty for not doing so is fogged perception, stereotyped behavior, and a self you do not know, is the cure equally as troublesome as the disease? Perhaps it would seem so were it not that, as we sit, walk, read, talk, work, or interact, if not totally absorbed, some part or all of the mind is in any event preoccupied with the problem of the self, and this constant circling of the self, which is often distracting and frequently disruptive, might as well be put to constructive use. The somewhat paradoxical fact is that the only way to lessen preoccupation with the self is to engage in it intensively. Having written so ferociously about E____, for example, I have not given him a thought from that day to this. The splinters of the attack I felt from E____ were extracted in one intense, fifteen-minute session, and there was no festering spot to nag at my attention and pull me into preoccupation with myself.

The attempt to know yourself can be made alone or with the initial help and guidance of a professional. However you begin, it is a process which does not end until your life is ended. But gradually, gradually, it does become easier, and it is never, even when painful, without its truly deep compensations.

PART **II**

TO

BE

Life is not worth dying for

Six

TO CHANGE AND
TO BE

H
AVING discussed how one may come to know the self, it is logical to go on to consider how one may change the self. Indeed, I cannot imagine that anyone is reading this book with any other thought than to change the way he is, unless it is to change the way someone else is. But, as a psychiatrist of my acquaintance remarks, the customer is always wrong. The problem is not to change the self. It is exactly the opposite; it is somehow to contrive to abandon all efforts at changing the self.

The psychiatrist's comment that the customer is always wrong was made when I asked what he was planning to call a series of mental health centers being set up under his direction in a slum area of New York City. "Anything but mental health centers," he said, "because people always misidentify what their problem is. If we say the centers are for mental health care, we'll get all the people with housing problems and welfare problems, but if we say they're for housing and welfare problems, the people with psychiatric problems will come, and that's what we want." Perhaps I looked dubious, for he went on: "If you, for instance, tell me you can't start work on a new play because you have to do more research, I know right away that the problem is psychological. If you tell me, on the other hand, that the reason for your not writing is psychological, I can be perfectly certain that it is because you need to do more research. That's the first thing you learn in psychiatry, that the customer is always wrong. If a patient tells me his problem is in the present, I know it's in the past; if he tells me it's in the past, I know it's in the present. If he says he's sane, I know he's crazy; if he says he's crazy, I know he's sane."

I am overstating my friend's case, and he is quick to point out that when the tables are turned and the psychiatrist is the customer, the situation is no different for him than anyone else. But it is a vital point, one we intuitively take into account in our appraisals of other people but often forget about ourselves. The fellow who says, "I am a peaceable man, but . . .", we instinctively identify as anything but a peaceable man. The woman who says, "I don't like to gossip, but . . .", we silently mark as someone not to share confidences with. The person who says he is quite capable of straightening out his own troubles is the one we most wish would get professional help. And the problem we think is causing our own difficulties is quite likely not to be the problem at all.

The Angry and The Guilty

In no circumstance is this more apt to be true than when we say, "If I could just change this about myself, I would be all right." We have identified the problem as needing to change, but we are quite wrong: our problem is the attempt to change. Take the instance of V____. She told me over lunch that the two girls with whom she shared an apartment wanted her to move out and that she did not know why. "I've tried so hard," she said. "I was glad when they asked me to move in. I really was quite grateful because they're terribly attractive girls and I wouldn't have thought they'd want me. I wanted them not to be sorry, so I did more than my share of the cooking and cleaning, and I was careful to stay out of the way and not be a nuisance, but I seem to have gotten on their nerves anyway." She added, trying to smile, "It's the story of my life. All my life I have tried to be someone other people would like and want to have around, and all my life I have failed."

Is V____'s problem that she cannot change into someone likable or was it the effort to make herself over into a likable person that irritated her roommates? Clearly, she was not a nuisance to have around in the first place, else the roommates would not have asked her to move in, but apparently she succeeded in becoming one through her efforts not to be.

Implicit in so much social comment, and ethical and political and even psychological, is the assumption that people are too unaware or too lazy or too conservative to make attempts at change. But, when you stop to think about it, are not efforts at change the great national pastime? How many books are sold that are devoted to telling us how to change the way we are, how to become popular or successful or attractive or financially independent? How many sermons delivered? How many lectures given? How much conversation centers on how so-and-so would be a marvelous person if only he did not do this and did do that? How many dialogues are held with the self about the necessity to change? It seems to me that people cannot be divided into two groups on the basis of whether or not they are attempting to change, but that everyone is making efforts at change, with the only viable distinction being whether they are trying to change themselves or other people.

The people trying to change others can conveniently be termed the angry, while the people trying to change themselves might be called the guilty, although it would be just as descriptive to speak of the controlling and the dependent, or the paranoid and the repressive, or, inelegantly, the screamers and the criers. In some circles, attaching labels to people rates only a little higher than chicken stealing, because it is assumed that a label immediately ends attempts to understand the individual. But human beings emit a great deal of surface noise, and sometimes efforts to understand are jammed by the sheer amount of communication being given off. If the basic assumption is made that all people are engaged in efforts at change, the angry and the guilty then become useful labels, for they enable identification of where the main thrust at change is coming, whether it is directed at the self or at others. I had difficulty with one of my fellow playwrights, for example, until I realized that his tirades against producers and the state of the theatre were showers of sparks given off by one of the angry who identified the source of his frustrations as outside himself. And I am sure he has difficulty with me, which might be lessened if he understood that my argument that our plays are unproduced because they are not good enough comes from one of the guilty.

How did he come to enlist in the ranks of the angry and I the guilty? In the same general fashion in which virtually everyone joins up. The story of each person's childhood is the story of injustice, for, inevitably, there were hurts, mishaps, and disappointments, traumas, attacks, and accidents. When failed as children, some of us felt, obscurely, that it must have been our fault, that somehow we must have deserved to be failed, that we must have brought it on ourselves, either because we had transgressed in some unknown way or because we were, in and of ourselves, not worth *not* being failed. We joined the ranks of the guilty. Others, when failed as children, felt, obscurely, that there must have been some mistake, that no one could have intended letting such a deserving soul down, and that if attention was called to the error, a fitting correction would be made. They joined the ranks of the angry.

But whether angry or guilty, the attempt to change remains. And it is the attempt to change that perpetuates the problems it is meant to solve. V____, for example, would like to change into a likable person. Her definition of a likable person is to be nice, helpful, and self-effacing, but it is not always appropriate to be these things, and when she is these things inappropriately, she is not likable. If her roommates say, "Would you like steak for dinner?" and she replies, "Whatever you like," her wishy-washiness can soon become irritating; if she always does the dishes, the roommates may come to feel guilty and dislike her for producing this feeling in them. V____, in an attempt to be likable, lays down a party line of behavior which she requires herself to follow regardless of the demands of reality, and thus her behavior becomes as maladapted, contradictory, and occasionally downright ridiculous as that of a Communist following the Moscow party line. Leaving aside questions of terror, it is perhaps this ridiculousness of pursuing notions instead of evidence that has most discredited Communism in the eyes of the pragmatic West, but it is a th:ng we all do in our personal lives. We have a notion that we are unlovable, or stupid, or inane, or whatever, and we decide we must change. We decide to behave in lovable, or bright, or sagacious ways, which means that we decide to behave in fixed ways. And fixed ways of behavior are, by definition, inflexible, repetitive, and ill-tailored to the circumstance; in short, neurotic. The effort to change that was intended to be the solution to neurotic behavior quickly leads to its intensification.

Because we are so imbued with the desirability of changing the way we are, it is not easy to accept that what is presented as the cure is really the problem. But think back to the last time you took stock and faced the fact that you were behaving in unrewarding, inglorious, and self-defeating ways. If you are among the angry, with the best will in the world you located the source of the trouble in someone else and said, "If I can just get him to change, then I will be able to behave as I should." And you set about trying to change him and, consequently, you engaged in unrewarding, inglorious, and self-defeating behavior. If you are among the guilty, you said, "I behave stupidly because I don't have enough self-confidence, so I will change and act self-confidently." And you set about acting self-confidently and this led you into unrewarding, inglorious, and self-defeating behavior. All of which brought you up short and made you feel you must change. Cause becomes effect becomes cause.

To Be and To Change

One evening, a few years ago, I was sitting on a kitchen stool talking to a husband and wife while he put the steak on and she mixed the salad. Their unfed dog was underfoot, and when the wife stepped on him and he yipped in pain, she knelt to hug him, apologizing for hurting him. When the husband stepped on him, he gave the dog a well-aimed kick on the rump and yelled at him to get out of the way. When I was trying to understand recently why the husband and wife were getting a divorce, I remembered this and it illuminated their relationship: she the guilty and he the angry, she accepting blame and he placing it. It was not surprising that they were married to each other, for the angry and the guilty are like lock and key, but it was not surprising, either, that they could not stay married to each other.

Incompatibilities are absolutely bound to arise between any two people. When they do, they cause pain, and the two people look for the source of the pain. The angry one is accustomed to finding it outside himself; the guilty one is accustomed to finding it inside himself, so both readily agree that the guilty one must change.

In the instance of this couple, one symptomatic area was that the husband said his wife was undemonstrative, that he always had to be the one to initiate any affectionate exchange, and that he longed for her to make an occasional gesture toward him so that he too would have the pleasure of feeling warmly and spontaneously loved. The wife agreed that she should reach out to him and proceeded to make an effort to do so. The effort was a self-conscious one, though, because she was a person who could not act in the little, casual, and free ways that came naturally to him. It was not characteristic of her, and in trying to acquire traits she did not have, to replace her traits of reserve with traits of outgoingness, she behaved without spontaneity and with embarrassment. This was perfectly apparent to her husband, of course, who took her planned and stilted little gestures as a failure of love, was hurt and insulted by them, and ended by saying frigidly that he would rather she did nothing at all if it was such an effort for her to touch him. She protested that it was not, but the more she tried to behave in accordance with their notion of how she should behave, the more artificial her behavior became, until even the funny hidden warmth that had originally been natural to her was gone, and she was in an agony of self-consciousness and he was in a rage of rejection. He felt that she was deliberately withholding what he needed, deliberately trying to irritate and frustrate him, for she was refusing him a few easy gestures that he knew for a fact were

112

absolutely simple to make. She felt, for a long time, despair and inadequacy, but because one cannot live indefinitely with a disastrous picture of oneself, she came to feel resentment at the blame both of them had heaped on her, at the ever-present weight of guilt she had to carry. When the frustration and the resentment grew great enough, they went their separate ways.

They went their separate ways to give their scraped and bleeding self-images a chance to heal. Had she been able to answer, when first he said that he wished she could reach out to him, "I do, too, my dear, but that's my problem," and had he been able to say, when first she commented that she wished he could understand that she did not intend to frustrate him, "And that is my problem," perhaps they would never have initiated the efforts at change. And how much better if they had not, for attempts to change are, without exception and whether directed at the self or the other, ineffective and destructive.

Often, it is the failure of attempts to change that prod people into examining their pasts, hunting for the roots of behavior so that they may pull them out, since cutting off the visible vines has only led to sturdy regrowth. V____, for one, had done this. A second thing she told me over lunch was an incident that had taken place when she was five. She had packed a toy suitcase, marched into the living room where her mother was stretched on the couch reading, and announced that she was running away from home. Her mother had not looked up from her book. Rather than liberating V____ from her sense of worthlessness, however, this recollection of a past event had simply substantiated it: other people, of course, could not be expected to wish to have her around, for even her own mother had not. Since nothing can eradicate the event from V____'s past, is she forever condemned to her sterile round of supplicating behavior? There is no way in the world that she can unravel her life back to the age of five and replay the scene, saying, "Mama, I am running away from home," and this time have the answer come back, "Darling, I wish you wouldn't because I love you and I want you to stay with me." Is she, are we, each of us, because we are the products of our pasts, the prisoners of them?

We are our history, that is true. Things that should never happen to anyone have happened to each of us, and we are the consequence of them. But it is not the events themselves that go on influencing us, shaping us, controlling us. It is the attitudes derived from them. Without the attitudes, past events would have been long over and done with, ended in time as they began in time. But they achieve timelessness, deathlessness until the self's own death, not through some magic property of existing outside the laws of forgetfulness and decay, but because they are coated in the preservative of attitudes. The cause of V____'s maladaptive behavior is not that her mother did not look up; it is the conclusions she drew from her mother's not looking up. Thus, she need not change herself and she need not fret that she cannot change the past. Her problem, her solution, is to drop the attitudes she derived from the event.

Her problem and ours, her solution and ours, is not to change the self but to be the self. It is to divest the self of archaic notions formed in the past and acted on in the present in ways that have reinforced them. Her roommates did not see V____ as unlovable. It was she who deposited this old attitude with them. She projected this attitude to them, felt it as coming from them, and acted on it, saying, in effect, "I will now prove that you are wrong, that I am lovable." When her attempts proved the opposite and the roommates asked her to move out, V____ confirmed what she had known: no one liked her no matter how hard she tried.

If V____ were to recognize that the attitude that she is unlovable is in herself, not in others, and if she were to succeed in dropping the attitude, would she not change? Yes. Her behavior would be likely to change quite considerably. Is it sophistry, then, to insist on a distinction between to change and to be? I think not, for "to change" implies a remaking of the self, a forcible substitution of one set of traits for another, which is not only not possible but engenders a great deal of

114

harm, while "to be" connotes a ridding of the self of attitudes imposed by old circumstances upon the self. It is an emptying out rather than a redoing, a peeling away of notions that were always of dubious veracity since they were arrived at originally with the limited and self-involved mind of a child. What is substituted in the place of these notions? Nothing. Exactly nothing. The objective is "to be," not to be attractive, likable, gentle, aggressive, indifferent, charming, or any decided-upon adjective, but to be whatever is appropriate to the moment. To be nothing by previous and rigid definition allows one to be everything as it is appropriate. This is how stereotyped, automatic, inflexible behavior is ended: by not codifying oneself or one's behavior, by not attributing to anyone an opinion about the self, and by not having opinions about the self.

Hindsight and Insight

To drop attitudes is a task first of detecting them. They were established in the past, and this is why it is necessary to know the past: the characteristic features of the landscape of infancy and childhood and the idiosyncratic features of one's own life. But when some fruitful mound, such as V____'s memory of packing the toy suitcase is excavated, it is not enough to expect the exposure to air to turn the memory to dust; it will remain operative until it is examined for attitudes. That is, hindsight is not the sole answer. There must be insight. Hindsight is remembering events; insight is coming to recognize the attitudes deduced from the events.

V____ merely related the incident with her mother; neither of us commented on it nor explored it further; but the following guesses are probably accurate enough because emotions are not complicated, only the defenses against them. If V____ packed a toy suitcase but then went to tell her mother she was running away instead of just slipping through the gate and starting out, she must have been testing her mother and she must have wanted to be stopped. Why would she test her mother? Because she already had severe doubts of her mother's love. Why did she want to be stopped? Because she wanted her doubts proved wrong. What would she feel when her mother did not stop her? If she placed herself among the angry, she could guess that she would have raged and said, "You must care about me!" But since she placed herself among the guilty, she could assume that her feeling was, "If you do not care about me, you must be right and I must not be worth caring about." This is the point at which hindsight turns into insight, for now V_____ does not see just her mother's attitude; she sees the attitude that she took over from her mother. "I am not worth caring about" is an attitude that she has transferred to other people and has had echoed back to her all her life. It is, far more importantly, the attitude that she has had toward herself. Her behavior has been predicated upon it. Her life has been distorted by it. She cannot change. But if she can drop the attitude, she will change.

A friend of mine once remarked, in a phrase I thought so telling that I have never forgotten it, that we all have a thesaurus of clichés by which we explain other people's behavior and excuse our own. Insight begins when we stop quoting automatically from the thesaurus, open it, and honestly examine the clichés. Not one of them will be found to be invalid. But they are valid because we behave on the basis of them; we do not behave on the basis of them because they are valid. Hindsight can tell us where the cliché was born. But it is insight that lets us know it is simply a cliché and, as such, is perfectly open to being discarded.

Blame and Responsibility

At a dinner party, I was sitting next to a man, an artist, who was arguing with two guests who teach in the New York City school system that they were unfair to complain about the viciousness of their students in behavior and their apathy toward learning because the students undoubtedly came from backgrounds that might fairly be described as both deprived and depraved. The teachers did not disagree about the backgrounds; indeed, they cited with compassion individual histories that typically included events of a girl being raped by her uncle and a boy having no known father but a succession of transient ones; but they made the point that the children's behavior made it impossible to teach them. The artist was arguing that the cause—the children's horrendous backgrounds —was producing the effect, the children's unteachableness. While not disputing this, the teachers were pointing out that the effect, their unteachableness, was perpetuating the cause, lives of illiteracy, poverty, and degradation.

There is no question but that slums must be replaced by decent housing, poverty alleviated, and teaching methods improved. There is equally no question, however, but that the destroying circularity of a life must be broken by the person living it. It seems harsh to say that a delinquent raped by an uncle is responsible for her life. But, harsh or not, it is a fact. Each of us, no matter what our experiences, is in charge of how we live our lives simply because no one else can drop the attitudes we hold which dictate our behavior. A therapist may tease attitudes out of the matrix of a life and hold them up to be seen, or a wise and good person may contravene attitudes by steadfastly behaving at variance with them, but only the person whose attitudes they are can decide to let them go. The fact that they were originally inculcated by others is true but academic, just as it is academic, if I fall downstairs and break my leg in three places, whether I tripped or was pushed. It is not two places if I tripped and three if I was pushed. It is the same number of bad breaks, it hurts no less, and I am the only one who can see to the healing. I can take responsibility and do everything I can that is therapeutic, or I can point to someone else and say, "You are why I shall limp the rest of my life." There will be a certain satisfaction in pointing, but it will not alter the fact that I am the one who is crippled. In the same fashion, if we lead lives that are ugly and unaesthetic, cruelly disappointing and a burden, we can point to who and

117

what is responsible, but it becomes somewhat beside the point in view of the fact that we are the ones who are having to live the lives.

Very, very many of us who welcome Freudian theory as a way of opening the door to a different life, try to change, fail, and then use Freudian theory to close the door: whatever happened, happened; it shaped us; and we are marked forever by our experience. It is true that we did not perpetrate the events that maimed us. But we are the ones who preserve the attitudes that keep the influence of the events alive. And we *are* responsible for the attitudes. Though alien in origin, they are solely our own now, which means that we have a choice about them. We need not keep them. We can discard them. We are the only ones who can.

If the truth were known about the past of any one of us, no one would blame us for being what we are. But not being blamed for a distressed and diseased life is a far cry from leading a good and satisfying one. We may get pity and compassion from other people, as V____ did from me, but I could get up and walk away when lunch was over and she had to live on in her dismaying life. The delinquent, male or female, remains mired in every circumstance he rightly blames for his failure, is trapped in every misery he is screaming in protest against, until, or unless, he can say, "Okay, I have unarguable reasons for being like I am, it is not my fault and no one can blame me, but the life ruined by other people has to be lived by me and so I shall do what I can to make it livable."

We can win the struggle to avoid responsibility for our personal lives, but if we do, what we lose is our lives.

I<small>N</small> these pages, discussion of the deep requirement to *know* the self has preceded discussion of the equal imperative to *be* the self, but, in practice, they are head and tail of the same coin. Although different in aspect, their true value lies in being inseparably joined. To know the self is a task carried out internally, while to be the self is a task carried out in the world, but they are in completely reciprocal relationship. The way to be is to know. The way to know is to be. It is knowledge of the self that allows the actions of the self in the world to be appropriately conceived, and it is the actions of the self in the world that are the most accurate source of information about the self.

Insight and Action

Like everyone else, I have a few close friends with whom I talk things over. In discussing with two of them, one a man and one a woman, the belief that an enormous number of personal problems flow, not from people's unwillingness to change, but from their constant, failed efforts at change and that the answer is not to change the self but to be the self, I got enthusiastic agreement. This pleased me until I discovered that each had drawn partial, and quite different, conclusions from the discussion. P_____, the woman, took it as an endorsement to behave in every way she chronically had, and she called to report how triumphant she had felt, in a clash with her fiancé, to be able to say that, not only could she not change the traits he was objecting to, but that it would be destructive of her to try. What she had heard of my argument was: you cannot change; you make things worse when you try to; the answer is to stay as you are and accept yourself as you are. What she had not absorbed and held in mind was the matching necessity to know the attitudes she held about both herself and others, and to drop those detrimental to herself and to her relationship with others. On the other hand, what registered sharply with G____, the young man, was: you must not try to change; you must just be yourself, which he took to mean that you should live out your wishes and impulses. Accordingly, the following morning, he did not bother to show up at work until eleven and he dressed in slacks and a sweater instead of a business suit. He called to say exuberantly how liberated he felt, and I am afraid I said, rather drily, that what he was likely to be liberated from was his job, not his problems.

People understand what they can afford to understand and what they need to understand, I know this, but even so, I was distressed at this vanishing of the second side of the coin: the necessity to examine attitudes. P____, being one of the angry, simply confirmed her standard approach that it was not she who needed to change. G____, being one of the guilty and recognizing that he kept pushing and tugging at himself to behave in certain ways, decided to stop trying to change, that is, he decided to change into a person who does not try to change.

As my psychiatrist friend says, the customer is always wrong.

Insight sought by looking *into* the self is, at best, fragmentary. It must be matched with, and checked against, the view obtained by looking *at* the self acting in the world. Actions are based on attitudes (and the converse is also true: attitudes are based on actions), and so one must look at actions before deciding, as P____, the woman, did, that one has carte blanche to go on behaving in every familiar way, or, as G____, the man, did, that one has carte blanche to stop trying to behave in familiar ways. Both needed a very much longer time of simply looking at themselves in action before deciding anything at all. If, hopefully, they succeeded in identifying some of their characteristic ways of behaving, it would still not be the moment to decide anything but, rather, to ask what attitudes in themselves would seemingly account for their ways of behaving. With attitudes tentatively identified, their source can be hunted in hindsight, and the hindsight used to verify the insight. The sequence is this: What do I do? What attitude would be likely to account for my doing this? Where in the past might I have formed such an attitude? Do I still attribute this attitude to other people? If I dropped the attitude, would it make a difference in my actions?

Insight is theoretical and, for all practical purposes, useless unless it is verified in action. It is of some interest, but of no value, to know, for example, that you view older women as mother figures. The question is: how does this make you behave? If you come to know that you act toward older women in ways which indicate that you expect to be protected and coddled and accepted wholeheartedly no matter how much stress you put on the relationship, then the information is exceedingly useful, for it will allow you to know why you behave with uncharacteristic demandingness in the presence of an older woman and why you feel uncharacteristically hurt and bereaved by small actions that would not be perturbing if they came from someone else. This attitude must be seen first in action, for it will not be found simply by searching the self; then the insight must be verified by watching yourself in action to check that this is indeed your approach to older women. And then, it is in action that the attitude is dropped. It is not dropped by an internal decision but in behavior. If you can behave differently toward older women, the insight has been verified.

Touching the Bases

Hindsight is a useful but not a necessary component of insight. Attitudes can be detected, and dropped, even if it proves impossible to trace their source. But constant feedback between the internal and external self is necessary. The young man who went late to work in a sweater remarked that his boss reminded him of his father. "I would bring home a report card," G_____ said, "and my father would say, 'Why a C in music?', never once, 'I'm proud of you for getting so many A's.' " Hindsight allowed G_____ to trace the source of his troubles with his boss, but it did not give him sufficient insight to end his troubles because he had not explored how the resemblance of boss and father caused him to behave in action. His concentration was on: What is he (the boss) doing? His answer was: He is acting just like my father. Had he asked himself: What am I doing?, what might have emerged? I used to work in the same office with G_____ so I have some idea of what he did. The boss would appear in the doorway and ask when a piece of advertising copy would be ready. G_____ would answer, in a confused rush of words, that it was not easy copy to write, that he thought he had a really good idea but it was taking time to work it out, that he was sure the boss would be pleased with it, and that, if necessary, he would cancel his luncheon engagement and just have a sandwich at his desk so as to get the work finished on time. The boss would, by this time, have wandered over to G_____'s desk and been looking at the work sheets spread on it, and when G_____ came to a halt, he would nod and walk out without saying anything. G_____ would then curse the boss for implying that he was lazy, in-efficient, and not too bright, for snooping over his shoulder, for always criticizing what he did, and end by saying, "Why doesn't he just fire me if he doesn't like my work? Why does he always pick on me?"

G_____ knows himself to be a hard-working and com-petent person. He also knows that he feels criticized by the boss for laziness and incompetence. If he took his eyes off the boss and looked at himself in action, he might follow these steps in his mind:

The boss asked when the ad copy would be ready. I said it was not easy, it was a good idea, it was taking time, he would be pleased with it, I would work overtime. But this isn't what he asked. Why didn't I just say, "By five o'clock"? I was being ingratiating. As soon as he comes into the room, I think he is going to criticize, and I start in saying, "See what a good boy am I," and I pull out any number of plums for his approval. He says nothing, and I act as though I have been scolded. But it is reasonable for him to say nothing because he has asked for simple information. No wonder he is short with me and looks irritated. He probably walks in looking this way because he wants to forestall the nonsense, the supplication, out of me. I must stop being this way. I must just be myself, talk to him as though he were any other person. I shall show him I am not afraid of him by coming in when I please, dressed how I please. But why do I have to show him anything? Why can I not just be myself without deciding to be myself? How do I see this man? He is in a position of authority over me. He is my boss. He is older than I am. He controls my material well-being, whether I fare well or badly. He has power of decision over me. Who in my childhood is he like? Obviously, my father. What did I think of my father? I wanted him to love me, but he was busy, he didn't want to be bothered, he just wanted me to behave well, not be any trouble. I remember when I brought him a report card: I was so proud of it, but all he said was, 'Why a C in music?', nothing about the rest being A's. He looked for what I did wrong, never for what I did right. I guess he took it for granted I would do things right because I was his son and so all he noticed were the failures. What did I learn about myself from this? That I was a person who was somewhere inadequate but was not allowed any failures. That I must push myself but that whatever I did would not be good enough. And what did this teach me about anyone in authority over me? That they would be withholding. That they would deny me praise. That they would not let me derive any satisfaction from a job well done. That they would always be looking for an opening in which to criticize, while just taking it for granted that I would sweat and strain to do a good job. Like with my father, with my boss I am hunting praise and expecting criticism. I shall stop caring what my boss thinks. I shall come to work when I please, show him I have a sense of my own worth, prove, that I don't give a darn about his displeasure. But that is defiance. That is not being myself. It would still be seeing the boss in a special way. Arriving at work on time and putting in a good day's work is simply my part of the bargain, for which he pays me. It does not threaten my being myself. The thing is to accept this framework and be myself within it. How? By dropping the attitudes I have toward the boss and toward myself. Now that I know I expect him to see only what I have done wrong, not what I have done right, I shall try to remember, when he walks in, that this is what I think, and I shall try not to think it, paying attention only to what he actually says, not what I think he's saying, and answering only what he actually asks. Now that I know that I feel nothing I do is good enough, I'll try not to have an opinion about my work on behalf of the boss until he actually gives it. I'll listen to his words, emptying myself of words I ordinarily give him. I'll genuinely listen to him, hear only what he is saying and respond only to that. I shall stop looking for praise and anticipating criticism. And if I can do that, I shall be myself.

As remarked more than once in the course of this book, the self's most brilliant endeavors are in the service of concealing the truth about the self from the self. How can G____ have any assurance that by following this sequence of thought, he is digging around in pay dirt? The test of the truth of an insight is pragmatic rather than abstract. Does the insight work for G____? Does it make a difference in his behavior? Does it allow him to stop trying to change the boss and himself and permit both of them to be themselves? The insight which begins in the world is, after touching the bases of the past and the self, tested out in the world, and if it results in new ways of acting that come naturally and have nothing in them of exhortations to the self to be this or that, then that is truth enough. The objective is not to know the self truly and theoretically but to be the self accurately and comfortably.

Replacement of Parts

Insight is not one moment of revelation. The self is not a book that can be opened and read; it is a book with the pages constantly turning in a high wind, and only a word can be glimpsed here, a line there, from which, with persistence, some idea of the whole can be pieced together. The glimpses are enough to make most people slam the book shut altogether and substitute a work of fiction more to their liking, but for the ones who keep on with the task, there are rewards not to be earned in any other fashion. The dropping of even a small and peripheral attitude brings a lift, a sense of release, an exhilaration that comes from the discovery that it is safe to be the self. Even with just a few of the barnacles of old attitudes scraped off, the self rides higher, more buoyantly, and responds more sensitively.

And scraping just a few of the barnacles off gives the self permission to know more about the self. When G＿＿＿ observes himself acting nondefensively with his boss, even if, at first, he can manage it only for a moment or two, the success of this action allows him a more prolonged glimpse of just how defensive he has been. We assume that our thoughts govern our actions, but, as Emerson pointed out, it is quite probably the other way around, that our actions govern our thoughts. If, for example, you observe yourself behaving in a servile way, you think of yourself as a person without stature; but if you can have even a brief time of observing yourself behaving with assurance, you can think well of yourself; and if you think well of yourself, you can behave better. And so it goes, in the process of circularity that is so much a part of the psychology of life.

That the barnacles of old attitudes can be scraped off only one or a few at a time, not in wholesale lots, is not only because it takes patience and objectivity to identify them but because new ways of acting must be tried out. Let us say that there is a woman who has not married and who is unable to behave with ease in the presence of men. She is aware of this and has tried to change by forcing herself to appear casual, but she finds that the effort results in her giggling unexpectedly and saying arch and stupid things instead of the clever little remarks she had planned to have come out. This is humiliating enough so that she looks at her behavior objectively and identifies it as nervous and defensive. Why? Here she goes hunting for attitudes, but in a relaxed way, letting feelings drift up rather than quickly putting forth excusing explanations. What comes to mind is the conviction that men are thoughtless, self-centered, demandingly indifferent, that she is afraid of their trampling and contemptuous of their insensitivity. Having these thoughts, never too far out of awareness before but never bluntly faced, she cannot be disdainful of them. She may tell herself that the constancy is in herself, not in men, but this is an intellectual knowing, not an emotional knowing; and it is only emotional knowing, and acceptance, that brings about any change in behavior. No notion, no matter how foolish, can be dropped because it is a foolish notion. Its foolishness must be tested in action, and an action that does not incorporate this foolishness must be tried. This woman has been acting on her notion a long time, and the pathway that the notion follows is deeply engraved. She may tell herself from now to kingdom come that men are lambs, only to have the perception of a man go scooting down the lion path, until she deliberately and with effort suspends the attitude and makes herself wait to see what path the man blazes on his own. If holding her attitude in abeyance allows a sentence which earlier would have come out archly to come out intelligently now, she may get a sensitive response rather than the insensitive turning away she had thought characteristic of men, and the sensitive response is information fed back in, which allows her to make a further small adjustment in her behavior, with the consequence of this adjustment being further information about herself and her functioning to be fed back in.

The flow of information back and forth between the self and the environment is a process without end; it is, again, a way of traveling through a life, not a point arrived at in a life. You see yourself act in the world; you look for an attitude that might account for the action; you try suspending the attitude and observe your action when it is not operative; you make an adjustment in your attitude on the basis of the information; and with new ways of thinking, you try new ways of acting and reacting in the world. The self is heavy and intransigent if an attempt is made forcibly to replace one trait with another, but if insight and action are interlaced, it is lightened and begins to emerge from its higgledy-piggledy encrustation of attitudes and defenses.

The Leap of Faith

There is an assumption here that perhaps should be argued out rather than taken for granted. This is that the self is worth being. There is a philosophical dialogue that turns on the question of whether people are born good and become corrupted or are born evil and become civilized. My own opinion is that each is equally true. Thus, I cannot claim that if you strip yourself of the encrustation of attitudes and defenses, you are going to expose an angelic, euphoric, and expansive person. But, certainly, neither are you going to find the cretinous and willful monster that most of us fear is lurking underneath. There will be a human being, with the assets and limitations inherent in the definition of human being but, for the first time and most importantly, with the choice not to be ugly and cruel and stunted. If I look back at my own life, the hurtful things I have done have been out of defensiveness or an effort at adaptation or toward the end of becoming more comfortable with myself. Never once was the hurt of someone else gratuitous and unmotivated. Deliberate, yes, and wrongly motivated, but never gratuitous. Very, very few people are vicious without cause; and the cause, when the usual person is vicious, is archaic fear and defensiveness. It is the things that are not self, the pulp of notions around the self, that are the source of what we deplore and fear and long to change in ourselves. The dropping away of that pulp will not expose an ungovernable, reprehensible being but a self that can expand and afford to act with decency and generosity and courage. To give the self permission to *be* the self, a leap must be taken across the chasm of dread that the self is little and mean and nasty to a certain faith that it is a good thing to be and that spontaneous behavior can be trusted.

The Search for the Mother

And there is a second leap to be made: that to a trust in the mildness of other people. Both are leaps that must be made against a great deal of resistance, resistance born of the fear that the self and others may fail a trust in them and, equally, resistance born of the fear that they may not. The woman who finds men a problem, were she to lift the curtain of her attitudes toward men and hold them aside while she took a long and unbiased look, and were she to find that men neither menaced her nor were menaced by her, would be left without any known and automatic reactions in setting after setting. She would have to improvise. She would have to meet each man and have him meet her as an unknown quantity. She would not know automatically what to expect and how to act. Since it takes much more thought and energy to behave in unpatterned than patterned ways, just as it takes far more attention to drive a car than to run a train on tracks, it is simpler and less demanding to have a closed mind than an open one. One can long to be free and yet, when freedom is imminent, have it loom as a feared burden. Suddenly, there are too many choices, there is too little structure. One of the problems besetting mental hospitals is acclimation of the patients to the hospital; the patients talk of getting well and getting out, but they grow comfortable in the routinized setting where they need not cope with fresh and complex stimuli, where they know what to expect and what is expected of them, where the horizons are comfortingly close and the landscape completely familiar.

In all of us, while there is that within us which pushes toward health and freedom and expansion, there is also that which wishes to stay small and restricted and safe. We dream of virtuoso performances but we confine ourselves to the simple tunes we have danced to all our lives. If we did not, we would be responsible for ourselves. We would be responsible for an imaginative and varied performance of high standards. We could not say: "I cannot help it. I try but I cannot help it." We could not ask for sympathy, nor for understanding and help and tenderness and support. We could not so subtly blackmail others into granting us goodwill and pity. We would have to take our chances on having freely offered what we now sue for by exhibiting our sores. We would have to say: I am free to behave in the way I choose, and, therefore, I am responsible for my behavior.

And therefore, I stand alone.

The fear of standing alone, which is mistakenly equated with loneliness, is the seminal fear—the intuition that we would no longer have an excuse for flowing out like pseudopods to seek love and acceptance, retracting when we meet resistance, engulfing when we meet promise. There was a time when we lived in symbiosis, in identity with another, and we have not forgotten and we have not lost the craving to have it come again. We want to be accepted just as we are. We want unquestioning love. We want, unconsciously, union. There is no harder acceptance for a human being to acquiesce to than that oneness will never come again, that there is no merging, no big rock candy mountain, no arms, no breast, no womb, that there is no mother, that we are, each of us, a separate human being.

We are driven by the anxiety of separateness. We are propelled toward people or from person to person; perhaps away from people because the fear of a second loss is so great it cannot be risked again; perhaps into joining groups, into efforts to become a part of something; perhaps into creativity because the oneness comes in the identity between self and the work; perhaps into symbolic searches for kharma, nirvana, enlightenment, or peace. Whatever, in a thousand guises, it is the search for reunion with the mother. It is a search that has as its goal the obliteration of what Martin Buber has called the "in-betweenness," the space between people. It is a physical law that two bodies cannot occupy the same space, and since two bodies occupy separate areas, there is, of necessity, a space between. How we long to penetrate it! How, even more, we long to have it penetrated! There is no deeper reason holding us back from mature, responsible behavior. We sense, quite rightly, that accepting the in-betweenness would mean abandoning the search for the mother and bowing to the fact that we stand alone.

The search for the mother is not an unambivalent search. Accompanying the hunt for an end to in-betweenness is the almost equal fear that it will be successful. While nothing is more longed-for than to have the in-betweenness vanish, nothing is more threatening than to have it actually seem in danger of doing so. A merger of persons is like the merger of companies: the newspapers report that corporations A and B are planning to merge but that they intend to keep their separate identities and freedom of action, but quite quickly company B sinks out of sight and there is just corporation A left. Company B lost its independence of movement and decision, and, without autonomy, it disappeared. So it is with people: the promised land of merger is the quicksand of disappearance of the self. Because there is no more terrible threat than that of ego-annihilation, there is a fundamental ambivalence in us: the wish for the mother, i.e., acceptance, support, and an end to aloneness, versus the menace of engulfment, of annihilation of the self.

The anxiety over separateness is at the deepest, most primitive, most infantile level in us. The hardest thing to accept in all our lives is that there will never be an end to separateness, but the saddest thing that could happen to us in all our lives would be to have the separateness vanish, for then we would lose ourselves. We dread to acknowledge aloneness for we fear that it means living in loneliness. But acceptance of essential aloneness, of separateness, is the surest way of short-circuiting the terrible tug of loneliness, for loneliness is what is felt when the search for merger fails, as it must and repeatedly does, not when it is given up. If we can say to ourselves that there will never be the mother again, not the real, not the ideal, not the symbol, not the substitute, it is a release, not a loss. It is a release from anxiety about others, from bribing them with bits and pieces of the self, from the consuming maneuvers of trying to hold them close but not too close. Far from meaning loneliness, acceptance of aloneness, that is, singularity of identity and the undesirability of merger, means a choice of how and when to love and a deeper love because it is not built on infantile needs and a fear of loss; it means clearer and greater communication, for a mature and reciprocal dialogue replaces masked probing for dependent or controlling roles or a combination of the two; lastly, it means an end to alienation from the self, for when the in-betweenness is accepted and allowed to exist, the self is accepted and allowed to exist. It is release from trying to change the self or other to the incomparably greater ease of allowing the self and the other to be.

130

ou do not need to be loved, not at the cost of yourself. The single relationship truly central and crucial in a life is the relationship to the self. It is rewarding to find someone whom you like, but it is essential to like yourself. It is quickening to recognize that someone is a good and decent human being, but it is indispensable to view yourself as acceptable. It is a delight to discover people who are worthy of respect and admiration and love, but it is vital to believe yourself deserving of these things. For you cannot live in someone else. You cannot find yourself in someone else. You cannot be given a life by someone else. Of all the people you will know in a lifetime, you are the only one you will never leave nor lose. To the question of your life, you are the only answer. To the problems of your life, you are the only solution.

The Temporary Facts of Life

It is a superlative by-product that straightening out your relationship to yourself also happens to straighten out your relationship to other people. But even if this were not so, the self would nevertheless be the place to start, for it is more agonizing by far to live unloved by yourself than unloved by some number of people with whom you come in contact. Freud defined health as to work well and love well, and these two things do not depend on other people allowing you to do this but on your permitting yourself. This is not to underrate the pull of heredity and temperament nor to rule out the influence of chance and fate. We all function within limits, and we all live with greater or lesser luck. Nevertheless, if we can

131

find a way to be on good terms with ourselves, we can get on even terms with the world. A man from the West Indies, a would-be playwright, fortyish, who is supporting himself with part-time work while he writes, complains that people will not let him be as he wants to be; they scold him that his worth is beyond odd jobs, that he is wasting his life, and that he is writing the wrong type of plays for today's nihilistic theatre. "Why," he asks, "don't people just let me alone to do what I want?" People do let an individual alone if they sense that he is comfortable with himself and with what he is doing. There is a serenity and certainty emanating from someone at ease with himself which is clearly, if unconsciously, communicated. What other people are responding to in this playwright are not his convictions but his doubts.

It is rare that anyone receives advice or opinions without soliciting them implicitly because most people are too involved with themselves to be sensitive to what is going on in someone else unless their attention is somehow directed to it. Thus, any examination of how other people are responding to the self starts with what the self is doing to permit or provoke the reactions being obtained. And it not only starts with the self, it ends there. Once you know, accept, and like yourself, you will be recognized, accepted, and liked by other people. Your inner evaluation will match your outer evaluation; you will be all of a piece; and people will find it very hard indeed to fly in the face of that and treat you in a manner that disputes what you are. There is a man I enormously like and admire, and for no reason based on things held in common, since he is a most successful businessman and is decades older than I, but I find it a joy to be with him because he is so exactly himself. He knows so well who he is that he needs no reflection of himself from you and can go to the heart of interesting matters instead of putting out feelers to explore whether you are friend or foe and whether you are accepting his image of himself or are about to threaten it. I doubt that he even makes the assumption that you will like him because, if he thought about it at all, he would consider this your decision, not his. He is himself, for you to accept or reject as you wish. And because he needs nothing from you in the vein of tacit indications that he is a fine and likable fellow, he totally allows you to be yourself. Not doubting that he is a person, he does not doubt that you are, which means that, although he is a complicated man, his relationships are not; they are easy, varied, and deep.

It would take more temerity than the ordinary, pleasant person possesses to volunteer opinions about this man's choices concerning how to live his life. There just does not exist an area of uncertainty to move in on. Admittedly, there are individuals who go plunging in no matter how competent and integrated their momentary target is, but in that case the target, being without anxiety over what is thought of him, is aware that the problem is theirs, not his. A woman I know called me, and in the course of conversation about what she was doing and what I was doing, I remarked that I was having sixteen people for a buffet supper. She said, "I'll tell you what you do. You put three tablespoons of olive oil and three of water in a large kettle, and when those are hot, you add . . ." She went step by elaborate step through a recipe for I knew not what, and wound up with the statement, "Now, I know you've written all this down, but if you're not quite sure about it, I'll come over on Saturday and make it for you." There is nothing to do with such people, except to check whether you are leaving them openings to move in on you.

This is not to say that advice cannot be asked for, that problems cannot be discussed, that a frank request for help cannot be made. These things are sometimes right and necessary, and it would be foolish to pretend that they are never needed. But they must be asked for, not sued for, and in genuine circumstances of need. Someone else's interest and help should be taken for granted and honestly requested, not seduced by presenting the self as less than it is. The West Indian playwright, for example, can and should speak of his life and hard times, but as facts, preferably interesting and temporary facts in which there is humor to be found, rather than as an invitation to sympathize with him and admire his pluck and doggedness, for in the latter event the listener will indeed sympathize but will soon begin to add his opinion of how the circumstances might be changed. He will assume that since the playwright is complaining of his lot, he wishes to alter it, and the playwright will hear the comments made not as the approval and admiration he wishes but as a calling into question of the way he leads his life and, inevitably, a criticism of himself.

Alliance for Regression

It is characteristic to believe that those in need are given to, that the squeaky hinge is the one that gets the oil, but in the realm of emotions this is not so. It is the person who does not solicit liking and love, admiration and respect, sympathy and empathy to whom they are freely given. When we encounter beggars, we pull back; when we encounter choosers, we feel a certain joy because we sense that we will not be dunned, that we will be free to bestow or not as our own wishes dictate, that we will not be required to pour emotional sustenance into a sponge. If a friendship grows from such an encounter, it will be a friendship of equals, supporting each other when circumstances require but not chronically acting as crutches to each other, a friendship in which interest and caring are genuine because there is no subtle blackmail to draw them forth.

The person who conveys, "I am nothing. Make me something," may all his life have people trying to answer his hidden plea, but their answer will be in terms of, "I am trying to make you something because you are nothing," and, thus, the insult will be embedded in the response. It will be heard just as clearly as the attempt to help. And it will be hated. The hand held out will be the same hand lifted to strike. It is the person who says, "I am myself, and it is a good and upright thing to be," who will never hear, "You are nothing." It is this person, this person who does not ask, who will be given what we all long for: the respect and affection accorded a human being. It is this person, this person who does not sue for liking or approval, who has his own supply, who will receive it.

Where does the supply come from? Given a reasonable childhood, it was deposited then, and all that is needed is to remain aware of it and not to be ashamed of it. There is a current cult of humility that implies that one should not take joy in being alive, in being competent, integrated, and independent, but that is nonsense, of course. One must never, never apologize for being alive, and one must never, never confess to crimes that have not been committed. But if one's childhood has not been reasonable, what then? Well, then, a little self-brainwashing is in order, that leap of faith earlier discussed. It would be blind to deny that there are rotten people in the world, and stupid ones and vicious ones. But are you among them? It is not very likely. It is far more probable that you are no worse than anyone else you know. Your history is studded with inadequacies and failures, but so is theirs. You have old wounds that ache, but so do they, and the wounds are not still open, still raw; it is the scar tissue that is tender, tight, and throbs with a change in the emotional weather. Rather than defending and protecting yourself, you must accept yourself. You must accept your failures and integrate them into your picture of yourself. Denied, encysted failure can turn malignant, spreading, corrupting, destroying. If it cannot be excised, it can be acknowledged, acknowledged not in despair but in sensible recognition that none of us is what we wish we were and that to turn our backs on our despised portions is to turn our backs on the whole of ourselves. It is far more necessary to forgive ourselves than to forgive our enemies.

Indeed, the only way to forgive our enemies is to forgive ourselves first, for we hate in other people what we hate in ourselves, we fear in other people what we fear in ourselves. We fear and hate their ability to wound us, to deprive us of love and respect. We fear and hate their ability to expose and exploit our inadequacies. But if we stop tenderly guarding ourselves, if we accept ourselves for what we are, we can accept others for what they are and loathing drops away as defensiveness drops away. To say, "I am what I am," is the release that

135

allows us to know what we are and to be what we are. To have a picture of ourselves that accepts both assets and limitations is not to have to ask other people for a reassuring picture, and not to have to ask other people for a reassuring picture makes us free to be ourselves.

This is a true freedom. No one can question your right to be alive, and if you are alive, you have a right to respect yourself as a person. It cannot be denied you. But neither can it be given you. You seize it or not as you decide. To live a life worth living, this is the indispensable center: to accept yourself, to trust yourself, and to like yourself, for, from the relationship to yourself, everything else flows.

Not Less of a Boy, More of a Man

To know and accept yourself is to complete a jigsaw puzzle. Isolated, the dissociated pieces have a false importance. Integrated, they are simply a part of the whole. The acceptance that allows even ugly pieces to be blended into the mass is not resignation. It is positive rather than negative. Shadows fled from are turned and faced, and the energy that went into keeping them at bay is released to flow outward. Peaceful coexistence with all parts of the self turns one loose to go about the business of living with equanimity.

This is not to say that repudiated aspects of the self, once accepted, need be acted on. On the contrary, one of the prime reasons for accepting the self is to exert hegemony over all of the self. Poorly considered or damaging or reprehensible behavior is a danger only when the possibilities for such are not truly faced. It comes from panic or heedlessness and the slipping of controls. When I was typing reports for the psychologist mentioned earlier, I was struck by how often the psychological tests revealed that a fear of homosexuality underlay the tensions and anxieties of the patients. Were an individual to accept this fiercely rejected aspect of himself, would it mean living it out? Not at all, for what is strongly operative is the fear of, not the drive toward. It is when it is held out of the personality that it is troublesome, not when it is accepted in. Allowed in, it can be expressed in constructive ways. I remember a man being laughed at when he told his teen-age daughters that he had not only been captain of the baseball team in high school but president of the garden club. His daughters thought it was the mark of a sissy to be fond of flowers, but he said quietly, "It didn't make me less of a boy, and it's made me more of a man." He could enjoy and make good use of his feminine aspects—if it is feminine to grow things—because he accepted this part of himself.

As well as not suing for the nourishment of acceptance and approval, it is equally important to be indifferent to it. If you pay nervous attention to other people's opinions, maneuver to obtain their indulgence and to stand high in their esteem, you will be whisked about in their winds and you will lose yourself. You know how you ought to behave, and that is the way to behave regardless of the subjective views of anyone else. Many people try desperately to control the behavior of others by making them feel guilty or by blackmailing them with threatened loss, but it is not always a correct assumption that such people will withdraw their love and approval if they are not successful nor that it will content them if they are. I have found without fail that when I tuck myself into my pocket and bow to someone else's pressure, he is not mollified and, for me, it is the beginning of the end of liking and love. Somewhere, way, way back, there germinates the seed of fear and hate, for the denial of one's separate identity gives a fore-taste of engulfment and death, and, unconsciously, the battle to preserve the self begins.

There need be no insistence on the self at other people's expense. No aggressive maneuver is involved, but a standing still in the face of encroachment, a refusal to be manipulated by guilt or fancied obligation or fear of loss of the other. What is required, when under pressure to relinquish choice of action for the self, is the courage and the conviction to answer an implied threat of loss affirmatively with, "Yes, if you are willing to carry it that far, if you are willing to give me up if I don't do your bidding, then I, too, am willing to lose you."

137

Concentration and Indifference

The most satisfactory relationship I have ever had with an employer was in a job I decided to be fired from rather than accede to being bullied. As it turned out, I was the only employee who was not bullied. I should have learned the lesson of creative indifference then, of commitment to the standards of self rather than propitiation of the opinions of others, but it is said that one always learns to swim in the winter: the fundamentals are learned but then there is a long fallow period and it seems that the learning has been forgotten, until, come summer again, one goes in the water and is suddenly swimming with ease. Several years after this job, I was on my way one evening to what I knew was going to be a huge and noisy party and was walking the several blocks there alone because my intended escort had come down with flu at the last minute. In general, I dreaded such parties, and in particular I hated going alone, having the feeling that everyone would be thinking: "Look at that one. Can't even get a date." I idly wondered how a psychoanalyst, if one were to be in my shoes, would feel on her way to a large party alone, whether more confident and less concerned, and it occurred to me that a psychoanalyst could afford to be confident and unconcerned because the people she met would be too curious about what she was finding in them to expend time formulating silent criticisms of her. In that moment, I decided to concentrate exclusively on what I thought of the guests, as though, in fact, I were a psychoanalyst, and to make not a single assumption as to what they thought of me. I decided to school myself to be absolutely indifferent to the impression I might be making and to remain totally open to everything I could see about others, both words and behavior.

It was an extraordinary evening in comparison to what parties had been like for me until that time. No word I said was premeditated. No joining or leaving a group was planned. I extricated myself from bores easily and gracefully. I made no effort to keep anyone standing talking to me so that I would not be alone. I spoke without dread that I would not be heard or listened to. I genuinely registered and responded to what was said to me. This led to my seeing the other guests with unprecedented clarity. I saw attitudes of posture that communicated far more than I had ever taken in before, facial expressions that quite belied words, foot tappings, tense and awkward movements. I heard the insistence in a laugh, the bursting pressure behind words. I saw how busy everyone was in trying to get recognition for himself as a person, and I saw the grateful relaxation that came upon an occasional person when it became apparent that I was really paying attention, that I was grinding no axe of my own.

I saw one of the absolute truths of this world: each person is worrying about himself; no one is worrying about you. He or she is worrying about whether you like him, not whether he likes you. He is worrying about whether he looks prepossessing, not whether you are dressed correctly. He is worrying about whether he appears poised, not whether you are. He is worrying about whether you think well of him, not whether he thinks well of you. The way to be yourself, I knew from that time on, is to forget yourself.

I was trying to convince the other guests of nothing. I was genuinely indifferent to what they thought of me, and I had committed myself to going all the way: they could find me ridiculous or stupid or uninteresting if that was their decision. I did not require of them that they give me myself; I was myself, and they could make of me whatever they wanted to. As though I were a painting hanging on the wall, I made it their choice whether to linger, whether to respond, whether to make an effort to know, whether to have a good or poor opinion. A painting cannot reach out and say, "Look at me. Notice this and that about me." No more did I. And I was not changed, I was not lessened, if someone chose not to see, any more than a painting is changed or lessened.

While by no means passive as a painting is passive, despite my unaccustomed openness to the look and communication of others, I never made fewer judgments. Somehow, when one is not anxious and not defensive and not threatened, one not only sees with clarity but with compassion. I realized that an interruption I would ordinarily have thought rude was an effort to gain attention, a turning away I would have thought a rebuff was a fight to appear popular. A psychoanalyst's concentration on the other person is not a boring in, not an attempt to wrench away veils and expose another's laughable nakedness; it is a free-floating but undivided attention that is registering what is being done as well as what is being said, and what is being not said as well as said, and a matching of what is registered with similar feelings that have been experienced. None of it is for the purpose of putting the person down. All of it is for the purpose of taking him in. When you are truly trying to take a person in, it is hard to strike at him. Indeed, you have no impulse to. You have been there, you know how it feels, and your impulse is to say or do something reassuring. It is defensiveness that gives rise to unadmirable behavior. When it is dropped, much generosity can emerge.

The Indicating Actor

We have an opinion that other people will perceive us in a certain way, that they will, for example, see us as foolish or uninteresting or insufficiently educated or cultured or accomplished. Perhaps they will. But that is for them to decide. It is not our business to hand them ready-made opinions. Our job is to hold still, to remain neutral, to be indifferent while they decide.

"Indicating" is a theater term used to describe an actor who signals the audience that he is a lawyer by carrying a briefcase and talking rapidly or that he is a tough guy by letting a cigarette dangle from the corner of his mouth. The actor is indicating rather than being. In the same way, the person who makes many quick nods of his head and many small encouraging sounds while you are talking is indicating that he is listening to you. But he does not need to indicate. If he is listening, you will know it. Similarly, we need not indicate to other people what we are; we just need to be what we are.

Although there may be a sense of foreboding at the prospect of dropping defenses and leaving yourself open, does it make any deep difference if stray people find you not attractive and not likable? It is not probable that it will happen, but if it does, you would survive it perfectly well. We spend so much of our lives in dread of punishment and disapproval and loss of love from casual people, but if they were to manifest censure, we would simply walk away from them. It is our own regard that is vital, not other people's, so it is not only ineffectual but pointless to indicate to others what they are to think of us. The pain of being unloved is not the absence of love but seeing ourselves as unlovable. And that is an internal problem, one that is cured, not by indicating to people that they are to find us lovable, which will only alert them to the fact that we probably are not; but by achieving an indifference as to how they see us.

La Rochefoucauld commented that, "Nothing prevents us from being natural so much as the desire to appear so." Any other adjective may be substituted for "natural," such as lovable, interesting, generous, or kind, and the maxim loses none of its accuracy. People and the world are so constituted that, in the realm of feeling, what is solicited is withheld and what is unsought is conferred. Thus, it is not worth killing off spontaneity and joy and ease and healthy egotism to try to be what presumably might please and impress other people. Life is not worth dying for, and indifference in a creative sense is rewarding. It is not indifference to other people, but indifference to their opinions. If the latter can be achieved, it so strengthens the sense of self by ending self-consciousness that one can live at ease with oneself and, therefore, live at ease in the world.

Nine
THE
GOOD FICTIONS

ERHAPS it is because the Constitution guarantees us life, liberty, and the pursuit of happiness that we count happiness such a goal of life, and an attainable goal at that. But time is a river, with the current unceasingly bearing us along, and nowhere can we tie up, nowhere can we say, "Here I am happy and here I shall stay." Happiness, if we are to have it at all, must join us on occasion; we cannot stay with it. It is usually a fleeting companion and always an unbidden one. It comes when it comes, and it goes when it goes.

If happiness cannot be suborned, can none of the large abstractions be pursued? I have slid the words decency and goodness and uprightness and honor into this text often enough so that you will not be surprised to have them put forward now. They seem to me viable goals. There is no gainsaying the possibility that they may be analogous to the carrot in front of the donkey which the donkey stretches for but never quite catches up with, but the carrot keeps the donkey headed in the right direction. And if the direction of a life is right and the goal is worthwhile, happiness may fall into step alongside often enough to have made the journey, in retrospect, one not to be regretted.

I am desperately aware of how old-fashioned decency and goodness and uprightness and honor sound, but I prefer to believe that this is the world's problem, not mine. Such standards may be fictions, but they are good fictions, and if the test of empiricism is what is wanted, it is surprising how well they work out. Sidney Hook, the contemporary American philosopher, has remarked that ". . . there is no rock we can build on except the possibilities of what we may become . . ." These words are how I would define the possibilities. Pursuit of them is not the irrelevancy that the pursuit of happiness is.

Preceding any look at the possibilities of what we may become, as I hope I have made very clear, is a look at the actualities of what we are. To live with the terrible truths about ourselves is the only way of not living them out. A need denied has infinitely more power than a need accepted. Denied, it is the sink and source of anxiety, and anxiety dictates behavior as no other emotion can. It traps us into failures of spirit and generosity, draws us into defensive maneuvers, and engages us in the self-protectiveness that heavily disturbs our relationships to other people. Somehow, we must contrive to say: So be it. "I need someone to depend on me. So be it." Or, "I dreadfully need to be liked. So be it." Or, "I cannot be outgoing. So be it." It is the frantic nonrecognition of needs and inadequacies that causes us to behave ingloriously, that unexpectedly undermines our best intentions. It is their recognition that puts them in front of our eyes where they can be controlled.

John C. Whitehorn, in an article in the *Archives of Neurology and Psychiatry*, wrote: "Physicians, because of their professional preoccupation with problems of life and death, are apt to assume that the fear of death is the great common denominator of anxiety. This is probably not true . . . anxieties arise out of interpersonal relationships and interpersonal attitudes." Although in relationships with and attitudes toward other people is surely where anxiey is felt, exchanges with other people will seldom generate anxiety if the self is nonanxious. Someone like V———, the grown version of the five-year-old whose mother did not look up from her book, cannot hope for less tortured relationships until she can say: "I am unlovable. If that is true, so be it. I shall not try to change it." The acceptance need not, indeed it should not, be despairing. It can, and should, be accompanied by the shrug with which one might say, "I'll never learn to play a decent game of bridge." There is a perspective, an objectivity, an honest acknowledgment of limitations here that is necessary and right. It is a fact; one sees it and accepts it; and one sets about living a life that includes it. But is it not very wrong to compare, if only by juxtaposition, being unlovable and being unable to play bridge? A life, after all, can be very comfortable if one never sits down at a bridge table again, but being unlovable is at the core of a life and leaves a dreary prospect stretching ahead. A fact, just because it is central, cannot be made to disappear. And because it is there, one must force oneself to accept it as though it were of no more importance than not being able to play bridge. If this can be done, it is at this point that one can say, "All right, I am unlovable, but that does not mean that I cannot live a life that is decent and honorable and good. That *is* within my power." That is within everyone's power.

At worst, a life lived in accordance with the good fictions does not add to the anxiety already occasioned by attempting to conceal one's inadequacies from the world and oneself. We think it is because we are little and fearful and timid and we are afraid of being found out that we are anxious in the presence of other people, but really it is because we are afraid of not being appreciated for how marvelous we are. Anxiety is a great egotism. That party I started out to, I was full of anxiety, not because I was little and fearful and timid, but because I was afraid that other people would see me in that way and would fail to recognize my unusual attractiveness, intelligence, and charm. What nonsense it is, this desire to be without limitations, this wish always to be seen in the most flattering light. We are anxious, not because we think so little of ourselves, but because we think so much of ourselves. We are anxious, not that we may appear in the worst light, but that we may not appear in the best light. Anxiety is born of self-consciousness, and it is alleviated to the exact extent that we can drop consciousness of the self.

Since it is readily apparent just how concentrated people are on themselves, an assumption that can safely be made and can help to lessen self-consciousness is that other people are almost certainly as anxious as you are. There are exceptions, of course, in particular circumstances where one person is

144

clearly in a position of authority or in the instance of well-integrated persons, but, by and large, that person you are facing is highly preoccupied with himself and with what you are thinking of him. It is a poignant fact of life that we believe other people to be more competent, less anxious, more secure than we are, when the probability is that there is very little difference among us. All people worry about being liked, being accepted, being accorded dignity and stature, about feeling helpless or being abandoned, about experiencing loneliness, about being the target of hostility or controlling their own hostility, about receiving approval and applause. It is reassuring to become aware of this.

But even greater reassurance, I think, can come from sitting or standing alone and in a quiet place and feeling what it is you fear, letting the anxiety rise in all its intensity. Feel hurt. Feel unloved. Feel abandoned. Assume that the worst has happened, and let yourself experience what you would be feeling if it had. Can you stand it? Will it destroy you? Can you go on?

Were V_____ to let the feeling rise: I am unlovable, could she go on? She might indeed be in for a bad time, but it would be a hurt with an end, whereas to fight to keep out of consciousness the thought: I am afraid I am unlovable, is an agony without end, consigning her to the role of beggar, pleading for a dime of reassurance here, a nickel of refutation there, and, if she receives them, spending them so quickly on her insatiable self that she must go immediately back and beg for more. Were she to let the feeling rise, she would be face to face with the worst. But she would not go under—people become psychotic or commit suicide in flight from the awful truth, not from confrontation of it—and soon there would surge the secondary feeling of being able to count on herself. There would well up the feeling of an internal schism bridged, a strength found, a sense that, having embraced her fate, she could encompass her fate and set about doing the only thing that was ever open to her to do in the first place: living a life of decency and integrity.

It is the only thing open to any of us. The other chips

145

have to be allowed to fall where they may, for we have no control over them. But thinking about the unthinkable, testing the full depths and finding we can quite readily keep our feet, ends the anxiety that the chips are arrows and we shall be mortally wounded by them. It permits a nondefensive acceptance of the self, which, in turn, brings about the most useful of qualities: the wit to look at ourselves with detachment and humor, to be appreciative of the ironies in our lives, to concede ruefully that, after all, it is less than earth-shaking what happens to us.

The Invasion of Flattery

It also allows us to engage in far less self-expression, which is one of the more overrated endeavors of our time. When there is a solid, inner acceptance of the self, there is no need to thrust the self forward to be seen and reacted to. It is the person with a shaky sense of self who grabs center-stage and insists on attention for himself. The fellow who talks loudly and animatedly manages a great deal of self-expression by the end of an evening, but what he has convinced his captive audience of is that he must have very little sense of himself if he needs to make such a point of it. Paradoxically, the self is never more strongly present than when it is excluded. I was thinking of this when I came out of the Museum of Modern Art one afternoon; if I had been asked which painter I would like to meet, I would not have named any of the abstract artists whose paintings dealt with their inner lives but Andrew Wyeth, whose painting, *Christina's World*, was totally free of any plea to notice the artist. This painting, in which none of the man was present, was infused with the sense of a man worth knowing. And so it is in the ordinary circumstance. The security implied in being able to forego an insistence on the self is magnetic. People do not ignore. They are drawn toward. They want to know what is not put on display for them to know.

It is the person who has a strong sense of himself who is not driven to express himself, but it is also the person who

146

does not express himself who strengthens his sense of himself. To make an effort to abstain from thrusting yourself forward for recognition and acceptance of what you are signals yourself that you are secure enough to forego this. By allowing yourself to be judged without attempting to influence the judgment, by not throwing yourself on the mercy of other people, you become aware that you are not at the mercy of other people. You rid yourself of the anxious, clinging dependence that concern with the self engenders.

There is an unexpected and interesting point in this connection: it is as important not to accept recognition as not to seek it. It would seem that, were it to be freely offered, it would not threaten the sense of self, but it does. I had dinner at the house of friends where one of the guests was a museum director so secure that he could afford to be completely interested in the other people there, talking about himself when it was pertinent and he had something lively to say but not rapping on the consciousness of the others to draw attention to himself. His absence of effort immediately marked him as the most worthwhile person there. Another man, not so fortunate in his sense of himself, when he attracted no more than polite attention by his direct efforts, shifted to the effective, albeit transparent, device of dominating the conversation by announcing that he was going to recount the impressions he had garnered of each of us in the hour we had been sitting having cocktails. An insecure woman, first on the block, hung on his every word, but the museum director, when it came his turn, shunted the comments off with a quiet joke and an adroit rechanneling of the conversation; he was enough himself so that he did not need to yield to the temptation to find out what someone else thought of him. But, after dinner, the martinied man seized the reins again and, changing tactics, said to the director, "Now I am going to tell you the very favorable impressions I had of you when you walked in the door," and this time the director said nothing. He waited expectantly and listened carefully. And, under praise, he became dependent; he grew to seem an uncertain person, needing approbation. Unable to resist the bait of praise, that strong sense of self was lured out and demolished by compliments. The martinied man, who had been dealing with his better, had found a way to turn him into his anxious equal.

The museum director could not, of course, have said anything like: "I'm not interested in your praise," for it is not only impertinent to imply that one holds oneself above praise, it brings on attack. And if he had said the equivalent of: "I'm fascinated to know but I'm afraid it will be a bore to everyone else," it would have sounded like a false modesty designed simply to elicit protestations of deep interest. Perhaps he might have replied, "Did you guess that I was looking forward to dinner because I know what a marvelous cook our hostess is?" Some such thing, said lightly, lightly tosses the ball along. This is the best thing to do with praise: treat it like a game of volley ball and keep the ball in the air, neither clutching it when it comes nor praying silently that it will be tossed in your direction. A chap I know handled praise beautifully when, after a good evening of talk, I said, "It is always so interesting to be with you," and he replied, "Ah, but you make me more interesting than I am." We grinned at each other, liking each other, neither in the position of supplicant to the other. He had been interesting out of himself, not to win my approval, and he was right immediately to join me on the step above where I had stood handing down a morsel of praise.

A Disciplined Love

To take yourself out of the market for praise and recognition, to be unconcerned about expressing the self, to prevent yourself, quite consciously and deliberately if necessary, from paying attention to the impression you are making, might seem, in prospect, as though it would be a standing alone which would increase the sense of loneliness, but loneliness comes from a fear of being excluded, of being rejected, of not being recognized and responded to. Not to search for acceptance is to end the anxious fear of not receiving it; if you do not go out hunting for dollar bills in the street, you are not likely to return home feeling disappointed and depressed at

148

not finding them. The anxiety that drives you toward other people, hands outstretched imploring for kind treatment while, at the same time, shying at every sound and exploring every inch of the way for booby traps that might unexpectedly detonate and shatter the self, drops away and is replaced by a sense of freedom. You stand upright and tall, with an exhilarating sense of enjoyment at being alive and enjoyment of the world as it is. And you go toward the world as it is, not hoping for special treatment for the vulnerable self.

An editorial writer in *The New Republic* of September 26, 1964, remarked on the "redemptive power" of what Walter Lippmann spoke of as "a disciplined love of the real world." Although I do not know in what context Mr. Lippmann was originally writing, I take "disciplined" to mean a conscious and deliberate and continuing effort to accept that the world does not owe us fulfillment of our hopes, consideration of our sensibilities, nor immunity from personal tragedy. With acceptance of this, it is possible to proceed to a love of the world that is unblinking for what it is, unsorrowing for what it is not, the kind of love that exists for a mate when romantic love has ended but affection abides for the mate *qua* mate. The redemptive power of this kind of disciplined love works on the self and on the world: it permits one to behave well, which is the only way the world may be redeemed, and to accept that, no matter how well one behaves, the world is as it is, which is the only way the self may be redeemed.

There are two things that must never be said. The first is: I do not have the world I deserve. In a short story of great art written by Sylvia Townsend Warner, there were these lines: "Celia worked herself to the bone, and probably did a considerable amount of good, but her great service to Hallowby Juxta Mare [a town] was that she made the unemployed interested in their plight instead of dulled by it." There is wisdom here. It is always necessary to be interested in one's plight instead of dulled by it; and it is "a disciplined love of the real world" that keeps one alert and lively and seeking solutions instead of dulled, depressed, and impotent. It is the rare person who feels that his circumstances exactly suit his worth, but earth was always earth and heaven has always been elsewhere and we all take our chances. We fall ill or our child is killed or we lose our money. If we have not understood that this is a world where these things happen, there will be no love for it, and we will be mired in our plight and without heart for finding a way out of it.

The second thing that must never be said is: We have the world we deserve. Granted that the world is, in many ways, an ugly place, to count this as the entirety of the "real" world and to use it to justify ugly behavior is to underestimate the importance of the self. It matters how one individual conducts his life. It increases or decreases the ugliness of the world.

Unfortunately, the impulse to live decently and honorably, the desire to be a person of stature and substance, the wish to achieve meaningful accomplishments is perhaps as repressed now, and with as much shame, as the instinctual drives once were. The latter have become respectable and the former a source of embarrassment. It is not surprising since, as Henry A. Murray, Professor of Psychology at Harvard, noted, "Our eyes and ears are incessantly bombarded by a mythology which breeds greed, envy, pride, lust, and violence, the mythology of our mass media." In the face of the bombardment, in the face of repression, is it hopelessly outdated to quote Benjamin Disraeli: "Nurture your mind with good thoughts; to believe in the heroic makes heroes"? It might be so, were there not the figure of John Kennedy.

After his death, Mrs. Kennedy told Theodore H. White: "At night, before we'd go to sleep, Jack liked to play some records; and the song he loved most came at the very end of this record. The lines he loved to hear were: *Don't let it be forgot, that once there was a spot, for one brief shining moment that was known as Camelot.*"* Are the good fictions a foolish carrot? This man, who viewed himself with detachment and humor but committed himself to "the pursuit of excellence," followed them to Camelot.

* From *Camelot*, copyright © 1960 by Alan Jay Lerner and Frederick Loewe, Chappell & Co., Inc. New York, New York, publisher and owner of allied rights. Used by permission.

PART **III**

TO

ACT

*You are not yourself until you are yourself
in the world*

S

INCE the world is where you must live, it is how you live in the world which convincingly defines the self. You are what you are in action. And since to act in the world is necessarily to act in relation to other people, you must contrive to be and remain yourself not only in action but, more specifically, in interaction.

The areas of interaction which are simultaneously the most meaningful, the most rewarding, and the most troublesome are love and friendship and marriage and family. It is here that concerns about intimacy and distance, control and submission, and acceptance and rejection are most pronounced, that is, concerns about giving the self and yet being the self, adapting the self and yet asserting the self, being loved for the self and yet not buying love with the self. The question, more particularly in these areas than in any other, is how to be the person you are and still love and be loved.

A Strong Position in Love

Loving and being loved, judging by current literature, is the overriding preoccupation of our time, along with communication, which conceivably is another name for love. That emotions have become the object of almost single-minded concern may have more to do with the state of the world and the changed nature of work than with any change in the nature of human beings. It is the most common of observations that we live in a shrinking world, but it is less frequently remarked that we are shrinking right along with it in the sense that we have less and less feeling that we can intervene in events or exert control over their direction. Understandably, in reaction, we have pulled our gaze down to focus on areas in which we hope to be effective and find satisfaction. We look to human relationships to provide us with stature and dimension. Nor are we distracted from concentration on them by the necessity of work for survival. Not so long ago, work consumed virtually all of an individual's time and energy and virtually all of a family's time and energy, and in parts of the world where this is still true, there is not the intense involvement with feeling that we display; feeling is more known in the experiencing than in the examining, while here we seem to pay greater attention to the thermometer than to the fever.

When the family was a unit working together for survival, the work of the family was important and each member of the family had a place, a function, and a contribution. Caring *about* was implicit in the work of caring *for*. A man come in from the field, a child come in from the barn, and a woman come in from the kitchen were not likely to sit down at the dinner table and wonder: Am I loved? Do I love? Am I necessary to anyone? They were together, so what need had they to speculate about togetherness? But now the work of children has become nonexistent, the work of women downgraded, and the work of men remote. No one feels necessary, and so he must be made to feel necessary by love. Love is the only enterprise the family has in common, and thus it comes in for almost unrelenting attention.

Friends, too, are good for nothing but love. We speak of how enormously interdependent we have become, but our day-by-day dependency is on people unknown and unseen. We do not need friends to help with the haying or canning; they do not need us to put a new roof on the barn. We have fun together, but we do not work together, and since there is no point in trying to have fun with a person one cares little about, we spend some amount of time considering whether we do care, and how much, and whether we are getting a fair return on our affection.

All this attention to feeling may be having an unexpected effect. In scientific studies, it used to be assumed that it was

154

possible to observe a phenomenon objectively and that, if the observation was accurate, the phenomenon would be accurately known. But eventually it was recognized that the act of observation changes that which is under observation. This is Heisenberg's principle of indeterminacy, and it may be just as applicable to love as it is to neutrons.

There was told to me a story about a couple that began when the girl was seventeen and the boy nineteen. Against the wishes of both sets of parents, they were determined to marry and to come to the United States to study. They achieved both aims, but because the parents disapproved, they had to support themselves. The husband got a part-time job, the wife a full-time one, and they rented a large apartment and took in other students as boarders. My informant, who saw them at this time, marveled at both their enterprise and their compatibility and predicted a successful and happy life for them when they returned to their own country. Their return took place when they reached their goal of a B.A. for the wife and an advanced degree in engineering for the husband. The husband promptly obtained such an excellent job that there was no need for the wife to work, and she settled down to running the house and managing the servants. Six months later, she ran off with a painter, and when last heard from, was hard at work supporting him.

The husband, from all reports, is as baffled as he is desolate. All he can say is: "Why . . . just when everything was going so well?" Perhaps the answer is *because* everything was going so well. It is not uncommon to read in the newspapers about a divorce following fast on the heels of success. An actor or artist, after many a lean year, suddenly hits, and the couple soon after parts. There is a tendency to assume that the wife good enough for the struggle is being discarded as not elegant enough for success, but perhaps the important variable that has changed is work. Going uphill, two people tend to link arms; going downhill, they fly apart. With a goal, two people stand side by side; without it, they turn and face each other and begin to fret about the strength of the only bond holding them together.

155

Examining love is like examining a stocking: if you hold it up to the light and stretch it to search for snags, any snags there are may well run and ruin the stocking. In fact, if I may fashion Coudert's law from Heisenberg's principle of indeterminacy, it is this: Love is not only changed by observation; it is changed for the worse. Not the least of the reasons is that, to borrow the pet phrase of a businessman I know, we have taken such a strong position in love. With little else in our lives to give us a sense of self and success, we look to love to carry the whole burden. We invest in it almost exclusively; it is our income, our social security, our workmen's compensation, and our old-age benefits. We put all our eggs in one basket, and then we rivet our eyes on the basket. It is a lot to expect of love that it bear up under this intense scrutiny, particularly since, like children and flowers, it seems to thrive best given a warm environment and a sensible amount of neglect.

Falling in Hate with Love

"There are people," said La Rochefoucauld, "who would never have fallen in love if they had never heard of love." Well, we certainly, in these times, have all heard of love. We have heard that love is the answer, that love makes the world go round, that love closes the circle. We have heard that love makes it possible to like and live with ourselves. We have heard that love gives us ourselves. We have heard that with love anything is possible, without it nothing. Love has had a marvelous press, so much so that I suspect that for every person who would never have fallen in love if he had never heard of love, there are a hundred who would never have fallen out of love if they had not taken such a strong position in it and then come to feel that they had been sold short.

That love can work wonders is undeniable, as I lately saw with my mother. Her alcoholism over a period of twenty years so damaged her brain that she had to go into a nursing home, and there she further deteriorated so that she was transferred to a state mental hospital, where she was when I started writing this book. After three weeks in the hospital, where she was treated with indifference and neglect, she had aged thirty years: her head was sunk on her chest, she had become incontinent, she did not recognize me, and her speech was incoherent. The one clear thing she said was, "I am dying," and, indeed, it was apparent that she was. Not wanting her to die in such surroundings, her sister and I hunted until we found a nursing home where they would accept her in that condition, and we took her there. When we went back the following day, her head was up, her eyes were bright, she was no longer incontinent, and when asked how she felt, she said, "I'm fine. They love me here." *Re-Charh off*

In states of helplessness, love is certainly the answer, for, in such states, it gives a sense of the self, a worth and value to the self, which the self is unable to achieve for itself and unable to live without. When the sense of self comes from the outside, however, it can also be taken away. The young and the ill can only trust that it will not be, but the ambulatory adult must fear that it may be. That fear is always present if there is not an identity, a strong sense of self, which exists independent of being loved.

The person who looks to love to give him himself necessarily engages in a complicated series of maneuvers. He is trying to obtain from the person he loves the supplies he needs for self-esteem, and yet he must give up self-esteem, that is, the power of choice and decision and control over himself, in order to obtain them. He is trying to hold the other person close enough to reassure himself that he is loved, and yet not so close that he is engulfed and becomes simply an extension of that person. He is maneuvering to avoid rejection from the other person, and yet, to avoid the rejection, he must often reject himself. The individual seeking to shore up his sense of identity with love needs love badly but fears it profoundly because, for him, it is inextricably bound up with feelings of being manipulated, dominated, and humiliated. The love that bolsters his identity simultaneously undermines it. Just as much as it gives him permission to exist and to like himself, it takes away his permission to exist and to like himself.

157

Although highly ambivalent about love, such a person feels that he loves truly and deeply. He experiences how desperately he needs the other person, and he knows how much of his own autonomy he is surrendering in an attempt to keep the other. He is the one who adjusts, who gives in, who clings, who, like an outmatched boxer, tries for a clinch rather than standing firm and slugging it out. He feels that he loves greatly because he is in dread of abandonment and will give up himself rather than lose the other. Assuming that he loves greatly, he feels that love has failed him: it has not made him more but less; it has not reassured him but made him more uncertain; it has not made him strong but weak. He has put everything into love, and it has kept none of its promise to give him himself but, instead, has cost him deeply of himself. It is this person who, in E. E. Cummings's pointed description, "falls in hate with love."

The Terrible Compulsion

Self-affirmation cannot be found in love; it is a prior condition of genuine love. If you are first a person in your own right, you can afford to give steady and generous affection to another, unconcerned about preserving distance because intimacy does not threaten engulfment, unconcerned about questions of submission and dominance because intimacy does not imply control, unconcerned about the possibility of rejection because intimacy is sought as a good in itself, not in order to win acceptance for the self.

Acceptance of the self permits unreserved acceptance of the other as a person with equal prerogatives, wishes, and latitude. This is love, this love of a person who exists as he exists. The more you know yourself, the more you can know the person you love. The less you need his love to give you yourself, the more you can give yourself to him in love. The less you fear losing yourself in him, the less you fear losing him, and if you do not fear the loss of the other, you can wholeheartedly love. The person with a firm sense of identity, like a strong swimmer, has no fear of getting out of his depth and so he does not hold back, in contrast to the person with a weak identity who paddles about in the shallows of love, ready to break for shore when the going gets rough. It is only the person who can genuinely afford to lose the other who can afford to love genuinely.

If being a person in one's own right is the route to being a person who loves, so also is it the route to being a person who is loved. We receive love not because we deserve it but because we give it. Perhaps one of the most terrible compulsions under which we all labor is the myth that we must be likable and lovable. It is entirely wide of the mark. We do not need to be likable and lovable. We need to like and love. And we need to like and love out of ourselves, without ulterior motive, without any design to receive liking and love back. This is only possible when there is a strong sense of the self, when there is no apprehension that the self may be depleted by being prodigal with the stores of affection. The self can never be cheated by loving, for supplies of affection increase the more they are drawn on. The self can only cheat itself by not loving.

A friend described her nephew this way: "He is always at ease with strangers because he is always ready to like them. I suppose it is conceit, but he thinks he's a fine fellow and so he just assumes they're going to like him and goes right ahead and likes them." It is not conceit. It is self-esteem, and if self-esteem sounds like self-love, so it is, but it is not vanity. It is the self being strong enough to forget about the self and go out to others, not preoccupied with being likable and lovable and so being free to like and love.

The Story and the Plot

The temptation, upon falling in love, is to merge the "I" into an "us," to try to eradicate individual uniqueness and to fuse in a common identity. It seems natural to de-emphasize points of difference and to bring to the fore the delightful similarities. There is an impulse not to disagree, to hunt for common ground, to suppress quirks that hint at a potential departure from oneness. Nothing could be a greater mistake. "I" must remain "I" and "you" must remain "you" if love is to last. Love is spoken of as fusion, but it is fusion which is destructive of love, for just as powerful, although infinitely less recognized, as the basic drives of self-preservation, sex, and aggression, is the drive of maintaining self-identity.

When sacrifices are made on the altar of love, it is characteristic that the person with a strong sense of identity volunteers them and the person with a weak sense of identity demands them. The person with a flawed sense of identity intuits that the strong person's love is not built on need, and because his own is and this is the way he interprets love, he is fearful that the love will go elsewhere, and he threatens to do what he fears the other person can do, that is, withdraw his love. He attempts to produce in the other the apprehension he feels. He maneuvers to undermine the other's sense of self so that the other will become dependent on him and thus be bound to him.

The weapons of the weak are far more powerful than those of the strong. They are dependency and clinging and need. With these, the weak invade the strong, inducing in them pity, compassion, empathy. Although the strong can move freely in the world and find a variety of people with whom they can relate, it is this very mobility which makes them unwary. They feel able to give, so they do not object to giving. Aware of their self-sufficiency, they somehow suspect that that this may mean they love less, so they give up bits and pieces of themselves to demonstrate that they love as much as the other. It seems an easy sacrifice, but it is an insidious one.

D____, a man of my acquaintance, is an excellent, a fine and complete and generous man. That he has been married and divorced four times casts doubt on this description, for surely there must be some severe flaw, else why could he not have sustained any of these relationships? And why is he now seemingly in love with a rather helpless, rather pathetic woman who becomes demanding and tearful after a second cocktail? When I questioned a mutual friend, his comment was that D_____ had had bad luck with women, that each of his marriages had started out propitiously but had disintegrated in a confusion of sacrifices by D_____ and demands by his wives. D_____ apparently got locked into the familiar situation of the strong trying to save the love by sacrificing himself, the weak trying to save the self by sacrificing the other. This man did not have bad luck with women. He had the bad luck to have such a strong sense of identity that he did not take alarm when he met a woman with a weak identity. He allowed himself to be clung to, invaded, and hollowed out, until he had to pull free to prevent both of them from going under.

In love, one cares very much about the well-being and contentment and pleasure of the other, and if it seems that these would be enhanced by some change in the self, it is worthwhile to make the change. Certainly, one cannot refuse to make adjustments and accommodations and necessary compromises, for love can no more survive the absence of these than it can the opposite: sacrifice of self. But how are reasonable alterations in the behavior of the self to be distinguished from destructive attempts to change the self? The problem is analogous to that which a playwright faces when the play he has brought to maturity in solitude goes into production. The producer, the star, and the director all request changes in it, for various and variably respectable reasons, and the playwright must decide which changes he can make without harm to his play in order to keep his cohorts happy and which he must refuse no matter how much pressure is brought on him. Robert Anderson has commented that he meets this problem by always being willing to change the plot and always refusing firmly to make any changes in the story.

In a play, the plot is what is happening, the action; the story is why it is happening, the fundamental make-up of the characters. It is as though, traveling to Chicago, you might readily change your route at someone's suggestion but you would not change your reason for going. The road by which you get there does not make any particular difference, but your purpose for the trip is a part of you. In the same way, I think it is fair to say that in a life, it is valid to make any changes in the plot that seem a good idea, any change in actions that might make life smoother, but it is necessary to be adamant about refusing to change the story, the person you are. For instance, it is perfectly reasonable to learn gin rummy if it pleases the other to play, but it would be a mistake to engage in intensive gambling if you have a conservative nature. It is reasonable to be asked to be affable in company, but it would be a mistake to spend all your time partying if you have a solitary nature. It is reasonable to be asked to be thoughtful, but you have a perfect right to refuse to be required to be intuitive.

I loved someone once, very much, and I did not know that I had a right to be myself—more than a right, an obligation—and I kept trying to follow all his directions to be someone different than I was. The more I struggled to change, the more I failed, for the reasons outlined earlier in this book, and the more I failed, the more resentful I grew. I found a phrase continually recurring to me; it was Winston Churchill's remark that he had not become prime minister in order to preside over the dissolution of the British Empire. Eventually, the translation came to me: I did not fall in love in order to preside over the dissolution of myself. It is an accurate phrase. You cannot find yourself in love, but, also, you must not lose yourself in love.

Strangeness in Love

What may seem to the other like selfishness is, in the long run, the only thing that will preserve love. If I had resisted incursions on my legitimate right to be myself, if I had resisted affably and courteously but implacably from the beginning, I might be living in the castle today and never have had to crawl out from under the smoking ruins. But I did not know that one could wish only the best for the other and still never have it be at the expense of oneself, of the sense of being a person of worth and value and dimension. I did not know that "in-betweenness" is inevitable and that love is not diminished by its acceptance, only by attempts to obliterate it. I did not know that a life in common is only mistakenly interpreted as an identity in common, that separateness is not separation, that strangeness is not estrangement.

"Lovers should guard their strangeness," remarked Emerson, for if they do not, ". . . all slides into confusion and meanness." The impulse, when one has fallen in love, is to abandon strangeness forthwith, to open oneself completely, to tell of dreams and high wishes and prideful assets, and, equally, to tell of shames and weaknesses and bitter events. Never will there be a more interested audience, and the pleasure of being *known* is intense. But it is illusory; one can never be truly known since a life is what it is but a person is all the things he might have become. And it backfires; initially it is a joy to be understood, but eventually it is always an irritation. The other, having been told all, acts as though he knows all, and the self knows that there is much more to it than that. The other begins to make assumptions based on what he knows, and the self soon comes to view the assumptions as premature and belittling. As much as one always behaves in the same way, one nevertheless knows that, before an action has been decided upon, many alternatives have been thought of and discarded, and it is maddening to be viewed as completely predictable.

This is not to advocate a withholding of the self or of information about the self. I am suggesting that, first, the search should be for understanding and acceptance of the self rather than for someone to understand and accept the self, and that, second, when love comes into being, there be a quite conscious reminder to the self that merger is not possible, is only at this time tempting but in the long run a mistake, and that identity and strangeness, kept inviolate, are the nourishment of love. What remains exciting and lively is two people constantly opting to walk together, out of admiration for and delight in each other, not two people struggling in the net of a confused mutual identity. The arithmetic of love is unique:

two halves do not make a whole; only two wholes make a whole.

The person who knows and accepts himself, who is able to be and remain himself, is the person who deeply loves, for he is able to allow the other to be and remain himself. He confirms in the other the other's sense of identity. Instead of chipping away at the other's sense of worth and dignity and respect for the self, he enhances it. He loves the other *because* he is the other, not in spite of it. He knows perfectly well the difference between joining up together and joining together. He knows that, though they have chosen to join up together, they are each individuals, and that, though they may rejoice in each other, they are not responsible for each other's behavior in the same fashion as they are for their own.

A Scornful Look

A couple I occasionally encounter at parties are unfortunately not atypical. The husband gets a little drunk, and the wife sprinkles her conversation with: "Oh, R____, they've heard that story." "R____, nobody's interested in that." "You're making a fool of yourself, R____." Far from having her comments reform him, however, R____ is driven to drink more and to clown more as the evening wears on, both to retaliate for his wife putting him down and to gain a little amused reaction from the other guests. It would be interesting to see what might happen if the wife persuaded herself that her husband's behavior was his own and that, although married to her, he was no less a person in his own right. For one thing, her own behavior might improve. In calling attention to his to demonstrate that she is clever enough to see his boring foolishness and does not intend to be tarred with the same brush, she turns herself into a nag and as much of a bore as he is. For another, the husband might be less inclined to play the jester. As André Maurois noted: "In many cases people are what you make them. A scornful look turns into a complete fool a man of average intelligence. A contemptuous indifference turns into an enemy a woman who, well-treated, might have been an angel." Criticism, silent or stated, never mended a fault, for it undermines self-respect, and to the degree that self-respect is flawed, so will behavior be. Paul Valéry made this admonition: "Don't forget that I see myself in your attitude, and I don't want to see anything unbearable."

Both praise and criticism are reinforcing, but praise reinforces good traits, criticism bad traits. To criticize with the thought that pointing out deficiencies will cause them to be repaired is illusory. Criticism produces defensiveness, and no one acts well out of defensiveness; he is rattled, shaken, and hurt. Criticism causes the personality to shrink, to be diminished, and not only the personality of its target but of its deliverer as well, as R____'s wife is diminished by her criticism of R____ and he is not aided by it. While criticism is toxic, praise, in contrast, is enhancing. It is an expression of generous feelings which expands the area of warmth in the giver and gives rise to confidence in the recipient.

It happened that on two evenings this week I played bridge, both times with a partner whose game was superior to mine. On the first occasion, I played very well indeed, quite over my own head, and on the second, very badly, not nearly as well as I can play ordinarily. My first partner said such things, when my hand went down, as, "I see why you stopped short of game. You couldn't have known that I had the ace of diamonds." The second spoke along the lines of, "You should have gone to game. You might have known that I had the ace of diamonds." I played with confidence the first evening, none the second. I had a grand time the first evening and could not wait for the second to be over.

When someone is deprived of his self-esteem, he is deprived of the only thing that makes him a person worth loving. For one's own benefit, if for no other reason, the effort should be to build self-esteem in the other, to confirm rather than to assault it. This is achieved, not by flattery, but by a generous appreciation of the other's strengths and a generous de-emphasis of his weaknesses, by speaking to his good points and as rarely as possible about his bad ones. People who are good to each other make each other good.

Love can drain away just as readily through multiple pinpricks as through large wounds. Much of the impulse to criticize comes from a sense that to make the other person less is to make the self more. It is as though we sensed in ourselves a limited supply of approval, admiration, and liking, and we feel we must spend it on ourselves rather than give it away. But these things, like love, increase in the bestowal. The more there is given, the more there is to give.

Let Love Die

Love is a gift that one person makes to another. It is a gift of the heart, and the heart, as E. M. Forster commented, "signs no documents." It does not sign a lease, a mortgage, nor a bill of sale. It offers no warranties of service nor guarantees of faithfulness. It is well to remember this, both that you have no inalienable right to another's continued affection and that you have no obligation of your own always to love someone you once loved.

Sometimes, if your own life is to add up, you must subtract yourself from someone else's life. This time comes, I think, whenever you find that the affection or love of someone else can be kept only at the cost of yourself. If you are on the receiving end of much criticism, if the other has nothing but dissatisfaction with you, if you have lost the sense that to be yourself is a good and decent thing, it is time to get out. If love lessens you, if an undeclared war is being carried on in its name, if it is an excuse for destructive demands, if it is painful and joyless, it is time to let the love go and save yourself. You will find another love but never another self.

I know this is easy advice to give but agonizing advice to follow. If there were nothing to it but to get out, you would need no advice from me. You would pull free in a quick, convulsive gesture of self-preservation. But relationships that are deeply distressing are also deeply needed. I have not defined love because I am unable to, and I would certainly hesitate to define it wholly in terms of transference (that is,

166

infantile needs acted out in present-day relationships), but one simply does not fall in love unless there is an interlocking of needs and an implicit promise that the person will act toward you in the way that you unconsciously define as love. That definition, which will be based on the archaic experience of childhood, may involve tenderness, but it may equally well involve hidden contempt, abuse, hostility, exploitation, or pain arousal. Thus, although you may feel hurt and threatened in the relationship, that is also, to some extent, its lure, and the situation is not so clear-cut as saying: I am mistreated; therefore, I will get out. The very qualities that distress you may be the qualities that you need in order to feel that you love and are loved.

You may rage against the clinging dependence, the devouring weakness of your partner, and yet need this dependence to make you feel complete. You may fear the engulfing, denying qualities of the other, and yet only feel alive and loved when you experience this fear. You may rebel against being blackmailed with loss of love if you do not consent to being dominated, and yet only know love when you somewhere dread losing the one you love. You may long for more generosity, and yet unconsciously define love as having demands made upon you. You may rage against coldness and indifference, and yet only be attracted to persons who manifest them. You may loathe selfishness, and yet fail to be attracted by altruism.

That you may come to find that you do not *want* what you *need* is where love goes awry. I have heard a friend of mine say incredulously: "Why did I marry her? She has every trait I despised in my mother. Why didn't I see she was just like my mother!" He unconsciously did see, of course, and that is why he married her. He may have despised his mother's traits, but he had his definition of love from her. And this is why the observation is made that the person who remarries weds the same spouse over again; the name and the face are different, but the personality characteristics are strikingly similar.

Recognition of the similarity of a present love to an earlier one, to an earlier adult one or to a childhood one, always comes too late. First there is what Edmond Cahn in his book, *The Moral Decision*, calls "the chemistry of rapture," and the chemistry of rapture is blinding. Unfortunately, rapture does not last. It is reputed to in fiction, but it does not in fact. Affection may be abiding and love may be abiding, but the state of being in love is transitory. When it ends and the penalties of the relationship become apparent, it is not that something new has been added but that there has been a shift in the balance of ingredients. So often, one feels that one has been misled, that facets of the loved one have been concealed, only later to come to light. But that is not true. The facets were always there, and one always knew they were there, if unconsciously, and there would have been no falling in love without them.

The penalties may be minor and nonthreatening, and love may be not lessened but deepened by the burning out of the chemistry of rapture (which has nothing to do with sex but only with that uncritical, almost other-worldly state of being in love). The scales may drop from your eyes and you may delight in what you see. But if they drop and you are frightened, threatened, disappointed, or angered, then the problem is twofold. One is the problem that you need what you see, and it will be a prolonged and painful struggle to end your own love as well as to walk away from the other's love. The other is the problem that if you do manage this, you will walk into the same type of relationship all over again.

At least, that was my experience, and if I were back there now, I would do it all differently. I would have asked where my definition of love that included and required the traumatic had come from. What, in the total I defined as love, was transference? How much of what I hated did I need? I would have tried, that is, to know myself, and then I would have tried to be myself. I would have tried to see what my contribution to the mess was, and then tried to withdraw my contribution, on the theory that if I withdrew mine, his would be bound to be modified; he could not, for example, snap me into line by threatening to withdraw his love if I stopped fearing loss of love. I would have tried for a sense of myself that did not depend on being loved, and I would have tried to make the problem of what I was his problem, not mine. I would have tried to convey this: You have told me all the things I must do if I am to hold your love, all the ways I must change, all the things you dislike in me, all the things that make you unhappy. But I do not dislike them, I am not made unhappy by them, and so they are your problem, not mine, just as what you are is my problem, not yours. But they are problems to be lived with, not changed. We must find a way, not to change each other, but to let each other be.

And if I could not manage that and he could not manage that, then I would have gotten out. For that is when, I think, love must be allowed to die.

To be the self and still love and be loved is an equal problem for men and women, but it is not the same problem. The problem men characteristically must solve is that of not losing their identity in love, while the problem women characteristically must solve is that of not finding their identity in love. The basic fear experienced by men is whether, in opening themselves to love, they make themselves vulnerable to being drained of strength and effectuality and directness and decisiveness and independence and individuality, whether in lending their support, as a tree does to a vine, they end by being tangled and sapped. The basic fear experienced by women is whether, in opening themselves to love, they make themselves vulnerable to disappointment and denial and belittlement and contempt, whether in lending their substance, as honey in the comb, they end by being digested and discarded. In fine, men fear impotence; women fear abandonment. Men fear being used; women fear being used up.

The Relapse

There is no topic currently more discussed than the definition of the male and female roles. If a definition, any definition, cannot be readily arrived at in positive terms, it may be possible to say what something is by saying what it is not. Requested to define the color black, for example, you might find it easiest to remove from a room all the objects that were not black; you could then say confidently that black was what was left. Suppose there were two people in a psychoanalyst's office and you were asked which one was the patient and which the analyst; you would be correct in saying that the one who was not the psychoanalyst was the patient and the one who was not the patient was the psychoanalyst. In a marriage, who is the husband and who is the wife? The one who is not the husband is the wife, and the one who is not the wife is the husband. Since x cannot both be x and not-x, exclusion of the not-x is a means of identifying x.

In considering the male and female roles, a possible approach is this type of definition by exclusion. Reasoning in this way, the male role is that which does not include the not-male; the female role is that which does not include the not-female. But the present problem is, of course, that fewer and fewer activities have a not-male or not-female label attached. The dropping of not-male and not-female labels is a phenomenon of the recent decades. Before the first World War, it was characteristically not-female to vote, to own property, to run a business, to work in a profession, to live outside a family setting, or to be dominant. Similarly, it was not-male to run a house, make clothes, wash dishes, raise children, or to be submissive. But after World War I, as women commenced to vote and work and acquire property, the not-female label, if it did not come completely unstuck, at least began to loosen from various activities that had formerly been exclusively male. With each activity that in whole or part lost the label not-female, the definition of the female role widened, and as it widened, specificity was lost and the possibility of confusion increased. There were prolonged colloquies on the place of women, the threatened loss of femininity of women, the duality of women in work and home. On the other hand, there was no comparable confusion about the role of the male because the label not-male remained firmly attached to virtually all areas traditionally so designated. Men may have worried about their prerogatives, they may have worried about competition from women in the marketplace, but they were not worried about their masculinity, for they had not extended their sphere to include household and child-raising concerns, and with this large area still strictly defined as not-male, men kept their role definition simply by staying out of the not-male area. There was some question whether women were becoming masculine, but there was none that men were becoming feminine.

That apprehension awaited the end of World War II and the sudden, striking immersion of both sexes in home, hearth, and family. Women raced back into the home and childbearing, and men were right on their heels. As women had invaded male preserves after the first war, so men invaded female preserves after the second, and as women had forced down the signs of not-female from so many occupations, so now did men sweep aside not-male labels to participate in child-rearing, domestic, and home improvement chores.

It is interesting to speculate why the male radar, traditionally turned outward to bounce off the world, reversed to concentrate on family signals. Perhaps it was because, turned outward, it necessarily reflected, as never before, the immensity of annihilation, the impersonality of injustice, the anonymity of corporate endeavor, the monstrousness of the absurd; and the one sound that seemed able to compete with these cold signals was the cozy static of the family. We did not, either men or women, contemplate the cataclysmic times and become prophets and reformers and monks and saviors. We became parents, for children as sources of surface noise are the one socially unimpeachable distraction from fear and emptiness and anxiety. We did not espy the coming of the deluge and abandon ourselves to irresponsibility and frenzy and orgy. We filled the house with children and played their games while waiting.

Not the least important and certainly the most apparent result of this retreat to the home is the almost total confusion in male and female roles which has ensued. With virtually nothing any longer defined as a not-male activity and virtually nothing defined as not-female, it has become extremely difficult to know what the definitions of male and female are. This is not a comfortable state of affairs, and both men and women have been struggling to formulate a restructuring of their roles. Curiously, both have chosen to go about it by the same route, that is, by concentrating on a delineation of the female role.

There is a general assumption that men were men when women were women, and women have guiltily tried to identify a narrowed female role so as to leave men free to be men. And men, seemingly unaware that they themselves have blurred their role definition by incorporating in it much that was formerly not-male, attribute their confusion to the lack of specificity in the female role and try similarly to identify a narrowed female role.

For any restructuring, a fixed starting point is needed, and the indisputable fixed starting point in male and female is that it is women who give birth to children. From that starting point, the progression has followed some such course as this: women give birth to children; children require mothering; mothering is provided in the home; women's place is in the home; and if women's place is in the home, their fulfillment is in the home; if their fulfillment is in the home, their happiness is in the home; if their happiness is in the home, they are dependent on the provider of the home; if they are dependent, they are passive; if they are passive, they are not competitive; if they are not competitive, they are supportive; if they are supportive, they live through another; if they live through another, they are not persons in their own right; if they are not persons in their own right, they do not have a separate identity.

Women, who struggled long and hard to establish that they did have a right to a separate identity, might have been expected to cry out against the re-imposition of this restricted definition of the female role, but, in general, they have concurred in it enthusiastically. Even women who for circumstantial, psychological, or financial reasons have been unable to fill the role do not reject the concept but, instead, feel apologetic that they find themselves outside it. They feel that they should and must find their identity in a man, and that if they fail to do so, it is a life failure and failure as a female. Again, it is interesting to speculate why this may be so, and certainly it is bound up with those reasons earlier touched on of the changed nature of the world and work, as well as with the fact that when the male definition was steady, as it was prior to World War II, it was rather more exciting than unsettling for the female to be in a state of flux, just as it is fascinating to travel from home but travel turns into aimless wandering when there is no home base. Women were traveling before the war, but after the war, when the male role was no longer a point of reference, the travel grew to seem like wandering and they became as anxious as men to reorient themselves. But there may also have been an additional factor, a phenomenon analogous to an occurrence in therapy. When the patient has worked through to new and mature ways of behaving and the therapist suggests that it is time to consider termination of the therapy, the patient characteristically experiences a flare-up of all the old symptoms, a flare-up unconsciously designed to demonstrate that he is by no means ready to be on his own, that he needs the continued support and protection of the dependent relationship. This relapse is short-lived because the patient *is* ready to function as an independent and responsible person, but it is intense and it must be worked through until the patient arrives back at the point, not only of confidence in himself, but of eagerness to exercise autonomy over his life.

Will women's hasty flight back into the old dependent ways be as short-lived as the patient's relapse in therapy? It is to be hoped that it will, for it has had astonishingly paradoxical and thoroughly unwelcome results.

A Gentle River Becomes a Torrent

The picture in the thirties, with women moving into the professions and business, may have been of a somewhat beleagured male. But the picture now is of a castrated male. The authorized explanation is that men were men until women came roaring out of the home, like Indians coming off the reservation, but it would be sad if that were true because then it would have to be assumed that masculinity is such a fragile construct that, after several thousand years, it collapsed in forty with a few huffs and puffs. Fortunately, the explanation

174

cannot be correct, for the castrated male is a postwar phenomenon and came into being at exactly the same time that women were squeezing themselves back into the narrowed female role. It is not women not being women that has undermined men, but women being emphatically women.

The energy and intelligence and competence of women that became common knowledge in the pre-war and war years and conferred on them a certain density, a specific gravity which had been lacking before, did not vanish with the return after the war to the narrow definition of the female role. It had been made respectable for women to be effective, and their effectiveness did not cease when it was channeled into family life. They returned to their restricted role but with all their liberated capabilities intact. And as the waters of the gentlest river run swift and powerfully when confined between narrow banks, so did women become rather frighteningly forceful. They agreed that the fulfillment of women was in children and home and husband, and they threw themselves into these things. They agreed that the identity of a woman was to share her husband's identity, and they gave up pretensions to their own. And men applauded this in the belief that it would solidify their maleness.

Instead, it has threatened them as they have never been threatened before. The target of so much energy and interest, men feel manipulated, maneuvered, prodded, and pushed. The outlet for so much ambition, they feel driven, flogged on to achievement and accomplishment. As the identified source of identity, they feel, in trying to share their identity, sapped of it. As the identified source of pleasure and fulfillment, they feel inadequate, impotent to supply the full quota demanded. Men are in the position of executives of a long-established corporation who, thinking to end the threat of an upstart concern, buy it out and persuade its managers to work for them—only to come darkly to suspect that they themselves have been kicked upstairs, where they are in danger of becoming desiccated figureheads on the board, clothed in the trappings of authority and power but, in truth, puppets of the managers behind the scenes.

Women, for their part, dazzled by the bonuses promised, went to work for the old corporation with a will and then found themselves accused of unbecoming aggressiveness and intent to seize control. They disclaim such intent, and the disclaimer is genuine, but when a woman seeks to live her life through a man, her investment in him is great, her stake in his activities is enormous, and her concentration on him is undivided. She may well seem manipulative, and not only seem but be.

It was remarked at the opening of this chapter that the problem men have with love is the anxiety that they will be made impotent by it. They are apprehensive that the flow of the sweet transfusion will reverse and empty their veins of life and energy, that it is a seduction into sharing which will not enhance but dilute their powers. The present situation amply substantiates this fear. It was also remarked earlier that the problem women have in love is the anxiety that they are opening themselves to abandonment. They fear that love is a ruse to draw support and gratification from them, to stroke nourishment for another's ego from them, to lure them into making deposits in an account that is in someone else's name. Nothing now happening disproves the basis for this fear. But it is not inherent in the nature of love that men should be used and women used up.

In science, if data are trimmed to fit a theory, the theory is bound to be wrong, but if the data are left to sort themselves out, a theory will eventually present itself which covers the facts without doing violence to them. With a strict definition of the female role, women have trimmed themselves to fit the theory and have, in the process, grown attacking, dominating, and castrating. Men, attempting to hone the masculine role by means of definition by exclusion, have become castrated, dominated, and defensive. It is apparent that the more we have defined the male and female roles, the less male and female we have become. And the less male and female we have become, the more we have tended to blame love for the castrated and castrating results. Perhaps it is time to drop our attempts at definition and simply go about being what we are.

176

If a man has a sense of identity that does not depend on being shored up by someone else, it cannot be eroded by someone else. If a woman has a sense of identity that does not depend on finding that identity in someone else, she cannot lose her identity in someone else. And so we return to the central fact: it is necessary to *be*. Male and female, as basic as these adjectives are, are nevertheless adjectives, and to attempt to live in accordance with a set of adjectives, in whatever way they are currently defined, is to be engaged in attempts to change the self and/or the other. Such attempts in any direction, as I hope I have earlier shown, cannot be successful and can be highly damaging. Surely, it has been unfortunate in recent decades for men to try to change women in accordance with a definition of female and for women to try to change themselves. A woman who is able to be, who has a firm sense of identity, will be female because that is what she is, and a man who is able to be will be male because that is what he is. The basic problem in love, in the relationship of male and female, is not role definition but self-definition.

An End to Typecasting

Were we to leave off our attempts at role definition, would we not run the risk of male and female blurring together into one indistinguishable mass? An indistinguishable mass is not far from what we have at the moment despite the flood of scorecards, in the form of books, articles, and panel discussions, designed to tell us how to keep the players straight. We could scarcely be more confused, and it is quite possible that we would sort ourselves out if we suspended judgment on the ways we should behave as male and female and looked at the data of the ways we do behave. On such a point as whether or not a woman should work, for example, the stricture that a woman with a career is competitive and unfeminine may shake the feminine identification of a working woman and make the housewife feel smug. But I have known, as I am sure you have, many an appallingly aggressive housewife and many a nonaggressive careerist. The variable is not whether a woman works but whether she has a good sense of herself. Some women need work to give them the solid sense of their own worth that allows them to be noncompetitive; it may provide the exact reassurance that allows them to refrain from controlling and manipulative ways in their homes. The books written to inform women how to be women, both those that assure women they are dissatisfied with just being wives and mothers and those that sing hymns of praise to the incomparable satisfactions of being a wife and mother, while not uninteresting and occasionally provocative, are nevertheless worthless as guides. No one can say whether a woman should or should not work, should or should not have a career, should or should not be content to stay home. Each woman must find her place, not be put in her place. Her place is wherever, as the particular person she is, she feels necessary, effective, absorbed, and involved. To tell her that she does feel these things in a situation in which she does not or that she must not feel these things in a situation in which she does makes for a great deal of confusion and unhappiness that would otherwise be avoidable.

An instance of avoidable disaster made unavoidable was a most feminine woman who was lovely and delicate-looking, had unerring taste in her clothes and home, and was a marvelous housekeeper and cook. She was married to an extremely nice man who was intelligent, kind, witty and even-tempered. The only way in which they did not fit snugly into the male and female stereotypes was that she had a talent for managing a business and he did not. In the early years of their marriage, when he was having no success at holding a job, she started a small tea room. It was enough to keep them and their only child fed and housed, and eventually he joined her in the business and they prospered to the point of owning a large country club. It was his vision that moved them along, but it was she who had to do the day-to-day ordering, planning, and handling of the money, for he landed them in a mess in ways unfathomable to both of them whenever he held the reins. Despite their knowing this and his accepting it philosophically, she again and again insisted that he take charge, saying that it was the man's role to run a business. When the inevitable happened, she would step back in, but with bitter imputations concerning his masculinity. "If you were really a man," she would say, "you wouldn't let your wife work," and she said such ridiculing things in public. He left her finally, and she became an alcoholic. It was ironic that because she could not accept that male and female were what they were, not what they did, she subverted the very male and female identifications she believed she was upholding. It is easy enough to say that there must have been basic problems of identification already present, else they could have managed their limited role reversal better, and it is possible that I was blind to this because she was my mother and he my father, but, still, I think it was the world's rigid definition of roles that so troubled her. They functioned together well in other spheres, but she had not the serenity and sureness within her to buck the common view. As, indeed, few women have.

Were the world to accept the data as given, that is, were judgment to be reserved about what is masculine and what is feminine until it was seen whether a woman engaged in a particular endeavor was nevertheless not one whit less female and a man engaged in a particular endeavor was nonetheless male, men and women might become more secure in their sexual identification. I was startled when someone remarked that the hero in a play of mine seemed unmasculine because his hobby was gourmet cooking. Had he been a real person, should he have begun to doubt himself, should he have given up a hobby he loved, or should he have told the world to mind its own business, that he knew what he was and intended to do what he liked? I plump for the latter.

I know a real person, T——, who was a lively, confident, and competent person when she married fifteen years ago and resigned her job as a personnel director because, "My husband is going to wear the pants in this family." Her four children are attractive boys, but one is a compulsive stealer, one has a school phobia, and one presented difficulties in toilet training, continuing to soil himself until the age of seven. She herself has twice been briefly hospitalized with severe anxiety attacks,

179

and she will not go out of the house unless her husband is with her. Her psychiatrist suggested that, since she complained of feeling useless and worthless, she might think of getting a job, but she reiterated her fear that it would threaten her husband's masculinity if she worked. It could not be more apparent to even the most casual observer that she has emasculated both husband and sons and that what she is is a far cry from the femaleness of being life-enhancing, nurturing, maternal, and benign.

But the world defines her good housekeeping as female, and she has the seal of approval on her denying ways, while another woman, holding down an executive job, is made defensive about her feminine identification, for, with the slightest move of self-assertion, legitimate as it may be, the whisper will start: "She's rather masculine, isn't she?" The latter may wonder herself and may force herself to behave in ways artificial to her in an attempt to conceal the fact that she is intelligent and organized and effective. Her sense that to be herself is a good and worthwhile thing is shaken; and to the degree it is lessened, to the same extent is she lessened as a person and are her relationships with others disturbed.

Once when I was in Boston with a musical comedy trying out there, in the general hysteria prevailing in such a setting, one of the principals told me that, after a party the night before, she had ended up in bed with a young male dancer and that he was "the sweetest lover I have ever had." He had thanked her gravely, saying that she was the first person who had not assumed that, because he was a dancer, he was also homosexual, which he had suspected was not the case but had never had a chance to find out before.

My plea is for no particular mode of behavior but for an end to typecasting, or at least a temporary moratorium on it while we look at the data as given and see how, as men and women, we do behave and whether behavior that carries the label not-male or not-female may not be quite compatible with maleness or femaleness, and, conversely, whether behavior that is labeled male or female does not allow non-male or non-female behavior to be carried on under its guise, as in the case of T____. This is a difficult time in male-female role relationships, and this generation and the next are the ones who will, hopefully, work it out. We have tried going backward, that is, to women being weaker and men stronger, and found it has had the opposite effect. Perhaps we can go forward to allowing both to be strong, in the sense of allowing both to be what they are. A woman now, if she has a mind and independence, must conceal it. A man, if he is unsure and has an occasional need for dependence, must hide it. A great deal of manipulation and bewilderment results, and a great deal of personal unhappiness, and a great deal of failure genuinely to love. Definitions stand squarely in the road of self-definition, and where there is faulty self-definition, there is defensive and ungenerous behavior, which tangles male and female love, sex, and living relationships.

Twelve

THE MARRIAGE OF LOVE
AND MARRIAGE

HE following situation involving a man and his wife was recounted to me by a friend of theirs, who prefaced his description with the remark that he was of the opinion the husband was in the right but that a woman to whom he had told the story was convinced the wife was justified in her stand. The circumstances were that the husband purchased a car and registered it in his wife's name because she was a physician and he could thereby obtain M.D. license plates for the car and solve the New York City parking problem. Although he did this without his wife's advance permission, she ratified it as a sensible move, and it worked out perfectly well, for his office and her hospital were in the same direction and he drove her to work each day. So far so good, but then she transferred to another hospital at the opposite end of the city and a slaughterous dispute erupted, not over who should have the car—he was willing to buy a second one for her—but over who should have custody of the M.D. license plates. Since they were in her name, she believed she should have them. He, not wishing to give them up, claimed that she had been content with taxicabs before he acquired the car and could sensibly go back to taking them.

Asked which one I sided with, I could not think of a thing to say except, "When are they getting divorced?" I was told to stop trying to be clever and give an opinion about the "realities of the situation," but the freight of hostility, rivalry, and contentiousness that the story carried struck me as the reality of the situation. Granted that it is a tricky problem—he being the possessor of the plates but she the possessor of the M.D.— the fact that both are bitterly adamant in their stand and neither will entertain the thought of compromise suggests that they are not fighting over the plates but that the plates are the battleground on which they have chosen to fight out their relationship as male and female, husband and wife, businessman and doctor, person and person. That they are doing it with such an absence of grace, of generosity, and of kindness augurs a battle to the death of their life together.

Can Love Survive Marriage?

Although one marries for multiple reasons, to engineer another's destruction is not one of them, so it must be assumed that this couple started by loving each other. If she, for example, had married him for his money and he her for her looks, they would not now be in such a battle for control, for neither would be so deeply involved as to be so deeply threatened. There would be a portion of themselves that had never been committed to the relationship and that would now be providing an anchor of indifference. Only love comes to sharply acid strife. The time it is most likely to do so is when the honeymoon is over, not the literal honeymoon but the day when the fever of love returns to normal. The reason it is most likely to do so is that neither partner can forgive the other the cruel clarity with which he begins to see him. The let-down is a normal transitional descent from the heady, high ground of romantic love to the mature landscape of ripened love, but many spouses are taken by surprise by re-emergence of the separate identities they had thought blended into one, and they react with anger, fear, disappointment, and, perhaps, a quick grab for the controls. It is in such circumstances that role definitions become stickiest, prerogatives are suddenly nursed, and ordinary events thicken with symbolism.

A let-down, a reaction setting in, is a perfectly customary phenomenon in any area of life. The phrase, "the honeymoon is over," is part of the language; we use it to refer to the President and the press after the former has been in office for a time, and the President and Congress, and the end of an employee's breaking in period in a new job. Why we should be surprised that a reaction happens in marriage, whence came the phrase, I do not know, but we seldom are prepared for it. This is a pity, for it need have no ravaging effects if it is expected, recognized as inevitable, and coped with undefensively. It is the latter, a willingness to cope and an effort to do it undefensively, that are crucial to love's survival of the let-down.

Theoretically, the willingness to cope should be greatest in marriage because there is most at stake, most to be preserved, but, in practice, the majority of couples step into the same boat, set sail, and then refuse to bail, feeling that the marriage ties hold them together and no further effort is required on their part. For this reason, love has no greater enemy than marriage. I know of only two or three loves that have survived marriage, but I know several that have survived its absence in admirable style. I was taken for dinner on a recent evening to the apartment of a couple who have been together for twelve years, together but not married because he has a wife with whom he still retains a family house and form. This sounds a little racy, but it was anything but. They were a couple well beyond middle age, and they gave every indication of being an old married pair except that they so clearly liked each other. Each listened when the other spoke, each cued the other into his or her best stories, each was as polite to the other as they were to their guests, with not a trace of an undertone of impatience or criticism in their voices, and each had a lightness of spirit that allowed them to laugh a lot together. Do you know a couple who have been married a dozen years whom this description fits? I can think of just one.

I remember so clearly a vignette from several years ago, a dinner at a country inn where I happened to be sitting facing a table at which there were a man and woman and two small children. My companion glanced around at them toward the end of our meal and remarked what an attractive family they were. I said unhesitatingly, "They're not married. The children are her daughters, but he and she are not married to each other." My companion objected that I had no way of knowing that, but then he watched them for several moments and said, "You're right. He's really listening to her." This has stayed in my mind because it seems such a commentary on marriage.

I am not about to advocate living in sin, but there is much to be said in favor of living in a marriage as though one were living in sin. The let-down in love arrives under either circumstance, but when there are no marriage vows to have turned the key in the lock and either half of the couple is perfectly free to walk out the front door, both halves guard tenderness, guard affection, guard the sensibilities of the other. They cope because they have to cope. Nothing else is going for their relationship except the effort each is willing to make to preserve it. This effort involves continuing to value the other through the time of let-down even though it may seem that there is little of value about the other; it is the willing of an effort at suspending judgment, criticism, and dismay. Of course, quirks, traits, short-comings, and defects will rise to the surface. There will be the small, surprising failures of taste or tact or generosity, the startling vision of self-centeredness, the lapses in humor, the gesture that seems derogatory, even a show of cruelty. But these things happen when two people are living in closeness, and it is to be remembered that they are not one-sided. Both will display them. Neither will value himself less for doing so; he will treat his own lapses as understandable, forgivable and forgettable, knowing that they have nothing to do with his central core of decency and goodness.

People who love each other really owe each other at least the amount of forgiveness each grants himself. The unmarried pair have to find a way to manage it, and, actually, they have the advantage because they have no choice if they wish to go on together. It may cost each of them a well-bitten tongue, many swallowed tears, and private moments of difficult grief, but this is what it takes for love to survive. If the married pair cannot manage it, or if they believe that because they are married, they do not have to try, they may not part but they will have lost their chance at richness and ease together.

There is a phrase used in the theatre, the "suspension of disbelief," which is used to indicate that the audience at a

185

play must be willing to suspend their disbelief that what is happening on stage could actually be happening. When the let-down comes in love, this same willing suspension of disbelief is necessary. It does no good to say, "This can't be happening." It is happening. You are seeing things about the other person that you never saw before, and they are real, they are a part of him, they are not going to vanish. Criticism, accusation, or aggrieved complaint will not erase them. They must be believed. They must be accepted.

It is frequently observed that a prime requisite for a psychoanalyst is a complete openness to seeing the patient as he is. The psychiatrist cannot ignore or argue against aspects of the patient which displease him or do not jibe with his theoretical notions or strike him as unfounded. He must accept the totality of the patient, with the patient's incongruous bits and pieces of behavior and beliefs, if he is to be a fit companion to the patient in his attempts to grow into maturity. The only aspects of the patient certain never to change are those which the analyst does not accept about him. This requisite might well be borrowed from psychiatry by lovers. When the delirium clears, if love is to survive the let-down, an effort must be made to hold quite still and recognize the data about the other person: there is this and this and this about him. Wishing it were not so will not make it go away, nor will panic nor attack. The only maneuver that may succeed in making it go away is accepting it and integrating it into a total picture of him.

A friend of mine married a man whom she knew to be careful with money but she was startled to find, when they settled into the routine of married life, that he was obsessed with knowing where every penny went. He would not open a joint checking account nor allow her to have charge accounts, and he required that she keep each cash register receipt from the grocery store. Ridiculous and unfair? Of course it was, but somehow she was able to refrain from screaming at him: "How dare you treat me like a child who's not to be trusted! How dare you act as if you're the only one who matters in this marriage!" Instead, she said to herself, "Good heavens, so that's the way he is. Well, that's the way he is." She remained un-defensive; she told herself that it had nothing to do with her, i.e., that it did not mean that he did not love her; and she set about living with him as he was. After some weeks, one evening when he was adding up the accounts, she remarked that she she had the impression the household expenses were averaging about forty dollars a week. He did some figuring and said it was almost exactly that. "If you would feel comfortable about it," she said, "now that we know what the amount is, you could give me that much each week and I could make certain of staying within it." He refused, saying he liked to keep an eye on things. "All right," she answered equably. "I expect that's what your father did with your mother and you're used to its being done that way." It was true that his father had been a dictatorial man, and he had not admired him for it. Apparently, he turned the resemblance in behavior over in his mind, for a few weeks later he suggested that he give her forty dollars a week to run the house on. A somewhat similar series of steps led to her achieving charge accounts and a joint check-ing account. She still considers money an area in which she must proceed with great caution, but by accepting him as he was and not trying to change him, she did change him, at least enough so that he was perfectly easy to live with, and their love survived their being married.

Oddly enough, her love not only survived but it grew. It is one of those quirks of human nature that you love the person whom you treat well, not necessarily the person who treats you well. Love follows the trail blazed by generosity. Lincoln once said something to the effect that if he wanted a person to like him, he asked him to do him a favor; that is, he asked him to lend him a book rather than offering to lend the other a book. So it is in marriage: instead of coming to despise the other for his faults, if you behave with tact and understanding and good will, your love will increase. You will become ever more fond of the person you behave excellently toward. Thus, although it would seem at first glance that forbearance and pa-tience and silence might exact almost too heavy a toll to bear, the opposite is true. The other will benefit, but it is you who

187

will benefit greatly, for you will love more—more, perhaps, than you thought possible, and that is an incomparable feeling. We all know we want to be loved, and we speak of this, but we are less aware of just how much we wish to love. We want somebody in whom we can put the immense amount of love we sense we have. We want somebody who is worth all that love. What we do not realize is that we can create somebody who is worth all that love by loving him well. Our customary experience is that we fall in love, and when the let-down comes, we see the reasons why the person is not worth a great amount of love and the love begins to die back, sometimes just around the outer edges, sometimes all the way to its core, and it is our loss, even more our loss than it is that of the one who is loved. It is a loss that can be avoided by giving compassion and understanding without regard to whether the person merits it. It is not necessary to love so that we may give. It is necessary to give so that we may love.

Being generous is not as difficult as refraining from pointing out one's generosity. I remember once when I was about twelve or fourteen, I made a resolution not to say critical things. My mother walked into the room with a red blotch on her neck, and, resolution firmly in mind, I complimented her on how well her hair looked. She beamed and said how nice it was to get a compliment, and I promptly said, "Well, I've made up my mind only to say good things to people and so I said that instead of telling you about the blotch on your neck." I couldn't bear for her to be unaware of how gracious I had been.

As I have remarked prior to this, we all want praise and appreciation, and particularly do we want it when we have been big enough to overlook flaws in another or insults to oneself. There is almost a compulsion to point out that we have behaved well. What good is it to be a shining light if the light stays hidden under a bushel? But stay hidden it must. All is undone if gratitude is expected. An air of righteousness and that highly unattractive quality, self-sacrifice, creeps in, and it is better to be plainly attacking than to display these sly and mean traits.

188

Another of my friends, happily married for some years, was unaware that she and her husband would ever have a problem about money, but it turned up unexpectedly one day when she mentioned to him that she was thinking of renting loft space and moving her hobby of weaving out of the house. Perhaps, she ruminated, she would buy a larger loom, and if all went well, she might try to market her fabrics. "What are you going to use for money?" her husband asked. She was taken aback, for he was a generous, easy-going man who was proud of her accomplishments as a weaver and had never made the slightest objection before to her spending money on looms or materials. When she pointed this out, he said that he had had no objection but that he considered a hobby one thing, a business another, and he had no intention of paying the rent on a loft. Both tried, over a period of several weeks, to make their points of view clear. Not only did they get nowhere on this subject but other minor hurts and disappointments each had experienced at one time or another began to be rung into the argument, and the disagreement seeped into all areas of their life. A sense of estrangement grew. At no time did they actively quarrel, but their relationship became clouded, and this so distressed them both that they agreed they must simply accept that each had a blind spot on the subject and they would not talk about it any more.

All writings I have seen on marriage have as a central piece of advice: Talk things over. Air your problems. Do not let grievances fester. Work out compromises. But the longer I live and the more I observe, the less sure am I that this is good advice. These two people had the luck and the wit to recognize an impasse and the generosity and mutual respect to be able, finally, to leave it alone, but much was said in the weeks before they let it lie there that, while not permanently damaging, would have been better left unsaid; and nothing was said in those weeks that had not essentially been said in the first five minutes when she stated her wish and he stated his opposition.

This is almost invariably the case: the first five minutes are meaningful and necessary so that each knows the other's position, but everything after that is repetition and elaboration and, ultimately, the dragging in of irrelevancies. One person does not change another's mind with words; only the person himself can change his mind, and he is not likely to do so under the pressure of argument. He may give up or give in, but he honestly reverses his stand only when, in silence and within himself, he plays back the arguments on both sides and truly listens to them. The arguments have not been heard during the discussion designed to elucidate them, for this is when the person is expending all his brainpower on defending his own position; he hears what is said to him only as points to be rebutted; and the more he is compelled to buttress his position, the more he convinces himself that it is the right one.

If, after the husband stated that he did not intend to pay the rent on a loft, his wife had simply said, "Oh," and then nothing more, the argument would have continued, but entirely within the confines of the husband's mind. Perhaps he would have said to himself: "I understand business, and I know it's not simple to get one started and that there are always unforeseen expenses. She'd need a second loom, and an assistant, and someone to make deliveries, and I'd be pouring money down a rathole." But then, feeling a bit ashamed, he might have added, "I've always praised her work and said it was more exciting and imaginative than the commercial variety. She must think now I didn't mean it and feel hurt. She's competent at managing money. She's got a practical streak. Maybe it isn't such a bad idea, and if it does go down the drain, so we don't take a vacation this year, that's all it would mean and that's not so catastrophic. It would please her if I backed her, and I would come out of it looking pretty good either way."

We always feel compelled to state our own case, but the truth is that the most ringing advocate we have is the other person's mind. Left to his own devices, the other will get around to arguing our case more brilliantly and more persuasively than we could ever manage, and he may very well win it for us where we would have failed. This is not intended to be a subtle suggestion on how to get your own way, although it may come down to this. Rather, it is meant to say that expressed arguments are never won, that only the first several minutes of any discussion can be counted on to involve a calm elaboration of points of difference, while every further moment increases the danger of the argument degenerating into angry accusations and hurt defense, and that, in all probability, you can count on the other fellow to see your point of view if you give him the silence in which to do it. Even if this does not prove to be so, even if, despite seeing your reasons, he continues to find his own more cogent, nothing is lost and something is gained. This wife, for example, might or might not have gotten her loft and loom if she had stayed silent, but she did not get it by arguing and the argument itself made something go out of the marriage.

A caution must be entered here, however. An icy or reproving or hurt silence is abominable. The silence, so as not to be ugly, must be intelligent, thoughtful, and noncommittal, and it is silence on the particular topic, not on other conversation. A moment or two of really registering what the other has said, of coming to the conclusion in your own mind that an impasse has been reached or is unmistakably in the offing, and then an easy transition to another subject is best. Or there is a handy phrase that can be used; I once read that a man who got derogatory letters about his work invariably answered with a one-sentence reply: "Dear Sir (or Madam): You may be right. Sincerely yours." An interested, "You may be right," indicates that you are taking the trouble to think over what the other has said, which is flattering and disarming, while at the same time it allows you to reserve judgment. What often comes in response is the comment, "Of course I'm right because . . ." and then a restatement of the other's opinion. There is a gentleman who handles me at this point by raising his hand and saying benignly, "I hear you. You're getting through. Just let me think over what you've said."

It is completely human to be convinced that, if you could just make your feelings clear, the other person would be bound to understand that you have reason and cause on your side. The difficulty is that the other person believes exactly the same of his argument, and so both of you endlessly restate your positions, trying to get past what appears to be a failure in communication. While there has been a failure in communication, it is not in the sending but in the reception; it is not because the right words have not been found but because neither has been listening.

There is a natural desire for closure, that is, for a rounding off, whether of a task, a conversation, or an argument. You wish a conclusion to be reached, an end to be made. But think back over the arguments you have had. Did they end with agreement? It is more likely that they petered out or were broken off, only to flare again at a later date. Closure is seldom achieved. If you can persuade yourself that pressing an argument rarely, if ever, leads to a resolution of it, it is easier to steel yourself to abandon attempts at closure and go on to speak of something else as casually and good-humoredly as possible. You can count on the argument to continue turning over in the other's mind just as pervasively as it does in yours and to come up again. The husband of the weaver, if his wife had dropped the discussion, is certain to ask within the week: "Have you given up your idea of a loft?" And the wife can easily reply. "No. I'd like very much to do it, but I haven't come up with a way of managing it. What do you think?" The husband might restate his objections, but if he has had second thoughts, his wife has given him a graceful opening in which to offer his help.

The Sandpaper of Anger

A close friend with whom I occasionally used to become seriously annoyed taught me the creative value of silence. When she had said or done something I considered thoughtless or rude or unkind or selfish, I would behave in an ill-tempered or aggrieved way to convey that I was out-of-sorts with her and to provoke her into inquiring why. But she never asked. She just went along as though I were my usual self. I suppose she knew what was the matter, not only because she herself is intelligent and perceptive but because one always knows. But she never probed, and eventually my irritation would fade and we would slip back into the good ways of our friendship. We are now devoted to each other, for the reason, I think, that she has never alluded to things about me that irritate her and has never given me an opening in which to criticize her. This is in contrast to another valued friendship that was lost because the brow of either of us had only to cloud slightly for the other to ask: "What's the matter? What have I done wrong?" Unfortunately, the one asked was always able to give a full bill of particulars, and the other quickly responded defensively in kind. We chronically talked out our differences and aired our grievances, until finally we had so bruised and bored each other that we grasped an excuse to go our separate ways.

The problem in human relationships is that people accept, in themselves, the affection or love they feel for the other, but they cannot accept the dislike they also feel, and so they feel obliged to inform the other of the existence of the flawed actions which they perceive to be the source of their dislike in order that the other may remedy them and thereby make whole and unambivalent the love given. There is inevitably an aversion to some facets of the other, a hostility felt because of some types of actions, a hatred of some qualities; and an acknowledgment of this is necessary, for when hate is completely shut out of love, it may come in the back door and take full possession. In suggesting that the better part of wisdom may lie in not speaking of the disliked qualities in the other, I do not mean to imply that awareness of them should be suppressed. On the contrary, they must be recognized, but as much as possible only in dialogue with the self. To confront the other with them will not act as sandpaper to smooth off the rough edges of the relationship; the effect will be to cause an abrasion through which love will hemorrhage.

This does not rule out quick, instant anger flashing in response to momentary provocation. Spontaneously expressed, such anger is neither dangerous nor destructive. It is when anger is allowed to build and attracts to itself, as a magnet does filings, slivers of words and looks and incidents that its bursting is ugly and contaminating. Suppose, as an example, that a husband and wife are returning from a party at which the husband drank a little too much and danced a little too often with someone else. The wife restrained herself from flaring up at the party, but in the car and on the way home is not the time to pour out her irritation either, for by now she is so angry and hurt that her words will be a shrewish attack, not a legitimate expression of annoyance. What can she do? Admit to herself that she is furious, this is necessary, but then she must force herself to swallow hard and struggle past the moment in which she longs to explode; and because a silence can be as vicious as words, she must hunt for every positive thing she can think of to say about the evening. Better still is it if she searches for a joke or twists a happening into a small, funny story. Humor, in such circumstances, requires an enormous effort, but if it can be contrived, it is remarkable in its effect, like switching a barreling freight train onto a siding. It drains the tension from the angry one and the hostile defensiveness from the guilty one.

To avoid having the anger hemorrhage internally, the wife does well the next morning to stab the words she might have said on to paper, writing out her attack until she has exhausted the force of her feelings. This has cathartic value, and, still more, it may expose the narcissistic wound at the root of the anger. One is angered by events that threaten the self, by actions that imply, in however concealed or seemingly remote a fashion, some derogation of the self. If the wound to the self can be exposed in writing, it may heal rapidly with the application of common sense. At the root of this wife's anger is her feeling of having been humiliated, but when she has unearthed that, she also knows that it had been a long week, her husband was unwinding, he did not behave as he did in order to hurt her, and that if it had been someone else's husband, she would have thought nothing of his actions.

If anger still burns despite having been set down on paper,

it can be an intriguing and enlightening exercise to take a fresh sheet of paper and go over the same material, this time writing the other's side of the story, climbing into his shoes, borrowing his mind to reason with, and assembling his arguments as he would present them if he were doing the writing. If as strong a case is made *for* him as would be made *by* him, it may be found that he indeed has a case. The effort must be, not to set down both sides of the story objectively, but to write each equally subjectively, pouring out the other's grievances and hurts and irrational feelings with all the emotion felt for one's own. When the other's angers and fears and defenses have been lived in this way, their sting is surprisingly pulled. The self becomes less guarded, less tender, for the worst is known, and the worst has turned out only to be human, not annihilating.

The Paper Weapon

When I was in college, the mother of a friend came to visit and took several of us out to dinner, including a girl who planned to marry at the end of the semester. The mother said she had just one piece of advice to offer the engaged girl, and this was that she and her future husband make a pact to bring up unpleasant matters in the form of notes to each other. Her point was that the tone of a note can be controlled, even if it requires rewriting it several times, whereas a tone of voice and the facial expression accompanying it cannot be revised or erased. The words in a note can be thoughtfully chosen to get a point across without making it an attack. A complaint which has been humming in the mind like a wasp, when set down on paper, may look picayune. If so, the note can be ripped up and the complaint forgotten. Or if the complaint continues to seem justified after it is written, the note can be delivered, freeing one's mind of prolonged rumination.

My own system is to write an imperious, insulting note, such as: "Only a stupid, thoughtless, selfish monster would make a sandwich at midnight and leave the bread open and

195

the butter sitting out and crumbs all over. Clean up after yourself! I'm not the maid!" After I have savored it for a few minutes, I then tear it up and hunt for a way to phrase my gripe lightly, such as: "I know I'm bad-tempered in the morning, but you don't have to add to it by leaving the kitchen a mess." The most effective way of persuading someone to see your point of view is to introduce it with a thought with which he already agrees. Since anyone would agree that I am bad-tempered before breakfast, I have obtained fifty per cent agreement with my note immediately and have only fifty per cent to go; moreover, it is disarming to tie in a defect of one's own with mention of another's. The wife of the errant husband might write: "I had a headache last evening, which may account for my lousy evening, but your behavior sure didn't help." She need not mention that it was his behavior which gave her the headache. If it goes too much against the grain to shoulder any of the blame, she might alternatively write: "I was good and mad last night and I'm still good and mad today, but on the assumption that your conscience is giving you as bad a time as I might, I'll let it take over."

So that guests do not see them inadvertently, a bulletin board hung on the back of the bedroom closet door is a good place for the posting of notes. Their subject matter need not be limited to complaints, of course, but can include requests for things to be done, such as, "Please, when you have time, fix the Venetian blind in the kitchen." In this way, one does not run the risk of turning into a nag by bringing up the same matter over and over; the note simply stays there as a reminder until the job is done. Small things sometimes fray the nerves in marriage more than large things, like not putting the cap on the toothpaste or leaving the milk bottle standing out on the kitchen table. A note on the bulletin board or taped to the object itself can remedy the irritation.

And every once in a while, as a change of pace so that the sight of a note does not make the recipient's heart automatically sink, there can be one that reads: "I was proud of you last night," or "Thank you for being so nice to Mother," or, simply, "I love you." Hardening of the hearteries is the most serious affliction besetting marriage, and warm, good-humored, approving words are the only effective preventive. Joseph Addison long ago noted that, "Two persons who have chosen each other . . . with the design to be each other's mutual comfort and entertainment, have, in that action, bound themselves to be good-humored, affable, discreet, forgiving, patient, and joyful, with respect to each other's frailties and imperfections, to the end of their lives." One does not marry to become a judge of the spouse's behavior. If a marriage license is mistaken for a hunting license and disapproval, punishment, and threat of withdrawal of love are employed as weapons, all one bags is one's own unhappiness.

The greatest boon to marriage is a sense of fun, good humor, and light-heartedness. If they do not come naturally, they can be—indeed, they must be—cultivated, and in writing may be the effective place to start, for it is difficult to be spontaneously funny but it is possible and feasible to spend half an hour hunting for a humorous way to make a point. To use the hypothetical disgruntled wife again, she may end up with a note which reads: "After last night, if I had it to do all over again, I'd do it all over you." I believe that this was an Abe Burrows' song title originally, but whatever its source, it could scarcely make her point better, while at the same time providing her with the easement of a laugh in writing it and her husband with the cushion of a laugh in reading it. Everything there is to say has been summed up neatly, tersely, and wittily.

The practice at being good-humored and/or humorous gained in note-writing can carry over into conversation, and you will find yourself hunting for the light touch instead of flying off the handle. Remember, though, that the best jokes are the ones you make on yourself. It is better to be the butt of your own humor than to use someone else as the target. In the midst of an argument, you can say, "Let's get down on all fours and look at it from your point of view," but that is sarcasm and will do nothing to lighten the atmosphere, whereas if you were to say, "Let's get down on all fours and look at it from *my* point of view," then you will both laugh and the bitterness will go out of the discussion.

The best preservative of humor in marriage is outside interests. It is an enormous mistake to give up friends, hobbies, or individual pursuits when you marry, or to let them drift away because the marriage seems all the satisfaction you need. If there is complete concentration on the marriage, perspective is lost, and without perspective there can be no humor. Having other things to think about keeps the events in a marriage from getting out of proportion. Besides, it gives you something to talk about. This is no small matter, for marriage is a dialogue, and if one partner has nothing to say of interest to the other, the other eventually stops listening. Marriage is love, it is sex, it is family, but ultimately and essentially it is companionship. This may seem prosaic and unromantic, but it is the lasting value of a marriage. And it is a value which can be preserved. Almost nothing can be done to make love last, except to do everything possible not to kill it, but companionship can be tended.

It can be tended in the same way that friendship can be nurtured: by a generous interest in the other's concerns, by refusing yourself the luxury of being bored, and by treating the other with never-failing courtesy. This last might appear to be the least because, in friendship, politeness comes easily. But, in marriage, it seems to be the most frequently omitted ingredient. A friend of mine listens attentively to everything I have to say, including my less articulate pronouncements, encourages me with perceptive questions and comments, and remembers, on the next occasion we meet, to inquire into the further developments of whatever episodes I have recounted; but when his wife speaks, he cuts her off impatiently, makes fun of what she has to say, and if she mispronounces a word, he hoots sardonically and uses the word, in her mispronunciation, throughout the evening. My friend is a fool to treat me politely and his wife rudely, for her friendship is far more important to his well-being and contentment than mine.

Many people, if they were to treat other people as they

treat their spouses, would soon have not a friend in the world. Why it is assumed that marriage is more impervious to the effects of discourtesy than friendship, I do not know, but of the people I have encountered, only headwaiters, truck drivers, and married couples are consistently insulting. If I were to formulate a single banner to raise over marriage, it would be this: Love, let us be kind to each other.

"I've seen flagrant infidelities patched up, I've seen crimes and even murder forgiven by the other party, let alone bankruptcy and every other form of social crime. Incurable disease, blindness, disaster—all these can be overcome. But never the death of common humanity in one of the partners. I've thought about this and I've invented a rather high-sounding title for this basic factor in human relations. I have called it the Law of the Quantum of Solace." The rather unexpected source of this quotation is a James Bond short story by Ian Fleming. Bond himself replies to this comment: "Quantum of Solace—the amount of comfort. Yes, I suppose you could say that all love and friendship is based in the end on that."

Thirteen

THE BEGINNING,
THE END

HE worst piece of advice I have ever been given was: "Go ahead and get married. If it doesn't work out, you can always get a divorce." It made marriage sound so easy, like accepting a job that has been offered because if you do not like it you can quit and do something else. Even at nineteen, I should have known better, but, alas . . .

Marriage is not a job, and divorce is not two weeks' notice and out. There is no hell like a bad marriage; divorce, although it may be a relief when it comes, is a highly public and painful admission of failure; and after divorce, you are not simply single again, back where you were before marriage. If a nineteen-year-old were to ask my advice now, I would say the opposite of what I was told, that is, that marriage should be contemplated as though there were no such thing as divorce. The possibility should be shut out of mind completely, and all the years of a life with this person envisioned: locked in, no escape hatch, forever committed. Is it a bearable thought, or is the prospect of marriage only intriguing because there is a way out if the going gets rough?

If the latter, remember this: until you can squeeze through the trapdoor, you are locked in, and two people can do each other serious and lasting damage in the enclosed space of a marriage. Wounds are inflicted the scars of which are borne for a lifetime. Far more anxiety and depression are involved than could have been predicted. There is ugliness. There is unexpected trauma. It is impossible to escape unscathed, or even lightly scathed, from a marriage. Between in and out, there is a bruising road to travel, and it is infinitely preferable to reconnoiter the road sanely before setting foot on it than to embark on it casually and take a chance on what lies around the bend.

What To Do Before the Minister Comes

If saying to yourself: Remember, this is the person with whom I'm going to spend the rest of my life, gives you stern pause, this is not sufficient reason in itself for ruling out the marriage. The mistake lies in saying: Well, I'll marry and see how it goes. The wisdom lies in saying: Well, I'll marry and some of it will go badly. What will be difficult? And will it be more than I can cope with? It is not a question of not marrying because of problems, but of recognizing them, facing them, and making them a familiar of your thoughts. To rely on the reforming effects of marriage is not a sensible hope. Very few people does marriage improve. In the abrasively close quarters of marriage, the veneer of restraint may be scraped away. The man who drinks heavily before marriage is quite capable of becoming an alcoholic after it despite, or because of, the responsibilities of marriage. The woman who is hypochondriacal before marriage will not automatically abandon her somatic preoccupations; instead, they may increase tenfold.

An astonishing number of people marry for messianic reasons, deluding themselves that they will accomplish a rescue operation that neither the person himself nor other loving souls have been able to pull off previously, but the love of a strong man does not necessarily stiffen the fiber of a weak woman, any more than the love of a good woman necessarily puts iron in the soul of a bad man. In fact, the odds against saving another from himself are such that if you can persuade yourself to stay out of this particular trap, you are well advised to do so. People are dismayingly stubborn about being reformed, and it is far safer to assume that marriage will intensify any given person's problems rather than cure them. There are exceptions, of course, but it is better to go into marriage prepared for the rule rather than counting on the exception.

Since love is a notable corrupter of taste and judgment, it can be useful to give some weight to the opinions of other people about the person you are in love with. While they may be blind to the ineffable qualities that delight you, they may, by the same token, have a sharp vision for qualities or potentialities that have escaped you. The opinion of one's own parents, although it is easy to credit it as prejudiced, is not to be dismissed out of hand. At the very least, while believing that they are wrong in their predictions of a man's ability to earn a living or a woman's ability to run a house, it can be temporarily granted that they are right and the future of five years hence imagined; are you capable of being content with a marginal financial existence or of being sanguine about a neglected and unattractive home? If not, arrange for a pause in which to validate their judgment and your own further. The opinion of friends is another source of insight. I remember a friend of mine commenting off-handedly about a man I was in love with: "My, he sure doesn't want you to have any life apart from him, does he?" I was not unaware of this, but I had chosen to see it in the flattering light of devotion to me; after this remark, I began to be conscious of the pathologic insecurity behind it. Another chap I was going out with at another time seemed to me de-lightfully thoughtful because he would say: "We'll have dinner here. No, I think you'd like it better there. But you like seafood, don't you, so perhaps we'll go there." A friend of his asked, "How are you at getting him to make up his mind?", and that was the clue that forced me to re-evaluate his be-havior and consider whether I could face a lifetime of indecision.

While the parents of the person you love are not likely to point out their offspring's problems, they are quite apt to embody them. People have a way of being very like their parents or, in reaction, very unlike them, and since it is pos-sible to appraise the parents of the person you are in love with much more objectively than the person himself, it can be revelatory to take a close look at them. Patterns of thought and behavior are transmitted from generation to generation and are deeply ingrained, so deeply that, even though the offspring may consciously reject a trait in a parent, he may be helpless not to duplicate it. A friend of mine speaks with despair of handling his own children in the same way his father handled him; he can hear himself the minute the words are out: the same tone of voice, the same phrases, the same strictness and coldness. Another couple, each of whom was raised in an atmosphere of restriction and punishment, in reaction have brought up uncontrolled and uncontrollable children.

The form, shape, and ambience of the parents' marriage can give a clue to the offspring's definition of marriage, again either in replication or reaction. A gentleman I know traces his difficulties back to his mother's absorption in her career and consequent neglect of him, but, almost to his own bafflement, he has encouraged, prodded, and financed his wife into a business of her own, rather against her own inclination to have children and a large, old house in the country. If the parents' marriage has a striking feature, such as the husband expecting a good deal of waiting on and the wife providing it, this will give forewarning of how their offspring is likely, if unconsciously, to define the marriage balance. It is not that the person wishes to replicate in his own marriage the marriage of his parents but that it is difficult for him not to do so because he has had this definition of marriage etched on his mind. That being so, the best guarantee that an offspring will like and enjoy and be good at marriage is pleasantly married parents of his own.

The offspring's parent of the opposite sex can provide an answer to a most interesting but rarely asked question: Why does this person want to marry me? One seldom thinks to query another's impeccable taste and flawless judgment in falling in love with oneself, but the truth of the matter is that there will be a transference factor present. A friend of mine, aware of this, looked with care at her fiancé's mother and thought her to be an unattractively positive woman inclined to demand that her husband and son cater to her. This was not the image my friend had of herself, of course, but, in attempting to cope with the information honestly, she faced the fact that behavior of her own which she had previously defined as inability to resist taking advantage of her fiancé's good nature was, in truth, an inclination to manipulate him. At this point, she could say cynically that if that was what he wanted, why should she deny him his masochistic pleasures? Or she could take the long view and curb her own natural propensity in this direction so that, when the fever of love returned to normal, they could transit to a steady love, she without contempt for his accommodating ways, he without a sense that he had been taken.

As well as probing for the neurotic needs that attract the other to the self, it is sensible to explore the expectations that the other has of the self, for spading them up and examining them lucidly and unflatteringly can permit a glimpse of the future. As touching as the expectations are now, can you go on meeting them year after year or will they eventually conflict with desires you hold for yourself? If he, for example, wishes someone to spur him on, to care very much about his career, will you eventually come to feel that you wish to reserve some of your energy and interest for accomplishments of your own? Or if she wants a strong father figure who will tell her what to think and do, will you come eventually to feel impatient at her dependence? The traits which make one feel needed and wanted at twenty-five may be grounds for divorce at thirty-five, without a single change having taken place in them. Indeed, that they do not change is the factor that ultimately makes them impossibly irritating. A young man may feel puffed with tenderness and importance in the presence of a girl who leans on him and is obviously quite helpless without him, but helplessness is not charming in a person no longer young. It is a truism that the more things change, the more they stay the same, but it is equally accurate to reverse this: the more things stay the same, the more they change. For a marriage to stay the same—that is, for it to remain the enclosure of love and delight in the other— the people in it must be capable of growing and finding new ways of relating to each other, ways built on liking and trust and respect, not on dependency and need. If they cannot, the more they stay the same, the more the marriage will change, and perhaps deteriorate beyond the point one or both feel it is worth preserving.

The bait of feeling needed is almost irresistible, for it guarantees the importance of the self to the other person, but it can be a costly, and ultimately empty, bond for the self if the other person's needs are archaic, infantile requirements for being nurtured, mothered, symbolically fed, and totally accepted. No amount of feeding will satisfy the hunger of such needs, and the self will grow exhausted in their service. Unfortunately, such needs are difficult to identify, and a sixth sense must be brought into play to penetrate the façade of youthfulness and outgoingness and easy charm which is their most usual camouflage. A possible alerting clue is the attractiveness of such people to older people, who find them winning and respond to the mixture of deference and gaiety in their manner.

Concurrently with the attempt to make intelligent guesses as to what the other sees in you so that you can project his needs into the future and imagine whether an older you will still be content to meet them, it is enlightening to reverse the examination and question what you see in him. To attack the matter head on will give you a set of answers you already know, all the delightful reasons you are in love with him; thus, it is necessary to come at the matter obliquely. As his parent of the opposite sex can reveal something of what the other unconsciously responds to in you, so can your own parent of the opposite sex suggest his appeal for you. Surface similarities are not what is of interest, nor is their absence proof that you have fallen in love with quite the opposite type of person. What you are searching for are broad generalities. Is the other placid and your parent quick-tempered? This means little if, underneath, both have a quality of being withholding of love and approval. Have you always been unsure of your ability to please your parent? Look to see whether that same unsureness is not present in your love now. As well as comparing the other to your parent, think back to other persons you have been drawn to. There will be a common denominator, and if you can identify it, you will have some hint of what your own needs are. Catching a glimpse of them will permit you to ask the same type of question for the other which you have asked for yourself: will it have worked out well five years from now that these are the needs in me that he has met?

There is a last, and odd, question to ask: what would the

other's life be like without me? If you have a sneaking suspicion that it would be a perfectly good life, go ahead and marry. If you have an equal suspicion that you, too, would manage reasonably well, you can marry with double assurance, for you can assume then that you want each other more than you need each other, and wanting is a much better long-range basis for marriage than needing.

Look Before You Weep

To distinguish needing from wanting is not a simple matter, but there are a few guideposts which can be checked. One that has already been mentioned is seeking points of fundamental resemblance between yourself and the other's parent of the opposite sex. If you and the parent are inclined to handle the person in the same general way, it can be assumed that the other needs this type of approach. A fellow I know, for example, would have said that he in no way resembled his autocratic father-in-law, but, to his regret, he finds that the longer he is married, the more he is tempted unthinkingly to order his wife about and to treat her as though she were a slightly incompetent child. Had he attached significance, before marriage, to this approach of his father-in-law's, he might justifiably have assumed that, whether or not he was aware of it, somewhere there existed in him the propensity for the same type of behavior, which his wife had unconsciously intuited and which would become emphasized in him over the years by her need for it. Forewarned, he might have weaned her from this need by consistently responding to her fully but differently. It might be questioned why he should bother to, why, if he had a nicely submissive wife, he should trouble to train her to stand up to him. The answer is that he should, not for her sake but for his own, for transference love differs from mature love in one crucial and potentially destructive respect: it is inextricably linked with dependency, and dependency can be the fountain of dread and hostility. Dependency threatens the individual's autonomy, which is to say that it threatens his very existence, and what threatens existence will be feared and hated. Transference love is an ambivalent love, and ambivalent love carries the seeds of its destruction within it. This wife who needs to be ordered around will somewhere fear and hate the husband who meets this need. It may never come to the surface in strong enough fashion to break the marriage, but it will always be there to keep the marriage from being the easy, warm relationship it could have been. How might the husband wean her from this need? Not by forceful means, such as refusing her guidance and insisting that she make every decision on her own, but by consistently respecting her as an individual and again and again inviting her opinion and weighing it equally with his own.

The devilish pitfall is that the transference love of the other meshes with a characteristic of the self that is very hard to give up. This husband is bound to approve of himself for being able to arrive at quick, firm, and sensible decisions, and he will, if only secretly, enjoy the opportunity to demonstrate what he considers an asset of his own. My friend who became aware, by matching her behavior to that of her fiancé's mother, that she treated her fiancé somewhat sadistically would have to resist an almost irresistible opportunity to behave in a way that comes naturally to her. When someone is inviting you to behave in the very ways you would normally behave, it takes a certain amount of maturity and generosity to sidestep the request.

Another route to identifying whether there is a heavy load of transference in the love the other feels for you is your own sense that you are being lured into highly consistent actions. T——, the authoritarian husband, for example, might have noted before his marriage that he found himself behaving decisively on small and large points, more decisively than was his wont in varied circumstances with casual people. My friend, for her part, might have noted that she ordinarily kept her talent for ordering people about in somewhat better check. If you are becoming quite consistent in your behavior because you sense that the other wishes certain types of actions from you, and if you suppress other types of actions because you sense that they will not be valued, it is time to take a look at the mold you are being chivvied into.

The element of transference is particularly striking when you cannot find in your own behavior that which would seemingly account for responses of the other. If you are frequently accused of indifference, for instance, or of being disapproving when no thought of censure has crossed your mind, or of not being truly loving, you can suspect that it is not you who are being evaluated but an early love of this person which you now embody. When you hear over and over, "You don't really care about me," or "You care more about what other people think than me," or "You really would prefer to be by yourself, wouldn't you?", protest that it is not so, but after a while cease going in bafflement over your behavior hunting for what it is you do that triggers the persistent accusation. It is not you; it is transference.

Having detected elements of transference in the other's love and perhaps in your own, should you not marry? Well, if all of us waited for a love to come along in which there were no transference components, very few of us would not die single. The best you can do is hope to recognize the nature of the transference and handle it in such a way that it does not disrupt the marriage. And the best way of managing the latter is to recognize the other's need to be a person of worth and strength with a separate and valuable existence, whether or not the other person is himself aware of this, rather than automatically taking advantage of the other's infantile needs or, out of misplaced kindness, trying to satisfy them. Whatever the transference needs, this is the basic need, and if you can keep that in mind and try always to respond to it, it should be very difficult to come up with a bad marriage.

How Soon the Bells?

There is one type of marriage in which it can be fairly safely assumed that needing each other has been mistaken for wanting each other, and this is the teen-age marriage.

208

Such a marriage is likely to be defined by the participants as a true step into the adult world. After all, are they not willing to tie themselves down, to give up the free and easy life of fun and games, to take on unusual responsibilities for their age? So they may see it, and marry they may in the name of wanting each other. But it is need, not wanting, and it is need, not even for each other, but for the family. It is fear of responsibility, the particular and difficult responsibility of becoming an individual. The years from seventeen to twenty-three are crucial years for the acceptance of aloneness, and acceptance of the essential solitariness of every human being is prerequisite to maturity. The teen-ager who goes from his family directly into a family of his own is avoiding adulthood. He is duplicating, in haste, the situation he cannot find the strength to do without. Teen-agers marry to be mothers to each other, not to be spouses to each other.

At what age should one marry? As a rule of thumb, perhaps not until you are past the age of feeling strongly that you must marry. When you have gained assurance that you can cope effectively in the world, when you feel comfortable on your own, when you have had time to develop an awareness of the self as a quite separate person, and, more particularly, when you have been deeply lonely and felt the panic of loneliness ebbing, it is safe to marry, for then you can have fair confidence that you are marrying the person, not the institution. There should be a time of being unplugged from your original family before plugging into a new family for sustenance and support. If that time is cut short, you will be marrying for what you can take from marriage, not for what you can bring to it. You will be marrying as a defense against anxiety, not because you have found someone with whom you believe you can live for the rest of your life and like it. You will be marrying because you are afraid of being single, which is not a good reason for marriage. To be yourself, you must be yourself in the world, which means you must first give yourself time in the world.

This is not to recommend a specific term of holding a job and the experience of supporting yourself, nor of living alone for the assurance that you can manage an establishment of your own, nor of a certain amount of travel so that you know something of the world, nor of a certain number of more or less intense encounters with the opposite sex. It is a time indefinable in terms of either experience or duration but of that length and with that content which allows you to sense that your center of gravity is in yourself, that you are free of the gravitational field of your original family and that re-entry, this time into a family of your own, will be by choice, not by weak default. For some people, this requires only a short interval and limited experience. For others, much may need to be lived through before they become aware that they are persons with boundaries and that within these boundaries they can be self-sustaining and self-supporting.

Do you know those balloon toys which are weighted at the bottom so that the clown, when tossed, always lands on its feet? After they land, they are upright but oscillating, swaying from side to side and then slowly becoming still. It is when you finally become still that it is safe to marry, when you are no longer fleeing from the past nor running into the future, when you like your original family but do not need them, when you want to marry but do not need to. The qualities most to be valued in the person you marry: the possibility of further, steady maturing, resiliency, optimism, good humor, and perspective, are the qualities which waiting out the oscillation will allow you to find in yourself.

The Imperfect Script

Suppose that the love of your life turns up before you are ready? Life is not notoriously co-operative about such things. The timing may not be the best; the circumstances may not be the most propitious; you may, without prompting, be able to foresee some difficulties quite clearly. I have not meant to imply in any of this that you must have the perfect script before you go into production. As in the theatre, many a seemingly sure-fire hit closes on Saturday night. I saw this in my teens in the persons of a boy and a girl who were inseparable all through school and married the day after they graduated from college. It had been a twelve-year courtship, and the marriage lasted three months. Again as in the theatre, many a predicted flop has undergone revisions and been turned into a long-running hit. In all human enterprises, there is an element of risk and luck. But the fact remains that your chances are best the more you and the other are persons in your own right and the more you are able to penetrate to an understanding of the type of interaction there is between you. To recognize that some of the interaction has infantile roots need not abort the relationship; on the contrary, it is simply to be forearmed so that the interaction may perhaps be nudged in a healthy direction or, failing that, accepted with less discouragement and disillusionment. All problems cannot be foreseen, but the foreseeable problems should be within manageable proportions. If you are tempted to marry someone because he needs you, go ahead, but keep in mind the experience of this country with foreign aid; the recipient of your benefactions is not necessarily going to admire you greatly for your generosity and he may go to hell in a handbucket even more rapidly in order to prove his independence. People are as jealous of their sovereignty as nations, and sovereignty must always be scrupulously respected. Marriage is an alliance between equals, and if the equality is a fiction, it must be a fiction so carefully adhered to that it becomes a fact. Lastly, do not marry because you are afraid of losing someone, for you can only hold by letting go; and do not marry because you are afraid of being single, for you will never feel so alone as you will in an unhappy marriage.

Just as many people marry for neurotic reasons as stay single for neurotic reasons, and there are just as many people unhappily married as there are unhappily single. Edna Ferber's famous comment is that being single is like death by drowning: a delightful sensation once you cease to struggle. I cite this, not to commend to you the state of singleness, but to suggest that it is not necessary to be panicked into marriage through fear of it. Most men and women who truly want to marry sooner or later find someone they truly want to marry, and it is infinitely preferable to come late to a good marriage than early to a bad one. The trick is to persuade yourself to be un-selfconscious about singleness, which is no easy trick in our society, but it can be done if you refuse to view marriage as the sole passing grade in the test of mental health. The agony in being single, if such there be, is not inherent in the state itself, for a full and meaningful life is achievable outside of marriage; it lies in not being able to accept the single state as a viable entity.

Divorce, Any Style

When you fall in love, it may escape your attention that you do not happen to like the person, but even if you have thought to check on this and all the other queries you can essay before marriage, the marriage may nevertheless go awry. If so, divorce is available. Although it is feasible, and occasionally highly desirable, one thing it is not is glamorous. A man or a woman who is divorced is automatically viewed in livelier terms than someone who has never been married, and even may be secretly suspected of having the best of two worlds: the seal of approval of marriage and the reinstituted delights of singleness. But the divorced person is like a man with a black patch over one eye: he looks rather dashing but the fact is that he has been through a maiming experience.

Most discussions of divorce center primarily on its effects on the children of the marriage, but I am not persuaded that children are not sometimes more resilient than the grown-ups involved. As far as I have been able to observe, divorce is seriously harmful to the child or children when they feel that they have been deserted, when they have not been made to understand that it is no failure of love for them which has caused the separation. The small boy of a friend of mine came to me and asked miserably if I knew his father was not going to come back to live with them again. I said, "Do you know that it has nothing to do with you, nothing at all to do with you?" He burst into tears and admitted that he was afraid it did. It was possible to explain to him then that a man and a woman chose each other because they liked each other, as he chose his friends, but it could happen that they stopped liking each other, as he had stopped liking his best friend down the block after a fight over a ball, but parents and children did not choose each other; they were knit together. His mother had never ceased caring about her parents, nor his father about his, as he had had occasion to observe, and in the same way they could never separate themselves from him; it was a special, unbreakable tie. "Oh, well, that's all right, then," he said. He seemed able to accept his parents as individuals with a right not to like each other and a right to separate from each other as soon as he became convinced that they could not separate from him. All was not surely and simply easy for him after that, but when he lost his personal anxiety, he was quite quick at adapting to the changed circumstances of his life.

If the child feels secure about the love of both his parents for him, he may rather enjoy the special attention he receives from the visiting parent, and there is somewhat more danger of his being spoiled than neglected. A youngster of my acquaintance turned into an impossible child the moment he sensed he was in the driver's seat. The child of divorcing parents suffers most from feeling deserted, from feeling torn in his loyalties, and, in the long run, from the absence of a parent of the same sex with whom to identify or a parent of the opposite sex with whom to relate. But a broken home need not result in a broken child, any more than an intact home necessarily results in a healthy child. A home without bitter dissension, without ugly words and belligerency and clapperclawing, is the basic essential for a child, and if it cannot be achieved with both parents in it, then it is preferable for one to depart. In fact, if a couple are staying together for the sake of the children, for the sake of the children they might better separate.

If the truth were known, I wonder how many couples ostensibly staying together for the sake of the children really are staying together for the sake of finances? It is one thing to contemplate divorce, another to get down to the practicalities of the matter and realize that the expenses of a household in which there are children do not lessen with the departure of the father. The mortgage, the insurance, the car, the clothing, the school and medical expenses go right on, and the income which may or may not have been adequate to meet all these has now to be stretched to cover a separate establishment for the father, perhaps another car, a cleaning woman, restaurant eating, and entertainment expenses. A friend of mine is worrying himself sick over his ex-wife's finances because she spent unwisely, got into debt, and is in danger of losing the house which, as part of the divorce settlement, was put in her name. He has taken out a huge bank loan to bail her out, but he has no control over her spending and he can anticipate that, even if he manages to save the house in this crisis, there may be another, and another after that. He thought he had only to meet his legal obligations, which were worked out on a realistic basis; now he finds that his responsibilities in practice go far beyond this. "What can I do?" he says. "The children have to have a decent home. And I have no control over what she does because I am not her husband any more." He himself lives in a dreary hole-in-the-wall because it is all he can afford, and his children, understandably, are unhappy at having to visit him there. Another man I know has bought a house in the country he neither needs nor wants because his children were bored and restless in the city when they came to spend vacations with him. He found that he was having to make elaborate advance plans to take them to the theatre, the zoo, the museums; the easy companionship he had looked forward to had deteriorated into a series of efforts to keep them entertained.

I asked a divorced gentleman one day why he looked so tired, and when he replied that it was because of the number of parties he had been going to, I suggested he might stay home a few evenings and get some sleep. He said he would love to but he did not dare to turn down an invitation because that might be the very party at which he would meet someone he could marry. He had not imagined that he would be anxious to remarry, but he discovered that he very much missed a woman's presence in the house—the old-shoe intimacies that he had thought he would be glad to be rid of: the smell of her clothes in the closet, her stockings hanging in the bathroom, her voice vaguely heard as she gossiped on the telephone. He missed the comforts and conveniences he had grown used to: his meals on the table, clean shirts in the drawer, his suits taken to the cleaners, flowers in the house. Most of all, he frankly missed someone to sleep with. His physical needs drove him into affairs he did not want with women he had no particular feeling for, and he longed to be married again and be done with the ritual of dating and courtship and seduction. He had assumed that he would enjoy it, as he had in his twenties before marriage, that it would be fun and exciting, but he found he was only impatient, that the whole enterprise seemed adolescent and outdated, like the stately patterns of a minuet. He kept wanting to brush aside the preliminaries, but, of course, he could not because many women's deepest suspicion is summed up in the phrase: "You only want to sleep with me." He longed to say, "Yes, and why not?" but the jig was up if he let any hint of this slip through.

Because this man is a close friend, he has given me a glimpse of the problems of a man after divorce. It is not easy to meet attractive and intelligent women of an age close to his own, not easy to meet them casually in the course of an ordinary social life, and he has found that arranged introductions are painful. It is perfectly apparent that he and the unattached woman at a dinner party of married couples have been invited to meet each other, and he feels that he humiliates the woman if he makes no effort to see her again, that he is passing a judgment that he has no right or intention of passing simply by recognizing that she is not appealing to him; on the other hand, he feels that it is nonsensical to make a date just to reassure her about her attractiveness. Of his own attractiveness, he admits ruefully that he is no longer so certain as when he was in his debonair twenties. Perhaps he was rebuffed as often then and simply moved on more readily, but now he finds that he is hesitant about pursuing a woman without clear signs of encouragement. He is conscious of being in his forties and of probably never going to be financially better off than he is now and of having left some part of his emotional commitment back in his marriage.

Women whom he meets in the course of his business also present a problem. Some, knowing his available status, make a play for him, and he finds he must be extraordinarily tactful in his sidestepping if it is not to have repercussions in his business. Others, the ones he feels drawn to, cannot, for the same reason, be taken out a few times and then dropped if he feels no further interest. Altogether, the role of the divorced man is not particularly the carefree life of the bachelor that it may seem from the outside. Indeed, this man described, with sorrow and sympathy, a friend of his who got out of a bad marriage only to make a worse one the second time. His wife would not let the children of his first marriage in their house and in other ways made his life miserable, but he made little fuss because being divorced had taught him that he could not live without a woman and he could not face the same period of pursuit and search a second time.

It depends greatly on the circumstances of the marriage and divorce, but in more instances for women than for men, I think, divorce is a release because women have a greater problem of maintaining an identity in marriage than men do. They are more apt to feel basically threatened at the core of their selves than men, and divorce may be a true escape from being made to feel an appendage, a chattel, an undervalued creature. A man's reason for divorce may have to do with his peace and well-being, while a woman's reasons not infrequently have to do with her very being. A dominating man, or a cruel or indifferent or unfaithful one, makes a woman feel she is being treated as a possession, as a second-rate object. A friend of mine described her unutterable relief when she boarded a plane and left her husband, who was a man with many gifts and great charm but who had been genuinely unable to conceive of her as a person. To this day, he has not understood why she was not honored that he had allowed her to have a share in his life. He never knew that their battles were fundamentally over her sense that she was drowning in his sea, and when she tried to explain, he could only say in bewilderment, "But you're my wife. What more do you want?" If she said, "I want to matter too!", he replied, "But you do matter to me," and explained how his comfort would be lessened, his house less smoothly run, his social life less well managed if she were not around to run the works. Never did he fathom the distinction between a wife who mattered and a wife who mattered to his comfort and convenience.

Whether or not a divorce has the welcome effect of freeing the wife from the contempt implied by unfaithfulness or cruelty, she will face the same aftermath as she will if the divorce has come from an acknowledged incompatibility or a slow change of interests and direction or, simply, boredom and irritation which both may have equally experienced. If there are children, she has the obvious problems of raising them alone, of disciplining them alone, of having competition for their love from a father who provides treats. There are all the difficulties in meeting a suitable candidate for remarriage which a man has, plus the anchor of children, which decreases mobility. A divorced man may find it harassing to attend parties; a divorced woman may find it impossible. Baby-sitters are expensive, and invitations are not easily come by since single women do not delight a hostess's heart in quite the same fashion as single men do. A woman feels conspicuous going to concerts and the theatre alone; she may also, in these violent days, find it dangerous.

The man who repairs my phonograph claims that his women customers are more attuned to, more pleased by, the bass sounds than are men and that this is because women's ears are designed to hear men's voices. Whether or no his fancy is correct, it is true that having a man around the house provides a lovely balance, accoustical and otherwise. I am not of the school that holds that women do not enjoy the company of other women—I think they do and for the same reasons of ease and mutual interests and relaxation from sexually tinged complexities that men enjoy men—but the sexes are complementary, and as a man misses feminine sights, smells, and sounds, so does a woman miss the masculine.

The sexual needs of women are less taken for granted than those of men. They may not even be particularly anticipated by the woman herself, especially if sex was one of the shoals on which the marriage cracked up, but she can find to her surprise that she feels the deprivation rather more keenly than she would have surmised. In one sense, she should have an easier time than the divorced man in meeting her needs, for someone else's husband, although he may not be overanxious to repair the broken step in the front porch, is often a ready volunteer in this category. In fact, there will be all too many and all too insistent married volunteers, few of whom will be able to understand why the fact that they are someone else's husband disqualifies them. A divorced woman needs to be fast at diversionary tactics and occasionally fast on her feet. She has to be prepared to be considered fair game. She also has to decide whom she considers fair game: friends' husbands (not cricket in my book), strangers' husbands (caveat emptor), neighbors' husbands (cave canem), or only single men. To protect her freedom of choice and her reputation, she had best have excuses ready that hinge neither on her virginity nor her faithfulness, since her divorced status rules both out. And she had best do some hard preliminary thinking to be sure that she is doing what she wishes to rather than accepting salve for a scarified ego. A divorce, particularly if it has taken place because the husband wishes to marry someone else, can so undermine a woman's faith in her attractiveness and desirability that she seeks indiscriminate reassurance. A time of six months to a year after divorce is the minimum period for making a determined effort not to be panicked into ugly episodes. After that, hopefully, a natural, healthy egotism will have reasserted itself.

When it is the husband who wants the divorce against the wife's wishes, there is a custom of making the husband pay heavily for it financially. With children involved, they must be supported, of course, and in the least skimpy fashion commensurate with the husband's having enough left to manage. In the absence of children, there is still something to be said for a settlement or alimony because the wife has been, in effect, a partner in a joint enterprise. But punitive damages demean the person who seeks them. It is really not worthy of a human being for a woman to say, "I'll make him pay through the nose for what he's doing to me." The marriage has not been successful, affection and respect have drained away, the couple were in it together and now they are out of it together; let it end, and decently and well, not with a scourging price tag. A woman of my acquaintance said, "Why should I let him off easy? He walked out on me." She is young, healthy, and has a good job; in fact, she so little needs her alimony of one hundred dollars a week to live on that she is using it to play the stock market. Why did he walk out on her? She professed to find it mystifying, but she mentioned that he had seemed surprisingly hurt when he came home one day to find that she had moved her twin bed into the guest room.

So Be It

This listing of some of the ways in which a divorce is uncomfortable is not designed to be a recommendation against divorce if the marriage is strife-ridden or rotten, if it is degrading to one or both spouses, or if it is bitterly empty. Form does not take precedence over content, nor is a situation worth preserving if the only course open in it is to be long-suffering. But it is pertinent to keep in mind that divorce is not a restoration of the status quo ante; it is a return to a singular rather than the single state; and its enticements are more fantasied than actual. Thus, before the wedding, it is well to block divorce out of mind and estimate the marriage in terms of a life-long commitment, and after the wedding, it is well to work at the marriage as a life-long commitment. If the marriage nevertheless fails in spite of one's best foresight and one's best efforts, so be it. I have known some most happily divorced people, myself included.

K
Fourteen
AND
THE MIDDLE

_____ and C_____ married during the war in a city far from their home, parents, and friends, and the minister who performed the brief ceremony in his study was kind enough to speak gently to them afterwards about the difficult physical adjustment of married life and to give them a pamphlet, later read solemnly as they sat side by side on the edge of the motel bed, which was vague on details but emphatic in its warning on the necessity for tact, patience, and understanding. The next morning K_____ and C_____ tossed the pamphlet into the wastebasket, laughed, and asked each other what all the fuss was about. They had not found the slightest need for tact, patience, or understanding.

I assume that this is a true story. Some years after their divorce, I knew K_____, the wife, well, and I met C_____ once or twice when he came to visit the children, and they gave the impression of being well-matched. Also, although women are not given to discussing their sexual experience as directly as do, I gather, men, there is usually enough said occasionally and obliquely to allow one woman to make a pretty good guess about another woman's attitude, and K_____ struck me as having a vital and joyous approach. I therefore believed her comment that sexual adjustment had been no problem in this marriage, which caused me to revise an opinion I had previously held that, no matter the public reasons given for a divorce, the private reasons, were they to be revealed, would be found to be connected with sex. I had listened to many an elaborate rationale of what supposedly had gone wrong in a particular marriage always with a sense that the words were designed to skirt the central issue, and I still believe that this is more often true than not, but K_____ and some other examples I have encountered since have cut holes in my blanket assertion. Now, I would add money problems, covert mental illness, and identity problems to the list, as well as the factor considered earlier of the cruel clarity that can wash in when romantic love ebbs.

The Other Problems

The mother of a friend of mine inherited a sizable estate and watched quietly through the years while her husband poured it into his failing family business. When the couple were in their late fifties, the last of the money was gone, the factory had to be closed, and they both had to find jobs. Should she have insisted that what was hers was hers? Someone I have known since I was a child asserted this claim, and she is now a wealthy woman. She refused to give her husband access to any of her money, and the day she discovered that he had used some property of hers as collateral on a bank loan, she walked out on him, viewing it as an act tantamount to thievery, while he, for his part, had thought it enterprising and a bit of one-up-manship which established that his masculinity was not to be denied. He had experienced their money disputes as a male-female, dominance-submission tussle in which he did not intend to be bested and he was thoroughly astonished when she made what he considered natural assertiveness grounds for divorce. To state that the first couple are poor but still married is not to make a pejorative comparison between the actions of the two women; I do not know which woman was right. One assumes that there must always be some middle ground of compromise, that the first wife could have been generous with some but not all of her money and the second wife protective of some but not all of her money, but it is difficult to say where either of them might have drawn the line and whether the eventual act of doing so might not have proved equally disruptive. It is too easy to say compromise, for money is not just money: it carries heavy symbolic freight, and it has different meanings for different people, elicits different attitudes in them.

The fiancé of a friend of mine borrowed two hundred dollars from her, and when he did not repay it promptly, she broke their engagement; she is not stingy, but she felt it to be a cavalier disregard of her requirements, a symptomatic insouciance in him. K_____ and C_____ might have enjoyed each other in bed, but they did not enjoy each other financially. He was content to live in a catch-as-catch-can fashion, and she finally took his want of concern over their financial brinkmanship as want of concern for her personally. It probably was not, but the giving of money can become closely tied in with the giving of love. In another marriage, a stable, long-standing one hitherto devoid of money problems, one suddenly arose when the wife, who had been doing volunteer work, was asked to fill in on a paying job for several months. She opened a savings account of her own into which she put the salary, a maneuver which made her husband indignant, for, as he pointed out, through the twenty-five years of their marriage, the money he earned had gone into a joint account; there had never been any feeling that because he earned it, it was his alone to spend. The wife, however, was adamant that it was her money to do with as she pleased. What she finally pleased to do with it was buy a piano for him, but because this story came to me second-hand, I do not know whether that was what she had intended all long or whether she decided on it as a gesture of compromise.

Now that the interest on bank accounts is being reported to the Internal Revenue Bureau, many and many a housewife is having to reveal the existence of savings she had kept secret from her husband. On the face of it, there may seem something sly about taking part of the husband's earnings and hiding the money away, but I think men insufficiently appreciate that it is not easy for women always to be in a dependent position about money. Just as one needs a little piece of space in this world that is one's own, so one needs a bit of money that is one's own.

Most of the comments written about money are in the vein of money's not bringing happiness. But absence of money does not bring happiness either; in fact, when financial stress goes on too long, it can wreck the happiness there is. A few years of poverty at the start of a marriage may be romantic, but after that it becomes grinding. Some people manage to keep their gaiety, but they do it despite, not because of, being poor. To marry for money is not the answer, but it does seem a good idea to think about money before the marriage: the long-range prospects of there being enough to live on, whether there is agreement on what each considers a minimum standard of living, whether the saving and spending views of each are highly disparate, and the symbolic meaning of money to each. After marriage, money problems are almost more difficult to resolve than any other aspect of marriage, for it is unusually difficult for an individual to acknowledge that his approach to money may not be the only valid one. It is hard to shut out awareness of malfunction in making temperamental or sexual adjustments, and even the spouse who denies that he has a share in them will concede that there are possibilities of alternative behavior, but it is the rare person who recognizes that he has a problem about money. If he holds onto it tightly, he cites the virtues of thrift. If he spends it freely, he claims that is what money is for. If he budgets, he is thinking of the future. If he goes into debt, he wants his family to have the best. Any position on money is defensible, which often lures marriage partners into defending their positions down to the last gasp.

I know of nothing really helpful to do about money disputes except to listen to yourself and the other to see whether you can detect an undermeaning to the argument which essentially has nothing to do with money. The latent content may actually be: you want to control the money so you can control me; you are giving me money instead of love; you don't care enough or you would take better care of me; you want to bind me to you with money; money is more important to you than my happiness; you are wasting my money so as to exploit me; you are stingy with feelings; you are trying to buy me; you are trying to buy me off. If it seems that the words are about money but the communication is about a deeper attitude, it may be best to stop talking about money and face the real problem directly. The spouse who flares up when told, "You can't hold on to a cent," may be quite capable of listening sympathetically to, "It makes me feel you don't care about me when you seem not to care about the money." Other than this, and particularly if the ways of handling money are irritatingly but not vitally different, it is probably wise just to concede each other's foibles and live with them.

Only Their Psychiatrist Knows for Sure

It would not seem necessary to comment on mental illness being a disruptive factor in marriage, but I should like to make the one observation that it is not always as obvious as it appears on the surface which partner is the one with the illness. A psychologist working in a state mental hospital told me of a woman who requested her own commitment because she was doing such insane things as sneaking out of the house in the dead of night to meet a lover and then being without recollection of it in the morning. The psychologist found evidence of hysteria in the projective test results but nothing to substantiate the woman's feeling that she had lost her mind. When the woman was questioned more closely as to how she knew that she was going outside in the night, she said that her husband woke her and told her to feel how cold her feet were and that he had heard her go out to the barn and come back. It may be objected that a more sophisticated person would recognize that the illness lay in the mate, not herself, but even highly intelligent people can come to doubt their own behavior when persistently accused by a seemingly rational spouse of strange and inexplicable actions. A psychiatrist referred for testing to another psychologist of my acquaintance a woman whose test results did not bear out the severe disturbance that appeared to be present clinically. The psychologist, on a hunch, asked the woman's husband to submit to testing. The husband gave the impression of being the epitome of rationality and composure, and he discussed his wife's illness objectively and convincingly; however, the tests showed him to be the one in whom the psychotic process was at work. His wife's seemingly bizarre reactions were, in reality, a response to his illness. A person suffering from paranoia, as this man was, can be utterly convincing in his projections and so quick and so detailed that even an extremely intelligent spouse, which his wife was, can come to doubt her own reason.

It was once a tenet of psychiatry that the therapist never treat more than one member of a family, but with the realization that it is often the interaction in a family that is pathologic, psychiatrists are now beginning to insist on seeing entire families for diagnostic purposes and often for treatment. A psychiatrist described to me sitting in a room with a family in which the twenty-year-old son was what he referred to as "the designated patient" and being able to detect, when the content of the discussion threatened to touch on sensitive matters, that the mother unconsciously signaled the son to hallucinate, in effect, to go into his psychotic act. This is not to say that the son was not psychotic; he was; but he was giving expression to her disturbance as well as his own.

While it is said that the other fellow's shoe never pinches one's own foot, in the close quarters of a marriage it may. At least, it is a possibility to be aware of—unless you are already convinced that it is the other's irrationality which is causing the trouble, in which case it is almost certainly your own.

The Childhood of Sex

Such problems as the foregoing notwithstanding, marriage difficulties are more apt to revolve around problems of sexual adjustment than any other area. While I have the sense that whatever I may say about sex and sexual relationships is being written on the edge of a sexual revolution and in a few years may read in curiously dated fashion, that is the future and I am writing now and can only hope that enough people share a somewhat similar past to make some comments in this area useful.

Should it come, what may consolidate the revolution in practice that has long been underway in attitudes is the availability of oral contraceptives. Speaking in broadest generalization, sexual mores have always stemmed centrally from the fact that women get pregnant, and thus mores have always dealt principally with the conduct of women. Men were affected as accessories, and, more often than not, they were the ones who promulgated the rules, but the object of the rules was women. It seems inevitable that when involuntary pregnancy is no longer a consideration, the prohibitions hemming in women will greatly decrease and that women will have the same discretionary freedom that men are granted. The average parents who raise sons to behave with discrimination and responsibility about sex but do not make an overly strong point of prohibitions and are philosophical about transgressions, being willing to concede that it is the nature and the necessity of the male to seek sexual outlet and perhaps even covertly or overtly encouraging him to find it as demonstration of his normal masculinity, may find that they must make, and are able to make, similar concessions to their daughters.

It has been the case that daughters are given many prohibitions about sex, for their own protection, for the safeguarding of their reputations, and because sex in women was considered to be not "nice." This will not change overnight, and perhaps never completely, because it will probably always be necessary to inculcate some strong cautions in girls so that they will be forewarned to avoid situations of potential seduction or rape, but, hopefully, it will be possible to do this in such a way as to keep the warnings specific, in the same way that children are taught the dangers of crossing the street without picking up the notion that automobiles are dangerous and distasteful. As for an interest in sex being not "nice" in females, this idea is not necessarily more amenable to change, although it would seem on the surface that we have come far from the days when this was generally believed; but the unconscious source of the belief, the incest taboo, will always be in existence. The woman who is the boy's first object of desire is his mother, and she is, of course, deeply forbidden to him to possess. She is a "nice" woman, and many males grow into adulthood with the unconscious connection that "nice" women and sex do not go together. It is an idea they may readily pass on to their daughters; and in their attitude toward their daughters' explorations of sex, they may be far more rigid, harsh, and punitive than they are toward their sons'. Concerning protection of the girl's or woman's own reputation, virginity is already far less valued than it once was and soon should cease to be of any importance. It was, for all time until now, the logical first step in insuring that there would not be an illegitimate pregnancy, but other than that, its utility is difficult to defend. Certainly, as long as there is civilization, there will be standards, the transgression of which will damage reputation, but these standards should be predictably less double and strict than they have been in the past.

This is in the future, however, and will affect girls being born now. Those of us already adult have grown up in the shadow of more repressive views and have had to find our way to a solution of whatever problems this has occasioned. For some, the problems have been minimal or nonexistent. This was true for K_____, despite the fact that her parents are hidebound New Englanders, prim and proper people in whose presence the topic of sex is not mentioned, as it was also true for F_____, a wise and dear old friend now in her sixties who commented the other day that she left her home at the age of twenty to work and live on her own and never experienced a problem of sexual adjustment from that day to this. There were four of us sitting around a dinner table talking, F_____ and another of her generation, I and another of a younger generation, and F_____ was the only one of us able to make that statement. The other older woman admitted that she had been given to understand that it was a woman's duty to submit to the "animal side" of her husband's nature but there had been no hint that she herself might share this nature or find any enjoyment in it. F_____ confessed herself somewhat mystified that she had escaped contamination by this view, since her recollections suggested that her own mother must have held it; perhaps, she speculated, it was because her father had so loved nature and animals and had shared this love with her that she had acquired a sense that sex was normal, natural, and enjoyable. My contemporary, who grew up in Europe, reflected the somewhat more enlightened attitude of a later generation of parents in that she was not taught the duties of submission to a degrading act, but, on the other hand, she was not given any sense of the opposite: the acceptability and pleasures of sex. Whatever she was told was in the vein of warning her to resist the importunities of men, all emphasis going on their sex drives and no mention made of her own, and she found when she married that her own were not accessible to her.

It would be assumed, by psychoanalytic theory, that her sex drives had been repressed, that is, pushed down and held out of awareness, and I suppose this is technically accurate, but I am always a little uneasy when I read psychiatric theories about women and sex, for the majority of them have been written by men, based on theoretical considerations elaborated by men, and I suspect them to be extrapolations from male experience. There is, for example, the construct of penis envy in the female —the assumption that females feel deprived, castrated, inadequate, and inferior because they do not possess this delightful, pleasure-giving organ. While I agree that females may not feel as valuable as *people* as males do, I do not know that it is so specifically because this organ is absent but because they often find males treated as more valuable persons by the parents and by society. This appreciation that females are admired less may come to focus, by way of search for an explanation, on the absence of a penis, but I question whether it goes the other way around. Is the little girl likely to say: I have no penis; therefore, I am less valued? Or is it more probable that she would say: I am less valued? Why could that be? Is it because I have no penis? For the first to be the sequence, three assumptions have to be made: that the girl aged three, four, or five has seen a penis and is aware that the male population possesses this organ and the female does not; that she finds the penis attractive and feels that the body with one is more complete; and that she is aware of its pleasure-giving properties. These are assumptions automatically made by male psychoanalytic theorists and, so far as I am aware, rather unquestioningly accepted by female writers on the subject. I would think the first assumption tenable for the majority, if not all, little girls; they do become aware, even if they are the only child in the family or have only sisters, that the male is constructed differently from the female. But the second assumption is highly debatable, and the third stands a fair chance of being flatly erroneous. Does the little girl find the penis attractive and feel she is incomplete without one? I was an only child but grew up in close association with a male cousin, and my memory is that, as we raced around naked after our baths in the evening, I thought he looked a little silly with this extra appendage bobbing up and down on his front, certainly far less neat and compact and finished-looking than I. I did not feel incomplete but that he had an unnecessary bit of trimming, an afterthought, like a gewgaw on a building that interrupts the smooth flow of line. This is just one female's experience, and how widely it can be extrapolated, I do not know, but surely it is more legitimate to extrapolate from one female to other females than from the male to the female.

The male experience is that the penis is a pleasure-giving organ, full of rich and delightful sensation, which it would be a tragedy to lose, and when he discovers that half the race does not possess it, he assumes that they feel deeply deprived and deeply envious, but there is a salient fact not taken into account in this reasoning: the female, never having had this organ as a part of her, has not the slightest notion that it is the source of many a pleasurable feeling, and not knowing this, she has no basis on which to feel deprived. I have a large, square, rather graceless leather armchair which I assume anyone seeing it envies me because I know the blissful hours I spend in it, but other people do not know that it is a reclining chair nor that its cushions are down-filled and they may simply view it as an awkward object marring an otherwise attractive home. Were male and female to spend their early years as undifferentiated beings, developing primary sex characteristics only in their teens, for example, when there is cerebral knowledge of the pleasures of sex, there would seem reason for penis envy, but the little girl either remains unaware of feelings of sexual pleasure or discovers them in her clitoris, and if she is unaware of them, she

229

does not envy the male his experience for she does not know what he is experiencing, while, if she is aware of them, she has no reason to envy him because she has a source in herself.

How many little girls do discover sexual feelings as a source of pleasure? There is no way of knowing, but their number cannot come close to matching that of little boys because the clitoris is a much less visible, palpable, and apparent organ than the penis. It has as many nerve endings as the penis, and because they are crowded into a much smaller area, it is more sensitive, but the clitoris is not handled in the ordinary course of going to the bathroom, it is not rubbed against by clothing, it does not have visible erections, and it is not protrusive. Thus, its existence may or may not be known. The little boy cannot escape sexual feelings; the little girl has to seek them out. The sight of a little boy clutching himself through his clothing is common, while the sight of a little girl doing so is infrequent. It is apt to be taken for granted that a little girl's lesser interest in, and awareness of, sex is a result of repression, but it strikes me that it is more reasonable to assume, not that the little girl has pushed sexual feelings out of consciousness, but that they never, or only fleetingly, entered consciousness in the first place.

There is this—which I would call physiologic—lesser consciousness of sex in females. Add to this the factor of parents' being less permissive about sexual expression in daughters and of their offering warnings which are necessary for the girl's protection but can be interpreted by her as instruction to shun a perhaps ugly, perhaps dangerous part of life. Together, these two factors seem to me to account for the more pervasive problems of sexual adjustment in women than in men. The Kinsey Report produced the finding that the peak of sexual activity for women occurs around age thirty-five, while for men it is in the late teens. This has been cited again and again as evidence of the much later sexual maturation of women than men, with the implication that the maturation is on a physiologic basis, but it would not be far-fetched to assume that the discrepancy is due to its simply taking much longer for the female to get untracked. The male, if the oedipal period around age four has been negotiated without such severe trauma that the boy feels compelled to renounce his masculine identification, then progresses along a direct course to sexual maturation. The female, on the other hand, must negotiate a double, parallel but contradictory course, one foot planted in maturation, one foot planted in suppression. Conveyed to her explicitly and implicitly is the necessity for control, for keeping the fires banked, warm but never blazing up. The male can press forward; the female must be the one to hold back. The male has one goal: to win the female; the female has two goals: to win the male and to reject him.

Not having had to support a schizophrenic approach, the male arrives at physiologic maturity with immediate and ready access to his sex drives. The female, in contrast, has to contrive to shed one-half of her dual approach to sex. When she marries, she is permitted—more than permitted, she is expected—to tap the buried strata of her sexual drives almost from one moment to the next and let them well freely to the surface. But the layers of prohibitions can be many and tough, the sexual feelings can be very far underground, and not all women are so lucky as A____ and F____ as to find them waiting to emerge. Some women never gain access to them, and for the majority, if the report of age thirty-five is correct, it is a gradual process requiring years for complete freedom to be achieved. It would be interesting to know if the age of thirty-five holds for all women, including those who have not married, or if it is predicated on the experience of women whose sex life started in their early twenties. In the latter event, which is more likely to be true, it would be fair to say that it takes the average woman twelve to fifteen years completely to free her sexual drives from the restraints in which they were bound for the first decades of her life.

The Experience of Sex

The minister who counseled K____ and C____ on the necessity for tact, patience, and understanding was giving useful advice for, I would guess, ninety out of one hundred marriages in which the wife is twenty and a virgin. The average wife has a number of psychological barriers to hurdle, and she may be dismayed to find that they do not all vanish on command. If the husband is equally appalled or angered or affronted or, worst of all, indifferent, he may reinforce the barriers instead of aiding her to work her way past them. He, of course, may have his own problems of ineptitude, of anxiousness to prove his virility, or of grandiose notions about the commanding male, any of which may send him rushing thoughtlessly on, and then trouble is in the making, for initial intercourse for the woman can be physically painful, adding physical aversion to the psychological barriers. If she experiences the invasion of her body as hurtful, threatening, shocking, humiliating, disgusting, or unwelcome, which is neither particularly strange nor un-likely given her past teachings and every individual's sense of privacy and the keeping of the body inviolate, it may be a long time before the conflict between one or more of these feelings and the sexual feelings is won by the latter. And it may never be won if she has, in the recesses of her being, turned against the act, against men, against her husband, or against her own body if she feels shamed or if she first suspects and then becomes convinced that she is frigid.

Just as I wish someone had warned me about divorce, so I wish someone had warned me about sex, had said, "Look, you're getting married tomorrow and it's going to be bloody, painful, humiliating, and disgusting. You're going to be uneasy and embarrassed having a man in the room, perhaps undressing you, watching you get undressed, undressing in front of you. You're not going to be able to sleep with a heavy leg thrown over you and an arm under your neck. You're going to want to cry at what's happened to you. You'll give half your life to be back in your own bed in your own room. You're going to hate the whole awful business for a night, two nights, a week, a month, a year, two years, however long it takes to unlearn what you were taught all your life. But stick with it and you will get untracked. Hate it all you want. It doesn't mean you are unnatural. It just means that it takes time to become natural. If you turn on a tap that has been turned off for years, nothing happens at first, then there is a trickle of rusty water, then an occasional spurt, and only eventually a clear, steady flow. But finally it comes, and when it does, it is as though it had never been turned off."

If I had been told that and found not a word of it was true, that all had gone as joyously for me as it did for K_____, I would have awakened to a sun-filled room, patted the leg over me, smiled, and said to myself, "That idiot didn't know what she was talking about." But if I had not gone to sleep all night, I still could have faced the morning light and said to myself, "Well, as she said, it takes a lot of getting used to and I hate it now, but that's to be expected. There's nothing wrong with me that practice won't make come right. He, poor dear, and I are going to have to be patient, but it'll work itself out in the long run."

Maybe there are mothers or aunts or wise old friends somewhere in the world who have the sense to tell a girl that it is all right for her not to like sex for just as long as it takes her to get to like it, but I have never known any such. All I have heard people say is, "Don't" to a girl, and then one day, "Ah, you're getting married. How wonderful. You're going to be so happy." I should like to put in a plea for the painting of a black picture because, as I say, if it proves to be a false picture, so much the better—it can be dismissed with a snap of the fingers. But if the black picture turns out to be in any part accurate, then the female has been given permission not to like the sexual relationship, and with that permission half the battle is won. It is like being introduced to oysters. If someone says, "You've never tasted oysters? Ah, you're going to love them," the first oyster you swallow may be enough to turn you against them the rest of your life; but if someone says, "Well, you can taste one, but you're not going to like it," you may eat one and decide, "That's not so bad. Let me try another," and go on to develop quite a taste for oysters. The hardest part for a woman is to feel lonely, frightened, and freakish if she discovers that she finds sex repugnant. She cannot talk it over with her new husband, for he will take it as a reflection on him. She may be able to talk to her mother, but,

233

on the other hand, if her mother was without problems, she would probably be having far fewer adjustment difficulties. The novels she has read describe only two types of women: the the earthy and uninhibited or the frigid, and since she clearly does not belong in the ranks of the former, she may despairingly attach the second label to herself. The marriage manuals take sex very seriously and emphasize technique and hygiene and homilies, at least the ones I read did. I never came across a discussion of sex that centered on the two points I think it is vital to know: that sex is play and that the really vital organ of the body as far as responsiveness and enjoyment are concerned is the brain.

A Strip of Celluloid

To a girl growing up, it is made abundantly clear that sex is procreation. Not very often is it mentioned that, for humans, sex is recreation. Parents, for obvious reasons, do not wish to convey the thought that sex is in the same category as going skiing or for a swim in the ocean, and they are perfectly right when they are dealing with an unmarried daughter. Apart from moral considerations, premarital intercourse is not to be taken lightly, for if there are problems of adjustment in marriage, they are multiplied tenfold outside of marriage; there is the attendant guilt, the illicit setting, the worry over pregnancy, and the absence of the continuity often required before a happy relationship is achieved. Over the longer stretch of time, there is the consequence that the process of arousal has started; it is like smoking one cigarette: it may be completely unsatisfying, but the very lack of satisfaction leads you to smoke another, and then another, until the habit gets firmly established; while, on the other hand, it is no particular hardship to refrain from smoking if you have never taken the first cigarette.

Intercourse before marriage cannot be interpreted as just another way of enjoying oneself, nor can extramarital intercourse, but there could not be a better way of approaching it within marriage. It is meaningful, of course, it is satisfying, but it is not serious. It is sensual, playful, relaxing, and entertaining. It is not the end-all and be-all. It is enjoyment for the sake of enjoyment. It is not a test you must struggle not to flunk. It is a slightly ridiculous process that happens to be exceedingly pleasurable.

You can play a lousy game of golf and still get a lot of fun out of it. The less earnestly you go about it and the more ease and naturalness you achieve, the better you get to be at it. It is the people who tighten up, who go about it as though their lives depended upon it, who end up lost in the woods and fuming, loathing the game, themselves, and the partners who are witness to their inadequacy. And when they try again, they are tense and anxious even before they have begun to play.

Sex is a noncompetitive sport, to be engaged in for the sheer gusto of engaging in it. Granted that it is a basic drive, it nevertheless exists only to the end of preservation of the species, not to self-preservation. You have to breathe, you have to eat, you have to protect your body from harm if you are to stay alive, but sex is not crucial to your existence. If you never have an orgasm, it will not subtract one hour from your life, so there is no point in going about sex as though it were a matter of the utmost consequence for it to be successful. Suppose you spend an hour making love and an orgasm eludes you? While more exasperating than feeling you are going to sneeze, it is not one jot more earthshaking. The only harm done is if it makes you apprehensive the next time. In fact, if you frequently or invariably have trouble arriving at orgasm, tell yourself that you know it is not going to happen and that you are not going to try to make it happen, that you are just going to relax and feel whatever you do feel and not worry about what is not going to happen anyway. Getting there is half the fun, and there is no profit in spoiling one-half for the sake of the other half that is not going to work in any event, any more than you would refuse to enjoy the boat trip because you fear London is going to be a let-down. The less you look ahead to orgasm and live moment to moment for the pleasure in the moment, the more the pleasure of the moments may accumulate and deliver you quite unexpectedly to your destination. Nothing so drives orgasm out of reach as trying for it. Indeed, you will do better actively to try *not* to have one. It is like falling asleep: lie there and concentrate on going to sleep and nothing happens; decide to stay awake and you are asleep before you know it.

A friend of mine once remarked, so casually that it sounded like a fact that everyone knows, "Of course, sex really works in the mind, doesn't it." Everyone may, indeed, know it, but that everyone was once minus one: me. I did not know it. I thought the body sort of rose up, like a watchdog from sleep, and started to howl, drowning out the restraining voice of the master. Not so, I discovered.* There are times when the body initiates the process with a slight pulsating or a feeling of warmth or a prickling of the skin, particularly if one is unexpectedly touched. I used to work in the same office with a chap who would come up behind me and grasp my shoulders suddenly and strongly, and instantaneously my stomach would flip and my toes curl, but a moment later I would think, "Oh, it's only old so-and-so," and my mind would cut off the response. The mind is immediately involved because it must register sex feelings, else you cannot know you are experiencing them, and the minute they are registered, the evaluative centers go to work making choices and decisions. Unfortunately, the decision may always be negative, even if the person who has stimulated you is the appropriate person at the appropriate time, if training or circumstances have conditioned the mind to reject sexual response. Frigidity or impotence is the mind's work, not the body's, with very rare exceptions.

I once read in a medical journal a description of what was called an "elegant," because very difficult and delicate, experiment, the insertion in a cat's brain of a sliver of celluloid between the hypothalamus, which controls visceral activities, and

* When I started work on this book, someone to whom I described it asked whether it was intended for men or for women, and I answered that the question had not entered my head, that I assumed concepts useful for one would be useful for the other, but here I should admit that I know only about women in this area and there has not seemed to me any point in borrowing material from other writers which I had no way of validating. Any statements about sex, therefore, are only about women, and probably only about some women.

the higher centers of the brain. This had nothing to do with sex, but I have since thought of it as descriptive of what happens in sexual unresponsiveness: an invisible barrier slides into place to block communication between the visceral center and the higher centers so that feeling cannot be received and permission to enjoy the feeling cannot be returned.

In dealing with sexual unresponsiveness, the task is to extract the strip of celluloid so that it cannot slip automatically into place. You may have so little notion of, or be so little able to face on your own, the circumstances that inserted it that you will need professional help to remove it, but, on the other hand, it is possible that some exploration which you can conduct yourself will dislodge it, if not in one operation, perhaps by teasing it out a fraction of a millimeter at a try. The task is partially accomplished by remembering that it is there, that a part of your brain, without which enjoyment is not possible, is not participating. Sex cannot be left to the body; the brain must be engaged too, just as fully and unreservedly as possible. The battle to tease the celluloid free is further joined with some questions. What do you think of sex? If you were honest, would you say it is dirty and sinful? Okay, that is what you were led to believe as a child, but you are not a child any more and you know perfectly well, with the rational, adult part of you, that sex is just an ordinary part of life. Do you connect it with the excretory organs and filth and "do-not-play-or-touch"? That, too, is a very old notion, and you have lived with your body long enough to know that it does what it has to in order to maintain itself; the ridding of waste has no more value judgment attached to it than the breathing out of carbon dioxide, and there is no reason not to accept another's excretory orifices as matter-of-factly as you accept your own. I must confess that I have sometimes thought that if I were God, I would have tried my hand at redesigning the arrangement, but perhaps He did and found that, as in a trailer, aesthetic considerations had to give way to fitting the most into the least space. In any event, no one's arrangement is any different from anyone else's; we are well aware of the size, shape, and function; and the idea of one need not contaminate the idea of the other. Do you

237

fear that you have physical inadequacies in the size or shape of your sex organs? Such a notion is more likely to be psychologically than physiologically based, but check with a physician, and in the meantime remember that people's faces vary quite a bit too and you love them for what they are, not for the length of their nose or the width of their mouth. Do you believe that you may be undersexed, that your sex drives are less urgent than the average? If you can get past your psychological block, you will be as sexed as you need to be. Do you think that sex is for grown-ups? Yes, but you are a grown-up now. Sex is permissible now. No one will punish you now. Do you suspect that other people know more about sex than you do, secrets about sex that remain hidden from you? Mommy and Daddy knew more, but that was a long time ago and now you know just what everyone else knows. Sex is simply not that mysterious nor arcane. The position can be varied, but intercourse is intercourse and you already have a perfectly straightforward knowledge of it if you will let yourself recognize that you do. Are other people brilliant at making love and you a dud because they know techniques you have never heard of? The physiology is such that that much range and variety is simply not possible. Anything anyone else can do, you can do. Are you afraid that you are homosexual? Having problems of sexual adjustment to the opposite sex does not imply that you would adjust any better to your own sex. The most active homosexual of my acquaintance, a lesbian who turned to women after several unsuccessful affairs with men, confesses that she is equally frigid with both. Have you unconscious fears? There is the jackpot question, and the answer is yes, of course; there would not be any problem if you did not. Both sexes can have fears of being overpowered by the opposite sex. Men may fear a huge, engulfing, swallowing, or amputating woman; women may fear a huge, riveting, destroying man. We were all children once, small and vulnerable in a world of towering, powerful creatures, and many of us have kept that image; our bodies grew but our imagination is back there.

On the Rorschach test, a series of, in themselves, meaningless inkblots, a man may give responses with a theme running through them of an opening with teeth: the jagged edge of a mine shaft, for instance, a tiger roaring, showing its fangs, an eagle holding a rat in its claws; and from such responses there emerges the supposition that he unconsciously fears the "dentate vagina," a vagina with teeth that will bite off the penis. A woman may reveal her unconscious anxiety by a series of answers that have a common theme of a menacing weapon: a club, a totem pole with an animal's head, a riveting machine, a tree trunk about to fall and crush what is below, an enormous boot trampling, a chisel; and in such responses there is revealed her unconscious fear of the shattering penis. The common unconscious fear of men is castration, amputation in a trap waiting to spring shut; of women, it is of being riven, torn asunder, and bled of life. The fear of men is of being lured, consumed, and destroyed; of women, of being attacked, shattered, and destroyed.

Were a man to be asked if there was such a thing as a dentate vagina, he would say no, of course not. Were he to be asked if women ever literally castrate men, he would say no, of course not. Were a woman to be asked if there was such a thing as a pile-driver penis, she would say no, of course not. Were she to be asked if men ever literally tear women apart, she would say no, of course not. The rational mind knows these things are not true; it is the unconscious mind which harbors such visions far out of awareness. It has been interesting, in Tennessee Williams's plays, to see the progression from symbolic representation of unconscious fears to their literal statement and the concomitant reaction of audiences. When Williams wrote symbolically of castration, engulfment, attack, his plays were brilliantly successful and audiences responded deeply to them, for he was speaking to their unconscious minds. In more recent plays, he has written literally of castration, cannabalism, and coprophagy, and the audiences have turned away, for he has spoken to their conscious minds, and the conscious mind rejects such things; it knows them not to be true, or if true, true of such a remote few in such remote places that it is of no relevance to ordinary life. As an admirer of Mr. Williams's work, I think it is a pity that he has gone in this direction, but for a nonplaywright it is an excellent road to travel: to get hold of the symbolic visions, put them in literal terms, and estimate whether there is a shred of validity in them.

To do this, you must first admit to anxieties by discarding the rationalizations of them, such as: "I'm just not interested in sex," or "I just haven't met the right person," or "I have higher instincts." Visualize yourself, next, in a sex situation; stick to it; don't let your mind go blank. Imagine what would happen to you if you ignored every warning your brain gave you, if you attempted to protect yourself in no way at all, if you participated without thought. In what way would you be damaged or destroyed? Put it in the frankest, crudest, most irrational terms. Do not let your sensible mind scoff, and in scoffing, censor. Let the images well up that you would be brutalized, smothered, raped, torn, pounded into the ground, beaten, humiliated, desecrated, fouled; or let the images well up that you would be mutilated, broken, chewed, swallowed, shattered, punished; or that you yourself would crush and destroy and consume; or that you felt sin beyond bearing, an agony of guilt, and must brace yourself for mortal punishment; or that if you let yourself go, you would never be able to get the pieces back together again. It is one or more of these fears, or unnamed other ones, that slide the strip of celluloid into place. If you can verbalize them to yourself, if you can let them rise in all their wildness and intensity, you have a chance of saying to yourself, "But, no, this isn't true. This won't happen. I am a person, and a body is tough, resilient. And he is only a person, and only the person he is, not my father, not a monster, not a machine." Or, "She is only a person, not my mother, not a harpy, not a maw." And, "This is an ordinary activity, a game, a sport. There is no danger in it. Two people are playing."

When I was a little girl, about four, my father used to send me to the store after dark, and I was terrified of the back depths of the front hall. I knew it was my tricycle that was stored there, but still I was frightened of the shapes in the shadows. One night my father gave me a little round disk and told me to hold it in my hand, that it was a talisman which would keep me safe from harm. I didn't tell him that I knew it was just a disk from his tobacco humidor and that I wasn't one whit less apprehensive with it in my hand. I pretended it helped, but it didn't really.

I offer the foregoing with the knowledge that it may be only a disk from a humidor, that it may work no special magic, that it may be no more effective than turning a flashlight on a recess and identifying the ominous shapes, only to have them spring back the instant the light goes off. When my father saw through my pretense that the disk had protective power, he made me tell him what I feared, made me describe it specifically, not just mumble that I was frightened. As I described an enormous black ogre jumping on me out of the shadows, it began to seem less reasonable. He asked what I would do if it really happened, and I said I supposed I would scream. He answered, "And I am right here listening, and I would hear you, and I would come and save you, and then we would have hot chocolate and laugh at how we had conquered the ogre."

If you can name the terrible shapes in the shadows and make them utterly real, paradoxically they come to seem more like fantasies. And fantasies made real, fade. Only little by little, it is true, but each moment you can delay the celluloid clicking into place, that is a moment gained for feeling and response. And in that moment you can practice integrating mind and body.

A Two-Way Wire

The higher centers of the brain must be persuaded not only not to interfere with sexual response but to participate actively. Permitted to function solely as a passive reception center for messages, the brain is quite capable of wandering off to attend to an irrelevancy. It must be coerced by concentration into setting up a "hot line," a two-way connection kept open and humming between brain and body. A kiss is felt by the lips, for example, and is registered by the brain, but the reaction may remain local and of no particular interest if the brain does not become intensely curious about what is felt and immediately seek further information. The mouth may send a communication that there is pressure upon it, and the brain should quickly respond with: "Send details. Make me feel as though I am there. Is it hard pressure? Soft? Nibbling? Tickling? I want information from each nerve ending. Go ahead and feel, feel completely. Never mind what's going on up here. All attention is on you. Okay, now let it get through to the nerve endings that feeling is being sent from here. It is flooding warmly through the wire. It will arrive there in quantity." Ignore how fanciful this sounds and try it. As a matter of fact, try it right now: put the back of your hand against your mouth. Your brain registers the slight pressure neutrally. But now concentrate on your mouth so that a direct wire is opened between brain and lips. Does not the sensation in your lips immediately increase? They are not just passively accepting pressure but are moving slightly, are registering the feel of the skin of the back of your hand, its warmth or coolness, its dryness or moisture, and are discriminating differences in pressure from the center of the lips to the outer edges. Visualize your lips and let the picture of them surge up and occupy the whole of your brain, as though the brain were a camera zooming in on one detail until it fills the whole of the screen. Then, reverse the flow of messages and send feeling from the brain to the lips.

I have a friend of whom I often say to myself, "There she goes, rushing off into the future again." When I visit her in the country, I am engaged in eating breakfast but she is hurrying to the kitchen to make a picnic lunch; when I am half-dressed, she is waiting in the car with the motor running; when I am settling down to sun-bathe, she is opening the lunch; when I am eating a sandwich, she is packing up; when I think the afternoon is at its height, she is fussing about getting home to dinner; through dinner, she is hastening to get to a movie. During the movie, she falls asleep, exhausted. There has not been a moment in the day when she has done nothing but enjoy that moment. She has not registered the skill of her fingers slicing bread, the pleasant motion of the car, the warmth of sun on her skin, the smell of grass, the brush of a breeze over her forehead. She has hurried through the day to the next pleasure, and so pleasure eludes her because pleasure is this moment.

And so in love-making. Pleasure is this moment. It is everything that can be felt in this moment, not what may or may not be felt in the next moment. It is pointless, when being kissed, for instance, to ask yourself whether you feel anything in the genital area. Forget about it until it is its turn; it will have taken care of itself. It is like being at a concert: if the strings are playing but the kettle drummer stands up and you begin to pay attention to him, wondering when he is going to come in, you stop hearing the music and start thinking about the mechanics; you lose the build of the music; ignore him and he'll come booming in on time, to your greater pleasure.

While you are concentrating on the moment and letting yourself deeply feel the moment, use your eyes thoroughly to take in your partner. See completely a patch of skin, the swell of a muscle, the sweep of a line. There is a lovely, sensual pleasure in utterly seeing, to the smallest detail, what presents itself to one's eyes, and it is a most effective means of ending distaste for another's body.

All of this adds up to being thoroughly *present*. Your brain will not be disengaged or preoccupied with anxieties if you sink yourself in the moment, if you look and feel with total absorption. Earlier on, I wrote of the anxiety-reducing effect in social situations of concentrating on what you think of and can take in about the other person rather than being concerned with what he is thinking about you. It holds equally true in sexual situations. Don't worry for an instant what he is thinking of your response, whether he is telling himself you are cold or passionate, clumsy or adept, prim or abandoned. Don't worry whether a gesture will displease him, whether he will notice an absence of reaction, whether, if you do this or that, it will disgust him. Do not, that is, if you are a woman. If you are a man making love to a woman, on the other hand, while you should also shut your mind to guesses as to what she is thinking of your equipment or technique, you should be responsive to clues of what she finds pleasurable and the rate of progression she wishes. It is better to be a jump behind, so that feeling is there and waiting, rather than a jump ahead so that it must be laboriously stimulated. And there is no reason for progression to be in a straight line; a light foray, a retreat, a side excursion, another foray and return, leaves a stronghold eager to be taken rather than resistant to being overpowered.

There is no reason not to talk in the process. A portentous silence punctuated only by heavy breathing makes the whole undertaking so earnest and sober that a lot of the fun goes out of it. Words are intensely stimulating, and more can be accomplished with them than with any number of caresses. They make two people feel close and warm and affectionate and lighthearted. Despite, or perhaps because of, their physical proximity, two people can feel quite lonely while making love if they are silent, for silence connotes self-absorption; it suggests that the self is turned inward and is indifferent to the partner. Silence is a breeding ground for nasty little worries about what the other is thinking, while intimate jokes are delicious and scatter any reserve or strain in the atmosphere, and a language of special phrases creates a special world in which two people feel very close.

The Fake and the Truth

It is usually the case that the man's experience exceeds the woman's, but whichever partner is the more sophisticated, he or she should attempt to attune the love-making to the level of the less practiced participant. Some men seem to feel it incumbent upon them to display a virtuoso technique, but the effect may be more to disconcert or repel the woman than to send her into transports. Too, if there are practices which one or the other considers out-of-bounds, the reticences must be respected lest all be spoiled; with time bringing ease and trust, the reticences may disappear of their own accord. This is not to say that there should not be variety; there should, indeed. Always to know what is coming next makes love-making an unexciting routine. Sometimes, to have nothing come next is a most effective maneuver, particularly in a new marriage in which the wife is having problems of sexual adjustment. Five minutes of love-making that is gently broken off, and this repeated fairly often, can reassure her that every caress is not necessarily going to escalate into full-scale involvement; her unconscious mind is disarmed from automatically slipping the celluloid into place, and the suspense piques her interest. I have sometimes been grateful, and sometimes sorry, that few men realize that there are occasions when the most seductive thing they can do is to do nothing. The man who paws you on a first date arouses nothing but your defenses, while the man who deposits you untouched on your doorstep five dates in a row makes you infinitely curious and eventually quite eager. So it is, too, in marriage. If the wife knows her husband is going to pat her fanny every time she walks past, it is of no interest and may be an irritation. If he sometimes does, there is the pleasure of expectation. If, further, he sometimes follows up the pat by pulling her into his lap, another possibility has been added. If the lap is sometimes followed up by bed, but not inevitably, there is the spice of variety and the interest of speculation. It is dull to read someone's intentions from the first moment, and, besides, if the wife is not given time to hear in herself whether her response is yes or no, she is quite apt to decide that it is no.

Given exploratory time to make a choice and knowing that to respond does not commit her, that she will be allowed gracefully to leave the lap, makes a woman feel that she is a person, not an object, a person whose desires count equally, not an object required dutifully to submit. It increases, instead of attacks, her sense of herself, and this is extremely important, for the stronger a woman's sense of identity, the more she can let herself go in sex. Sex is often feared as a powerful force which may explode the self into pieces which cannot be regrouped. The woman who is uncertain of her own boundaries, her own worth, her own strength, her own self-ness will struggle against letting feeling take over in her; she will be too unsure to let her hold on herself slip for an instant. If she feels that sex for a woman is a passive act, she may be made anxious that someone else is in charge, not she, and resist what she feels to be a dangerous surrender of self.

Women are often compared to cats, and, being fond of cats, I think it is not a bad comparison. A cat can surrender completely to the delights of being stroked, purr with pleasure, bask in warmth, wriggle to have just the right spot reached, while not surrendering an iota of its sense of being a marvelous, separate, and independent creature. Nothing can persuade a cat that it does not have a mind and a will of its own, that it exists, not by tolerance, but by right.

But unlike cats, women are apt to propitiate the taller and stronger beings in their world. Unfortunately, women are able to fake a sexual response, "unfortunately" because they can resign themselves to going through the motions, admitting only to themselves that they have no talent for this activity. If their problem was less easily concealed, they would have to make greater efforts to straighten it out. In all my years of schooling, I flunked just one course: typewriting. I was totally incompetent at it. Had I simply been able to go convincingly through the motions, I would never have learned, but, of course, it is meaningless to pound away to no end, and so eventually I got the hang of it and I am now very good at it. For many women, sex is something they have to get the hang of, but it is difficult to give the advice that, until they do, they must not fake a response, for the ego of the male is deeply involved. There is a pervasive misconception that if a woman fails to have an orgasm, it is the fault of her partner, and it is the rare man who does not take a woman's frigidity as an affront to his masculinity. But no man has any control over a woman's unconscious mind, nor can he compel her to involve her brain in the process. There are areas to which he has no access, and do what he may, however adroitly and lovingly, to areas within his reach, it is she who must involve her mind and imagination. If this were better understood, the vanity of men would need less protection, and women could better afford the honesty that would allow them to work through their problems a step at a time. As it is, if a man detects that there is not a full response, he may be angered because he feels it as an insult or because he must use anger to thrust away doubts of his own adequacy; he may double his efforts; or he may curse his luck at marrying a cold woman, none

246

of which is of any help to the woman. If, on the other hand, he accepts it as her problem, one which involves him but for which he is not responsible, then he can offer his completely interested help and co-operation without feeling threatened by it. To talk about something, even to joke about it, makes it all so much less earth-shaking; it becomes, not a bleak fear descending between two people, isolating them in separate, anxiety-ridden worlds, but a temporary, admitted, shared problem that stays in its proper perspective. A husband may eat many a poor meal, but he and his wife both know that the wife will get to be a better cook with practice, and in the meantime they laugh about the mishaps. A botched episode of love-making is no more important than a botched meal. A husband would think himself a boor to grow tight-lipped and irritable over a burnt roast, insane to wonder darkly if his wife were deliberately trying to starve him, unreasonable to expect her to be an accomplished chef without any training, stupidly pessimistic to resign himself to unpalatable food the rest of his life. Instead, he would tell her not to be upset, that it was not as important as all that, tease her a little, hug her a little, and convince her that they would both manage perfectly well to muddle along until she got her bearings and then they would look back and laugh at how serious and insurmountable it had all seemed way back in the beginning.

Can a wife tell her husband that she must win her own ground? If they are newly married, I think it is best to say openly and unashamedly, "Look, I'm lousy at this and I'm not going to pretend. But neither am I going to worry about it, and I don't want you to either. I've had instructions all of my life to shove my feelings down, and they are just not going to work their way to the surface all in a moment now. They're going to take their own sweet time, and until they do, I'm not likely to think this is the grandest enterprise in the world, but it's got nothing to do with you or loving you. I'll get used to it, and I'll get to like it, and it's time enough then to start worrying whether I have an orgasm or not."

But that is a newly married woman, and for her to admit to her inadequacies is endearing. I have noticed time and again, in an ordinary, that is, nonsexual, situation, when I have matter-of-factly confessed to some feeling, such as worrying that no one is going to talk to me at a cocktail party, the other person's face lights up and he says, "You, too! I thought I was the only one." People rarely, when you honestly say, "I don't manage this well," attack you for it; instead, they feel empathy and compassion and make an effort to be reassuring. And that is true in sex, too. A few men might feel challenged, but most are going to be exceedingly relieved that it can be talked about and will start in telling you it does not matter instead of protesting angrily how much it does matter. They will be patient and tactful as long as they feel their own prowess is not under attack.

This is an approach not to be employed in a marriage of some years' standing, however, by a wife who has been engaging in fairly consistent faking, for it is too much of a blow. Best she go about it gradually by now and then omitting the fake and saying unperturbedly, "Well, that didn't work out so well, maybe because I was trying too hard. Remind me next time to relax," the endeavor being to unaccustom her husband to a set response so that she can allow herself more leeway for searching out genuine feeling and for making a start on a franker, less routine relationship. He is likely to inquire on the next occasion whether she feels relaxed, and she can say, "I don't know. Give me a few minutes to find out," thus insuring his interest in her reactions and establishing the fact that there are two people involved. If she can get used to talking, to believing that her wishes matter as much as his, and to consider what she feels, she can begin to break through to a total, in place of a perfunctory, involvement. It is her task, as it is the newly married woman's, to accept her inadequacy, to accept her failure to feel, to accept her partial or complete frigidity, and to say that she is not going to worry about it and that she is not going to give a hang ever again in her life whether she has an orgasm or not, she is not going to try to change herself, she is just going to be herself. But she must say it silently. And believe it. She must genuinely stop caring about the end result and concentrate only on what she can find in each moment, for ridding the self of apprehension is nine tenths of the battle.

248

In Sum

All of this adds up to just two central points: the brain is crucial and sex is not serious. With whom and under what circumstances sexual relations are engaged in is serious, certainly, but if you keep in mind that sex is designed for pleasure, you can avoid moral mistakes in that intercourse which is illicit and guilt-producing, anxiety-provoking, or engaged in for such reasons as to prove attractiveness or popularity is clearly not a pleasure. The best advice I know of is this: outside of marriage, do nothing that will not bring you unclouded pleasure; inside of marriage, make sure you find pleasure in what you do. Sex is neither your passport to nor your exile from the world of mental health. It is simply a game, albeit the most satisfying game ever invented.

Fifteen
THE
SIMPLE DESIRE

ND in the end there is no desire so deep as the simple desire for companionship." So comments a character in a short story by Graham Greene in a rare, rare acknowledgment of a fact of life which overrides the facts of life. Passion may be absent from a life and still the individual manages, but let companionship be absent and the life is insupportable. Friendship is the enduring joy. It is not spectacular nor intriguing nor electric, which is perhaps why it is not used to sell soap or automobiles, why it figures only passingly in our literature, why no symposia are held to examine it. So much the better that it is a neglected topic; we deserve one area free of exploitation, corruption, and self-conscious exploration. But we should not be feinted, by the silence of the professionals, into underrating its importance in our lives. Add meaningful and satisfying work to meaningful and satisfying companionship, and no life, no matter how devoid of success, can fail to be a success.

The Friendly Effort

How does one acquire a friend? A chap whose opinion I asked said unhesitatingly, "By making an effort." He had long ago decided, he said, that when you meet someone you think you might like to know, you should make two telephone calls, the first within a day or two of the meeting and in the teeth of any and all qualms along the lines of: "He's too busy to be bothered with me," or "He'll think it's pushy of me to call," or "I should wait and let him make the first overture." Risk rejection and call, my informant said firmly. Use a matter-of-fact voice, neither diffident nor pressuring, and offer a concrete invitation but one with a built-in out, such as, "If you're not busy next Tuesday, would you have lunch with me at the Hungry Sphinx on 46th Street?" If the recipient makes use of the out by answering, "Gee, I'd like to, but I'm tied up on Tuesday," don't leave a silence in which you wait for him to name another day. Accept the excuse immediately, say, "Right. I'll try you again," and hang up. The possibilities are two: he is not busy on Tuesday but does not want to be bothered seeing you; he is busy on Tuesday. Do not try to decide which it is, and do not go back over the conversation looking for clues to warmth or coldness. In a week or two, when you make a second call and repeat your invitation, it is time enough then, if you get the same sort of response, to accept that the person does not share your wish that the two of you get to know each other. At that point, it is probable that you have been rejected, but is it so traumatic? It is just as conceivable that it might have gone the other way and been the start of a valuable friendship, and to have missed that because you were afraid to risk rejection by making the first overture would have been far sadder than your momentary sense of unease over being rebuffed.

Two of the people who are now among my cherished friends called me repeatedly before we slid into a relationship of equal contact and interest, and I am grateful to them for persisting with an occasional invitation and, in between, an occasional casual call having no purpose other than to say, "How are you?" Some people do this much more gracefully than others, and I must admit that I myself have no liking for the telephone, but when I think back on the friendships I have missed because neither I nor the other made the effort and the friendships made because someone else went out of his way to establish them, I am annoyed at myself for having hung back. The possibility of friendship is worth going out on a limb for, and if the bough breaks, you can cushion the fall by consoling yourself that it is the other's loss. After all, you were offering friendship and liking, gifts no one can receive in excess. Therefore, it is he who has been foolish in rejecting the overture, not you who were made to look foolish by offering it.

There can be more complicated situations, though, than an

overture to a like and equal person such as that the person is of the opposite sex or is in a position to do one favors or is a far more successful person. Judy Garland remarked to Jack Paar, in the course of some conversation on his television show, that she had just come from London, where she had sat alone in her hotel room, praying for the telephone to ring and someone's voice to say, "How about dinner tonight?" But the telephone was silent because she is the glamorous Judy Garland and everybody assumes she is in demand and would not want to be bothered with little old them. I once worked on a stage show which starred an equally famous woman, and during the weeks when the show was on the road, we did a fair amount of chatting while standing around backstage, and I often wished I had called her after we got back to New York and the show closed. We liked each other and we might have made friends, but the idea that she was somebody and I was nobody stopped me, which was not sensible because a somebody has as much need of friends as a nobody, and I was not nobody; I was somebody who might have been her friend.

As for the overture being to a person of the opposite sex, a certain delicacy is involved. A woman meets a man or a man meets a woman with whom she or he would genuinely like to make friends but there is just as genuinely no romantic notion in the background. On the whole, a man is usually able to proceed straightforwardly by stating his invitations as though they were the most natural thing in the world and by confining them to innocuous occasions. In the course of a few luncheons, if he remains casual but interested and friendly, while avoiding personal topics, it will become apparent to the woman that he would like just to be friends and she will relax and go along with that. It is pleasant to have friends of the opposite sex with whom sex is not a factor, but it is more difficult for a woman to manage it. There are some men whom she must rule out from the beginning because it is predictable that they will feel called upon to take up the challenge of what they will perceive as a come-on. Other men, however, will take their cue from her matter-of-factness. It has been my experience that, if I call a man and ask him to meet me for lunch, he will spend some part of the meal probing for my reasons: do I want him? do I want his advice or help? am I going to borrow money from him? If he finally cannot contain his curiosity and asks, I simply tell him the truth: I found him an interesting person and wanted to make friends, or I volunteer this if he seems either uneasy or eager. There is often a final probe on parting, on the lines of: "How about meeting me for a drink tomorrow night?" or "Shall we do this again next week?" The first is answered with, "I'm busy," without apology, so that it is clear that lunch is not the prologue to a series of rendezvous, and the second with, "Not next week. I'll give you a call next time I'm going to be in the neighborhood." And very quickly a pleasant routine of a now-and-then lunch is established that is without under- or overtones.

Three Faults

It is not possible, of course, to *make* friends, for, as Emerson noted, "We talk of choosing our friends, but friends are self-elected." The foregoing, then, has been by way of getting your name on the ballot; there is nothing you can do past that to force someone to elect you as a friend. You make yourself available. You indicate your liking and goodwill. You show a concern for the other's concerns. And then you permit the friendship to grow or not as it will. There are often factors involved over which you can have no control, even about which you can have no knowledge, for the other is not simply the person you see; he is his history, his present and past relationships, his problems, his transferences, and you may trigger in him reactions which are none of your intention and are prehaps irrelevant but about which you can do nothing. For this reason, most friendships probably come about through proximity rather than initiative, with circumstances contriving the repeated contact that allows the individuals to emerge as individuals, rather than referents to other people, other times, other traits. Such a framework as a classroom, a job, or a goal-directed group holds people in juxtaposition until they arrive at a discriminating knowing. While this process is going on, while you are waiting to become, in the eyes of the other person, the individual you are, you can reassure him and demonstrate your friendly feelings by not challenging his fictions about himself.

An unfailing means of alienating an individual is to assume that his circumstances accurately reflect his ability and personality. We are all so much more interesting to ourselves than to anyone else because we know how many potentialities are alive in us, and the person who considers them dead issues and insists on seeing us flatly as no more than we are is appreciated as an enemy rather than a friend. It is perfectly human to ferret out the other's inadequacies, for one reason because we wish to know in which direction he will attack or fail us, for another because we do not want him to be more whole and unassailable than we are. Once inadequacies have been unmasked to our vision, however, they should be concealed from the other's, for the offer of friendship is, in effect, the offer to love, honor, and support the other's fictions. The cruelest affront is treating the person as exactly the person he is. We all long to be understood, but not for what we are. We long to be understood for what we might have been had all been for the best in the best of all possible worlds and, at the same time, to be forgiven for what we are.

Of what someone is, how much can be forgiven? In a novel by Josephine Tey, *Miss Pym Disposes*, there appears the following bit of conversation: " 'My hairdresser,' Lucy said, 'who lectures to me while he is doing my hair, says that one should allow everyone three faults. If one makes that allowance, one finds that the rest is surprisingly nice, he says.' " Lucy's hairdresser is right. Three faults in anyone are allowable, short of such major ones as deceit or exaggerated selfishness, and it is rather a pleasant exercise to decide upon the three faults to be granted and not fussed about. I used to fume at a friend who is always late, but now I say silently as I wait, "Okay, lateness is one of the three faults I concede you," and I stand on the corner with reasonable patience. I grant another friend the fault of boring me, which she now and then does by requiring twenty minutes to tell an anecdote which could be recounted in two and is of no intrinsic interest in any event. On the other hand, I do not acquiesce to the same fault in another acquaintance because, for me, she does not have enough assets to make up for it. There has to be sufficient meat to the friendship to make it otherwise worthwhile when the three faults have been granted, but if there is, naming them to oneself, conceding them to the friend, and ceasing to brood about them makes for a strengthened, less ambivalent relationship. It is relaxing to realize that you are not compelled to like every trait in someone else, as it also is to accept that he is not likely to be delighted with every facet of you.

The one fault which you cannot permit a friend is attack by him on your right to be yourself. The friend who carps about who and what you are must be firmly requested to allow you three faults of your own and, unless they are horrendous, to shut up about them. If he cannot or will not accede gracefully, you are justified in withdrawing from the friendship, for anyone who chronically provokes anxiety or tension or defensiveness is not worth having as a friend. Do not be misled into believing that you are being subjected to frankness for your own good. Attack is destructive, and it must not be long accepted. The valuable friends are those who make you expand, who make you feel more decent and wiser than you suspect yourself to be. People will oppose your being yourself, particularly if you have spent any length of time trying to be what they want you to be. But go right ahead. If you offer a necessary tenderness, a willingness to understand even if you cannot always condone, and a pervasive confirmation of the other's right to be the person he is, you have done your share; you need not offer up yourself on the altar of friendship.

The Training of Friends

I used to believe that I could persuade someone to like me by letting him do all the talking while I listened, asking questions about his interests and dismissing my own as of no importance, by remembering what he had said and referring back to it, by approving of his opinions and relegating my own to the background. Although I realized that this was a successful approach only with people who proved not to be particularly worthwhile, I did not know why until it was done to me and I found that it was only momentarily flattering, that I soon wanted to say, "Look here, I find myself interesting, but not all *that* interesting." Friendship is built on reciprocity, and if the other gives nothing of himself, what are you to like about him? If he lets you appreciate nothing of his existence, how can you make him exist for you? It seems like a great politeness to leave the stage to the other, but it eventuates as stinginess, a refusal to spend the self in the friendship.

Even the person who is not spontaneously inclined to welcome a word slipped in edgewise will come to feel vaguely cheated and will drift on in search of another audience if you do not put yourself forward to be seen. Therefore, despite its being comfortable to indicate your interest in the other's events and let your own go by default, to state a contrary observation or to inject a happening of your own into the conversation is called for. It is not always possible—I know someone whose eyes glaze when I start talking about myself and who shortly says, "Well, let's have a cup of tea"—but it is worth a persistent try because there cannot be friendship when the interest is unequal.

Some people have to be trained to be friends. I let my tea-drinking friend go on too long using me as an object in her world, and now she cannot cope with any shift in the ground rules. The person who does not see you must be trained to see you. The person who sees you too exclusively must be trained to make his own contribution. It is not wise to acquiesce in a friend's being overobedient to your wishes, oversolicitous about your welfare, or oversensitive to your reactions, any more than it is wise to accept the opposite. A friend must be trained to value you or himself, as the need may be.

In an established friendship, however, there need be no adherence to an equal time rule. It is usual that, over the months and years, there is a see-sawing in the dialogue, with now one, now the other taking center stage, corresponding to whose life is the more placid and whose the more roiled at the moment, but where there is true companionship, it evens out in the long run. And if it does not, that does not matter because it is intuitively known that: I am there for you as you are there for me; I accept your needs as you accept mine; I welcome your singularity as you welcome mine. We are not dividing up the spotlight. We simply, always and truly, exist for each other.

Acceptance given to a friend does not require excessive interest nor unrealistic flattery nor agreement at every turn but tacit recognition that this is a separate person with individual ways of acting and feeling that may not be yours but are his. The object of friendship is not to eradicate differences but to have a continuing dialogue despite them, without challenge and with enjoyment, for there must be two people in a friendship, not a sound and an echo, two distinct individuals each of whom accepts the uniqueness of the other and does not push for identity of outlook or behavior. The necessary recognition in friendship, as in love, is not that you will banish my aloneness and I will banish yours but that we will be there for each other in our separate alonenesses—to hear, to reach out, and confirm our right to be separate people.

Most people ask of their friends that they understand them, but, on balance, I think I prefer a friend who understands himself. Such a person is not apt to be guarded and defensive, anxious to be in the right and to receive evidence of approval. A touchy, sensitive friend is a nuisance, not because one is unwilling to be careful, but because, no matter how careful one is, there is bound to be a nerve struck now and again. The person who can accept himself as he is can accept you as you are and will not be overly alert to evidence that you will think or do something subversive to his idea of himself.

Keeping Friendship in Repair

Great friendships are no more frequent than great loves. But having one strong and excellent friendship does not obviate the need for a number of additional friends. The circumstances of life change, and a friend for one period may not be adequate to another period or there may be unpredictable separation. Of my close friends of five years ago, one inherited a fortune and decamped for more sybaritic pastures, one was transferred to Europe by his company, one was called home by family matters, and with one there was a mutual diminution in rapport. Second- and third-rank friends have moved up to close the gap, and others have been added to take their place. Samuel Johnson has summed it up neatly: "If a man does not make new acquaintance as he advances through life, he will soon find himself left alone. A man, Sir, should keep his friendship in constant repair." A woman, Ma'am, should do the same.

It is not solely a question of not being left alone but of the asset of friends as sources of information and stimulation. I owe to friends an interest in subject after subject that I would never have explored had they not introduced me to them. I look at the city around me with different eyes because of a friend who reads extensively on the history of architecture. I am more knowledgable about art, organic gardening, baseball, bookbinding, the economics of running a ten-cent store, and myriad other small and large, useful and useless subjects than I would ever have been without exposure to the pursuits of friends. Friends are animated books. They are a completely delightful, absolutely painless means of continuing one's education.

It is rare to find one person who shares all one's enjoyments. A marvelous companion in the city may be out of his element in the country. A delightful dyadic conversationalist may be a total loss in a group. An otherwise understanding and empathic friend may be made uneasy by physical illness and be of no help at all, or the converse may be true: I have a friend who finds me of only passing interest when I am well but let me be sick and there is no one more devoted. I have heard people discuss the qualities they require in friendship, ending with a fair-sized catalogue of virtues, but I find it more realistic to have a fair-sized catalogue of friends, each with one virtue, than to hunt for one person who meets all the requirements.

With some friends, overexposure is just as deadly as it is to television comedians; they must be enjoyed on occasion, not be required to be a friend for all seasons. They must be liked at their best, not put in situations in which they appear at a disadvantage. The danger is not so great that you will cease liking the friend who lets you down as that he will cease liking you because he has let you down. It is far easier to be philosophical about another person's defects than it is about your own, so that, if you make a demand on a friend which he cannot meet or put him in a situation which he does not handle well, he will dislike you for having made him fail you. I, for instance, lost a friend who did not come to see me when I was in the hospital, not because I minded her inattention but because she felt guilty, while I kept another who called to say she was in the city but felt too tired to come; I told her to get in a cab and come anyway, which she did, and when the visit was over, she beamed at me and said, "I'm so glad you made me come. I'd have been ashamed of myself if I hadn't." There are times when you must not allow a friend to be derelict because, as wholeheartedly as you may forgive him, he will not forgive you for having seen his inadequacy. It requires a certain degree of seeming insensitivity to call when a friend has not called, to override a silence, to write when there has been no answer to a previous letter, to remind a friend to do something he promised but has not done. The impulse is to sit back and wait to see what, if anything, he will do to retrieve the situation and assure you of his good feelings. But if you wish to preserve the friendship, the better maneuver is to step into the gap just as though the next move had truly been up to you rather than to him. In the absence of massive evidence to the contrary, one should take for granted that a friend cares and act as though it were solidly and continuously true, not solicit, by hanging back, repeated evidence that it is so.

A Painful Friendship

An elderly family friend took me along to a dinner at which there were two other couples, one his contemporaries, the other a pair of fledglings recently engaged to be married. When the latter left us at the end of the evening, the host spoke of how

259

flattered he was that the "youngsters" had deigned to be his guests. It had been a superlative meal at one of New York's elegant restaurants, and the host, a witty and charming man, had provided extraordinary wines and excellent conversation. He was incomparably more interesting than the youngsters, who had only youth to recommend them and handled that awkwardly, and why he should have been honored that they accepted his company, I could not imagine. Friends are where you find them, regardless of age, station, background, or interests, and the other fellow is as lucky to have you for a friend as you are to have him. It is beside the point in which ways you are unlike as long as you like each other, and there is no reason ever to be grateful for being liked as long as you return the liking. A seventy-year-old and a twenty-year-old can be friends without marveling in the least over the discrepancy in age if each assumes that his own friendship is a valuable thing. One of the nicest aspects of friendship is that it does not in the least have to be plausible.

That plausibility has, in fact, little to do with friendship can be seen when one brings together, certain that they will like each other, two people who have much in common, only to find that they do not hit it off at all well. I was introduced recently to a man who is an editor, playwright, cat-fancier, and amateur sculptor. We had everything in common, except any great liking for each other. Having eagerly arranged such introductions myself any number of times, with sometimes neutral and occasionally disastrous results, it finally struck me that the secret of having people meet who will like each other is to introduce a close friend of mine, not to someone who resembles him, but to someone who resembles me. This is not conceit but realism in that, if my friend has chosen me, I am the sort of person he is drawn to; his friends are not people like him, they are people like me. With this discovery of the obvious, I have subsequently had better luck with my pairings.

When someone else is doing the pairing, you are under no obligation to like the person you are introduced to, any more than he is required to like you. The only reasonable basis for friendship is whether you give each other pleasure. Friendship is an absolutely voluntary commitment, with the possible exception of friends who date so far back in your life that there is almost the same tie as there is to relatives. Someone you grew up with or roomed with or went adventuring with may not have weathered the years well, may have become bitter and discontent or may have ceased to grow, but still you remain friends because you have a long shared history. Whether the friendship gives you pleasure is almost irrelevant in such an instance, for the friendship has an existence of its own; it just is. But for friendships not woven into the extended fabric of your life, the pleasure they give is the measure of whether they are worth preserving. "A friend," said Robert Louis Stevenson, "is a present you give yourself." To give yourself a handful of nettles or a leech or a screech owl is to undervalue yourself in an indefensible way. You should make yourself gifts of friends who do not need, but thoroughly enjoy, your company, and then keep those friends by not holding on to them.

The Demands of Work

Robert Louis Stevenson also had an observation to make about work, and it was this: "If a man loves to labor at any trade, apart from any question of success or fame, the gods have called him." The gods are not exactly tying up the lines these days, what with dominance of the American work scene by the great corporations which make cogs of workers in the lower echelons and nervous cogs of workers in the middle echelons. This is a pity, for work that uses and stretches the capacities of the worker is almost more satisfying than anything else in life. To be used, to be used well and fully and meaningfully by work, is a solid contentment. I have never envied the person who does not have to work, only the person who thoroughly enjoys his work.

It is so apparent that we work to earn a living that we are apt to overlook that work is living; it is not eight hours of the day paid in forfeit so that we may have the other sixteen to ourselves. We live in those eight hours too, and if we respect the work we do and do it with pride and competence, the hours are not taken out of our lives but add immeasurably to them. This is not to make a virtue out of necessity but to say that the necessity of work does not prevent it from being intensely rewarding if the work gives scope to our capacities and exercise to our mind and muscles. The requirement is, of course, that it be demanding work.

A frequent mistake is the choice of easy work. Nothing is more exhausting. It is a prison in which one idles all day, bored, irritated, and occupied only with thoughts of how to do still less and get away with it. In places where I have worked, the discontented members of the staff have been those most successful at doing the least amount of work. Curiously, it was they who complained of being exploited. Management was the enemy, the thief of their time and substance whom they had to battle constantly to keep from being taken advantage of. They were bitter about being underpaid, discontent about working conditions. They thought they had too much to do, but, really, they did not do enough. They may have been cheating the boss of a full day's work, but they were cheating themselves of a full day's satisfaction, which was by far the more important theft.

My publisher was telling me about a friend of his, also a publisher, who fell upon bad times and had to let go eight of the twelve people on his staff, preliminary, he thought, to closing down the business entirely because the skeleton staff would not be able to cope with the work. Instead, he found that, not only could the work be handled, but it was getting done more promptly and more efficiently and in an altogether happier atmosphere. For the first time, there was no grumbling about salaries, no clock-watching, no personality clashes. No one felt exploited; no one objected to staying late; in fact, they came in voluntarily on Saturdays. His only worry now, he said, with the business getting back on its feet, was that he might have to add more people.

The moral for the job-hunter is: look for a job where you will be overworked, not underworked; look for a place understaffed rather than overstaffed; look for a position you are not certain you can handle rather than one you can do with one hand tied behind you; look for work you can get something out of. And do this for selfish reasons. I have a friend who, like me, is a free-lance medical editor, and we feed each other work. He takes the manuscripts that need only light editing and are on subjects he knows; I take the ones that require heavy editing and are on subjects I know little about, being of the opinion that, if I have to earn money, it is a dividend to acquire some knowledge while doing the work. I like medical editing; my friend is struggling desperately to get out of the field.

That he is having great difficulty in getting out of the field illustrates an important point about a first job. The usual advice is to take any job you are offered in order to get started and gain experience, the assumption being that you can make a change later. This chap, who came out of college with a desire to get into publishing, accepted a job in medical publishing because he reasoned that it would give him editing experience that he could then use to obtain a position with a publishing house specializing in fiction, his real interest. But it has proved next to impossible for him to make a change. When he began looking around, he found that he was "typed" as a medical editor; employment agencies would not send him out on jobs for fiction editors, and employers would not meet his salary requirements because they said he was inexperienced in their facet of the field. When, in desperation, he said he would accept a beginner's salary, employers still would not consider him on the grounds that he would be discontent at making less money and would not stay long. The first job, then, is an extremely important choice. People do go from being secretaries to being copywriters, for example, or from being mail boys to being reporters, but the route is more certain if you can start out where you want to end up rather than trying to switch into it.

You do not always know where you want to end up, of course, but often you do know, or can know if you give it some thought, what you do *not* want. You can know whether you do or do not want to work for one man or for a corporation, whether you want security or change, whether you want to work with your head or your hands, whether you want to work long hours or short, whether you want to work anonymously or autonomously. George Bernard Shaw said of endeavors of his: "Behind the conviction that they could lead to nothing I wanted, lay the unspoken fear that they might lead to something I did not want." It is as necessary to avoid the latter trap as the former. It can have predictive value, when offered a job, to imagine that you have taken it, have progressed fully in the direction it seems to point, and after forty years in the field, are attending a dinner in honor of your retirement. Will you, while standing there waiting for the applause to die down before you embark on your exit speech, think to yourself, "Thank God, this is how I spent my life," or, "My God, is this how I spent my life"? To have succeeded at what you do not care about is no success at all.

And, sometimes, even to succeed at something you care very much about is not success. There are actors, for instance, who commit suicide at the height of their fame and writers who do likewise when they have achieved their goal. Having moved into their castles in the air, they look around and find emptiness. This is probably because they thought that to be a success they had to become a success, although the fact of the matter is the opposite: to become a success, one must be a success. That is, success is what one is, not what one becomes. It is being in possession of one's self and one's life; it is working well and honestly and enjoying the work for itself; it is confronting, insofar as possible, personal conflicts and anxieties rather than simply holding them at bay through work. It is not postponing living to some distant time at which it is assumed conditions will be right for living to be enjoyed.

Raises, vice-presidencies, pensions, retirement benefits are the trap. It is only sensible to look to the future and to store up against the future, but to pay for a time that may never come with the coin of present misery is a poor bargain. A man I know who works for a huge and benevolent corporation had a chance to go out on his own in a risky but fascinating enterprise. What decided him against it was that a thirty-five-year-old colleague of his had come down with a wasting nerve disease and the medical insurance provided by the corporation was taking care of the astronomical bills. "What," worried the man, "would become of me if the same thing happened and there was no corporation to pay the bills?" He would be put in a charity ward and be in for six months or six years of horror, however long it took him to die. And that is a grisly prospect, but the statistical order of probability that he will contract a chronic and fatal illness is infinitesimally smaller than the probability that he is consigning himself to the wasting disease of not being used at his best. *That* he can know he is in for, while he has no way of intuiting whether he is slated for a chronic illness at the end of his life.

Besides, playing it safe is just as risky as taking a chance. This same man, who stayed on in the corporation, believing himself certain of an orderly rise up the ladder, within six months had been outmaneuvered in a round of corporate musical chairs and shunted off to a static and unimportant department from which there was little chance for him to advance. Another executive of my acquaintance is a first-rate editor, really a gifted editor, in a small publishing house owned by a shrewd, amusing, but unscrupulous man who alternately cajoles and torments his staff, using the carrot or the whip as necessary to achieve his ends. The carrot he offered his editor-in-chief when another company tried to hire him away was a vice-presidency and more money, and the editor bit on it despite the fact that the boss made his life a misery. He now has "Vice-President" on his door, and an ulcer, a pronounced tremor of his hands, and a fragmented self-respect.

I have a newspaper clipping tacked up beside my typewriter which has been there so long that I have forgotten who is being quoted. This anonymous, sensible man said: "If you defy the system long enough you'll be rewarded. At first life takes revenge and reduces you to a sniveling mess. But keep sniveling, have the madness, the audacity, to do what interests you, forget about your pension, and eventually life will say all right, we'll let you do it."

Life will let us do what we want. The problem is to let

ourselves do what we want. Fringe benefits are aptly named; improved working conditions, insurance, stock options, retirement pay, shorter hours are fringe on the edge of life. What is central is good work worth doing and done well. It is a satisfaction in stable times, an anchor in bad times, and a reward in and of itself at all times.

RECAPITULATION

Every life is a dilemma that must be solved
by the person living it

Sixteen

CONFIRMATION AND
AFFIRMATION

W HEN I was in college, the professor of a music appreciation course was famous for his insistence on the necessity of identifying the theme of a work and then listening for its recapitulation. His words became such a catch phrase that when the school show came to be written at the end of the year, the big musical number was: "Good Lord, Where *Is* That Recapitulation!"

Here follows the recapitulation of the theme:

Self-Watching

We all make two wishes in life. We wish for the success of our relationship to other people, and we wish for the success of our undertakings. But, traditionally, three wishes are allowed. For the third, we had best make the wish to understand ourselves, since, if that wish can be made to come true, the first is certain to be fulfilled and the second is likely to be.

The initial step in understanding the self is observation of how we act in the world. Although it seems next to impossible that the self so indivisibly lived with could be in any recess unknown, in any impulse unfamiliar, in any action uncomprehended, it is exactly this terrible intimacy which renders the self poorly visualized. We are standing up too close. We must somehow contrive to grow distant to the self, strange to the self, if we are to come to know the self. That is, we must pull back and look at what we are doing as a first step toward knowing what we are.

This does not require vision of an order other than we characteristically employ. We are perfectly able to say of ourselves such things as: "I do a lot of traveling," or, "I don't form close attachments," or, "I change jobs often." These are legitimate observations, as reliable as those of a naturalist who notes that, in the field he is watching, a rabbit is bounding through the grass, a mouse is scrambling into a burrow, and a bird is singing. But the observations are an aid to the naturalist's understanding only if he does not attempt to understand them too quickly. If he says to himself, "Ah, that rabbit must be bounding away because it senses a fox and that mouse must be diving into its burrow to feed its young and that bird must be singing to defend its territory," he has learned nothing but what he already believes; which is to say, he has learned nothing. So it is, too, in self-watching. The person who says, "I travel a good deal because I like to see new places," has vitiated the usefulness of his observation by linking it with an immediate explanation, as has the person who says, "I don't form close attachments because I like lots of different people," and, "I change jobs often because I get bored with the same routine." Such explanations are not designed to explain, but to explain away, behavior, and rather than being an aid to understanding, they abort it.

Behaviors must be chiseled free of their rational excuses and left to stand unadorned until enough of them have been accumulated for patterns of consistency to emerge. That we find this extremely difficult to do is because we long ago became addicted to self-exculpation, hooked on the habit of finding a forgiving logic for our actions and reactions. I was in the company of a couple of small boys the other day, and when one hit the other, I rather stupidly asked, "Now, why did you do that?" The boy stammered, fiddled with his toys, and suddenly triumphantly shouted, "Because he was going to hit me!" He could not say, "I don't know." He had to have a reason, as we all have to give ourselves reasons. But if we are to substitute reason in place of reasons, we must allow ourselves to say, "I don't know."

With some characteristic patterns of behavior and feeling becoming apparent through self-watching, how are they then to be understood? Although they can be interpreted in the light of the present, it is a trap to examine them in this light because we are perfectly capable of distorting the present to make it relevant to the behaviors and feelings observed. What we must assume is that, whether or not we are able to find adequate present reason for our actions and reactions, we invariably have adequate historical reason. Our coping attempts in the dilemma of our lives are not arbitrary, any more than the information on the tape coming out of a computer is arbitrary. But we, and the computer, of necessity base our responses on previously programmed information. Since, as human beings, we were programmed by the experiences of infancy and childhood, it is only in their light that current clusters of behaviors and feelings can be creatively deciphered.

Of the early relationships and the events bound up in the relationships, some are accessible to memory, some are known by hearsay, some can be uncovered by exploring the charted landscape of infancy, but many are beyond all recollection and exhumation. This presents us with a problem comparable to the one that would confront the operator of a computer if only the sketchiest of records describing the computer's original programming were available. While the computer would not fail to click out some sort of a response to any situation put to it, the observing operator, late on the scene, might come to suspect that the answers were not as exact, as discriminating, nor as elegant as they might be. To penetrate to the unsophisticated or obsolete or erroneous data on which the responses are based, to distinguish these from data still useful and still pertinent so that the former may be eliminated and the latter preserved, the operator must read the tape produced by the machine and reason backward from it. If these are the solutions the computer gives, what type and quality and quantity of information stored in the machine originally might explain them? Such, also, is our task: to reason from observed response to the nature of the original programming being reproduced in the self's efforts to relive the past in the present.

This is the point, this dawn of backward vision, at which it is necessary not to lose heart. The more one uncovers and pieces together the past, the more one tends to feel helpless in the face of its programming. How can what was done be undone? The honest admission is that it cannot be. But what was done is done, over and done, gone, finished, dead. The past, if preserved, is preserved only in the amber of our attitudes. It has no life except the life we give it by keeping alive the attitudes it taught us: about the self, about the self in the world, about the world, about what to expect from other people and what to defend against. Thus, as we extrapolate backward from present reactions to past probable programming, we must attempt to drain the attitudes of their vitality by measuring them against a more objective reality and recognizing those facets of them which are ill-adapted to, and without utility in, current situations.

How Frequent the Self

Old attitudes are so deeply ingrained that they present themselves as the natural and inevitable route to follow. To conceive that they are simply attitudes, not truths, and that other approaches may have more accuracy and be more creative requires an effort of the will and imagination. And even when attitudes have been recognized and new directions found and proved to be appropriate and rewarding, the effort must continue. Like driving a car on a country road, it is necessary to fight the wheel to stay out of old ruts. The price of freedom from archaic, worn ways is, to warp a phrase, eternal vigilance. Self-understanding decays unless continually rediscovered and enlarged.

While the dilemma of a life can only be solved by the person living that life, it can never be *finally* solved by the person living it. Continued contemplativeness is required, the willingness to examine and re-examine, discover and rediscover, to review, integrate, and assimilate feelings, behavior, and events, to fit them in, digest them, and fatten on them. To believe that the self is fully known and finally understood is the best evidence that one is mistaken.

272

Contemplativeness is not preoccupation, however. If it were, the neurotic person who ruminates on his encounters and experiences would be a polished and complete individual. Contemplativeness is, instead, thoughtfully spaced attempts at self-awareness and self-review. It is not rumination but unblinking exploration: where is the self? what is it feeling? what is it doing? what response is it repeating? what response is it provoking? what is the common ground of this botched encounter and past ones? The questions are not constant, but they should be frequent, and they should be posed with a flat curiosity that is not intended, however secretly, to get the self off the hook. Excuses are comforting, but understanding is curative.

Meanwhile, between expeditions in search of the self, what is taking place? A perceptive doctor one day remarked to me: "Four and a half years of analysis? Don't you suppose it's time you did a bit of living?" That was the day I left formal psychoanalysis because I appreciated in that moment that life cannot be suspended for understanding. Early on in this book, I quoted Socrates's famous dictum that, "The unexamined life is not worth living." Let me now turn the phrase inside out: The unlived life is not worth examining. As Kierkegaard remarked, "Life can only be understood backwards; but it must be lived forwards." It must be lived in all its immediacy and with full involvement, with concentration on the reality around one, not on the self, with commitment to the reality around one. Self-awareness, self-examination, self-consciousness are for the quiet moments. In the arena they are paralyzing.

The self must not be held out of the arena until living skills have been learned. With the slow drip of psychoanalytic theory into the mainstream of thought, we have become increasingly aware in recent decades of how life traumatizes us, and this awareness has tended to blot out the fact that life can also be exceedingly therapeutic. Good experiences can be as instructive as bad and as influential as bad, and whether experiences are healing or painful, events and the self in action in events are the only raw material from which understanding of the self can be distilled. We need to live forward in order to understand backward skillfully, equally as much as we need to understand backward in order to live forward skillfully.

What that intelligent doctor was suggesting to me was, in short, that it was time to fish or cut bait. But when I followed his advice, I came to learn that he was only half right. It is essential to fish *and* cut bait: sometimes to be immersed in action, sometimes to draw back and attempt to understand, but never entirely to suspend one activity in favor of the other. Understanding is only of use if it is validated in action and found to lead to more sensitive response. And action prompts insight only if it is not considered over and done until an understanding of the self in the action has been reached.

The more frequent this type of feedback from action to insight and insight to action, the more rapid and more effective it becomes. The self's spontaneous actions grow in accuracy and relevancy, and insight into them arrives almost concurrently. Thus, the self has good experiences and is encouraged by them to venture into wider actions and deeper insights. Karen Horney, in remarking that psychoanalysis ". . . is not the only way to resolve inner conflicts," added that, "Life itself still remains a very effective therapist." I can only add: Learn and live; live and learn.

Infra Dig

If there is one concept that outweighs the others in this book, it is that one must not try to change the self. But I am nagged by the thought that it will be passed over because it is so contrary to customary belief. My pessimistic vision is of a reader who observes himself in action, perceives that he is, for example, inarticulate in virtually every situation, goes exploring and comes upon the finding that, as a boy, he was so ridiculed by a bright older brother that he became reluctant to express his thoughts. Probing further, he uncovers the great hostility to that brother that was thrust out of consciousness, recognizes the possibility that it is hostility that now ties his tongue, and resolves not to be hostile any more but, instead, to regard people affectionately. This resolve will stay in force for two weeks, and he will be greatly pleased. Then it will cease working and his old inarticulateness will overcome him again. Two weeks is about the length of time any resolution is influential, so, unless one is prepared to make a new resolution every fortnight, it is just as well not to go to the bother in the first place.

Sometimes it is just a bother, and there is no particular harm done by the fact that the effort fails and the change proves to be transitory. But sometimes the consequences are far more serious. So much of what is exhausting and heartbreaking in a life comes from repeated attempts to pry loose a behavior and force another into its place. The discouragement entailed when the effort fails can be enormous—the depression, the anxiety, the dismaying feeling of helplessness, the eventual sad resignation. It is preferable to do nothing, if this is the outcome, than to try to change by fiat.

There is only one way in which the self and its circumstances can be changed. This is by accepting the self and its circumstances.

The inarticulate man is proceeding excellently up to the point at which he resolves to replace his hostility with affectionate feelings. It is then that he goes astray, for the hostility persists, just as water goes on boiling after a lid is placed on the kettle and quickly builds up considerable pressure. The man's only workable course of action is to accept his hostility. He cannot uproot it or suppress it; he can only allow it in, accept that he feels hostile, know it, feel it, live with it, force himself to remain conscious of it. He need not express it, of course; he need not act on it; but he must keep it, so to speak, under his eye at all times. Let us say that he is called in by the sales manager of his office with whom, as with everyone, he has hitherto been inarticulate because of the necessity of screening his words in order to prevent any hint of his churning mass of hostility from slipping through. He has made himself aware now of the hostility, but if he tries to hold it in check by bracing a barrier of affection in front of it, he will continue to be just as inarticulate because now he has double the effort to make: he must push back hostility and push forward affection. Were he, on the other hand, to accept the hostility, to sit there and say to himself: "Look at the stupid beast pointing the letter opener at me and sniffing for a chance to catch me out. I despise him, from his ugly mouth to the hairs on his fat hands," he knows his hostility, he accepts it in, it is there in front of him where he can measure how deep and pervasive it is. Will it slip out? Must he guard his words? No, because now the hostility is under his conscious control. He is released to speak freely because he is no longer unconsciously afraid of what he might say.

The inarticulate man released to speak freely has changed, not because he has changed himself but because he has accepted himself.

The same thing is true of circumstances: they, too, cannot be changed except by accepting them. A striking instance of this is the common happening that childless couples who adopt a child often go on to have a baby of their own. I have known two such couples who tried hard to change their childless state, finally accepted it and adopted a baby, and then had children of their own. They did not adapt to their circumstances, but they did accept them, and when they had accepted them and done what they could in the light of them, their circumstances changed. It is important to distinguish that acceptance is not adaptation. To adapt to painful circumstances is not sensible because that can be as permanently deforming as adapting to painful shoes, but it is necessary to accept them so that the most constructive life possible can be achieved within them. The very constructiveness of the life managed may then bring about the change desired. In the instance of a woman who finds spinsterhood a painful circumstance, if she adapts to it, she may become rigid and drab; if she fights it, she may grow panicky and grab at any man, thereby frightening prospective suitors away; but if she accepts it with equanimity and sets about living a life of dignity and richness, there may come along a man perceptive enough to change her circumstance.

276

We all walk around in such very thin skins, desperately fearing an attack on our self-esteem, either from within or without. But there can be no severe attack on the self from within if its mechanisms are familiar and accepted, nor can there be an unexpected attack on the self from without if its deficiencies, incongruities, and circumstances are known and lightly conceded. If I have accepted, for example, that I have strong dependency needs, it cannot drastically threaten my self-esteem if I find that I am reluctant to leave the hospital after a bout of pneumonia. I quickly recognize why, am slightly amused by my maneuvers to stay put, pull myself together and get out. If someone else remarks, "You don't want to leave the hospital. You like being looked after," I need not become defensive and strike back angrily because of the blow to my self-esteem; I can say, "Oh, I'm doing that again, am I?" because I have accepted that mechanism in myself and the comment comes as no surprise, and therefore no attack.

The service the self can provide the self is not to armor it against attack but to divest it of the armor built up over the years by accepting, with neither fear nor defensiveness, what the self is. In such fashion is, paradoxically, the thin skin thickened. The self accepted is the self freed to act spontaneously and appropriately and generously. And when the self can behave in this manner, esteem for the self is present, both one's own and other people's. It need neither be anxiously solicited nor defensively maintained.

When one can accept the self, one can be the self. And to be the self is the only change in the self ever needed.

The Binoculars for Self-Watching

While it is far from easy to know and accept the self, and I have not wished to minimize the painful effort involved, there is one cheering fact. Unlike the case in physical dysfunction in which diagnosis is only a prelude to therapy, in the psychological realm, more often than not, the two are synonymous: diagnosis is the therapy and the therapy is diagnosis. To be able to diagnose the trouble may be all the treatment required to cause the trouble to disappear. If I have a high temperature and a rattling cough, I can call it a cold or bronchitis or diagnose it correctly as pneumonia and the symptoms will not abate one bit; but if I lie in the hospital feeling depressed and I can diagnose it as anxiety caused by the prospective loss of my dependent situation, the depression lifts.

To illustrate with an actual instance, I began this week at my desk staring out of the window at the rain, tired, indifferent, blank of mind except for a passing speculation as to whether it was the dreary weather or was I coming down with a virus. I picked up a pencil and wrote: "Where am I? I don't know. Nothing's happened. Yesterday was an ordinary day. I spent the evening with J____, who said nothing special, except that he did say. . . ." And as I wrote his words, anxiety came welling up, anxiety that had been held out of awareness by depression. The remarks had been trivial, but as soon as they were on paper, I recognized how they had triggered an old attitude. The depression overlying the anxiety lifted, and the anxiety, immediately it was diagnosed as anxiety, drained away.

It is because of its aid to diagnosis that a notebook is as useful to self-watching as a pair of binoculars to bird-watching; it allows the self to be viewed from a distance, yet in magnified detail. Attitudes, which can be enormously elusive on the wing, are caught in the notebook. As they appear and reappear in all their guises, it becomes ever more easy to identify them, and when the particular discomfort they are causing is diagnosed, often that is all the therapy required to bring about a cessation of symptoms. The cure is temporary; relapses are frequent, but persistent diagnosis achieves longer and longer periods of remission and renders the attacks increasingly milder.

There is a second type of notebook that can be kept, a very different affair from the ragbag of feelings, thoughts, dreams, undigested events, and thrusts at self-understanding that the first is, but a most helpful source of insight and amplification. This is a compendium of other people's thoughts and observations. There is nothing old under the sun; each of us must learn again, from the beginning, for ourselves; but the learning process can be hastened and deepened and solidified by a personal and creative borrowing of the insights of other people. The exactitude of a phrase someone else uses may sum up an idea hitherto dimly groped for. A writer's unexpected image or point of view may open a region which would otherwise go unexplored. The rightness of an observation may be so remarkable that an approach to an event or person can never be the same again.

"Truth, she thought, all the truths that anyone could need to lead an admirable, a nearly perfect life, lay spread out all round one all the time—but one had got to annex them, as it were, conquer them by force and make them one's own, before one could use them." I quote this, not only because it is beautifully apposite, but to illustrate that one need not look exclusively to profound sources to find wisdom. These lines are from Ann Bridge's romantic novel, *Illyrian Spring,* a pleasant evening's reading but the yield from it is at least one comment worth keeping in mind for the rest of one's life.

The Goal Standard

There has never been a generation in which men have not thought deeply on the living of a life. Choosing among their thoughts for the planks of a personal philosophy is akin to choosing among all the people whom one meets those who shall be friends: their nature must be fundamentally suited to one's own; their nature must confirm one's own. There will be many unconscious determinants of the selection, but this is unimportant because, whether it be friends or words, they are needed only to affirm the self, not change it.

No life, no matter how small in compass, need be trivial if decent goals for it are worked out and maintained. One cannot live someone else's life, but, oh, how easily one can fail to live one's own if there is no thought given to its purposes and intentions. "The absolutely imperative task of a democracy," wrote Ibsen, "is to make itself aristocratic." And so it is, too, the task of the individual. We are born equal, that is, we are born with an equal chance to become unequal, and if we are to become unequal in the direction of distinction and courage rather. than emptiness and meanness, we must hammer out a solid place to stand. Words, preserved and elaborated on, penetrated and recombined, added to and remembered, and lived by, can be a text of the possibilities of the self.

There is no single wisdom, there are many wisdoms, and each provides a gleam that, compounded, lights a life.

The Theme

So, in the end, it is this that has been said: do not mistake what your lifework is; it is your life. And in that life, all that truly counts is the relationship to the self—the self as deeply as it can be known, as fully as it can be accepted, as genuinely as it can be lived—for from that relationship all else proceeds.